CB135569

Gabriel Díaz Maggioli
Lesley Painter-Farrell

Happy Campers 6

Teacher's Edition

macmillan
education

Table of Contents

Contents

Student Resources

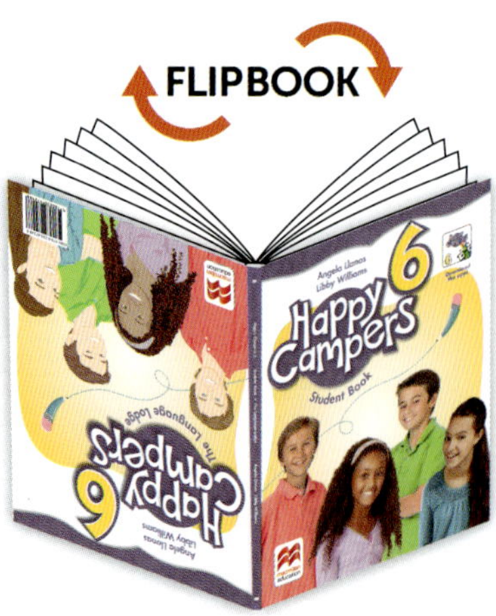

Student Book and
The Language Lodge Flipbook

Skills Book

Happy Campers app

About Happy Campers

Happy Campers is designed to provide a learning environment in which teachers and students feel a continuous sense of **achievement** and **satisfaction**. Lessons and activities are focused on simple, achievable goals that build confidence and encourage a **positive attitude** toward English language learning. By doing the activities in *Happy Campers*, students become part of a **child-centered community**—they work together to meet goals, sing, cheer, and echo while doing tasks and, above all have fun.

Positive Environment
\+ Manageable Input
\+ Practice

= **Learning English**

Teacher Resources

Teacher's Edition
Class Audio CD
Access code for
Teacher's Resource Center

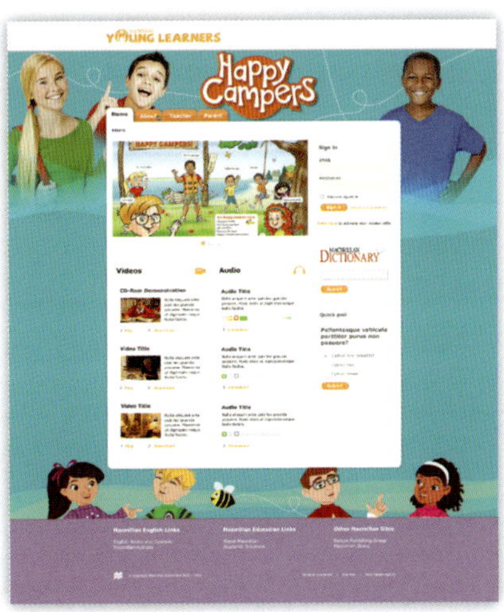

Teacher's Resource Center
www.macmillanyounglearners.com/happycampers

Scope and Sequence

Unit	Pages	Vocabulary	Grammar
1	8–15	**Circus:** circus, big top, ringmaster, parade, trapeze artist, tightrope walker, clown, unicyclist **Review:** Past tense irregular verb forms	We were at the circus. The big top was beautiful. There was a circus. There were tightrope walkers.
2	16–23	**Movies 1:** movie studio, director, cameraman, scene, cartoon, producer, movie star, script **Movies 2:** personal assistant, makeup artist, sound engineer, "Positions, please," "Action," "Cut"	I talked to a movie star. The director waved at me! She sat in the office. They ate pizza.
3	24–31	**Clothes:** sweatshirt, sweatpants, cardigan, vest, leggings, tights, hoodie, dress **Commands:** pay attention, go to bed, waste (your) time, rehearse a scene, be on time, learn your lines	I didn't take my wallet. Did you stay up late last night? Yes, I did. Did he learn his lines? No, he didn't.
4	32–39	**Types of Movies:** action movie, comedy, horror, drama, science fiction, western, documentary, musical **Adjectives:** serious, rude, polite, brave, grumpy, silly	Who did you go with? When did you go? What did you see? Where did you go? Was he brave? Yes, he was. Were they surprised? No, they weren't.
5	40–47	**Solar System:** universe, solar system, planet, Mercury, Neptune, Jupiter, Saturn, Earth **Astronomy:** astronomer, telescope, moon, comet, meteor, crater	The nearest planet to the sun is Mercury. The largest planet is Jupiter. Is it the nearest mall? Which is the smallest moon?
6	48–55	**Technology:** smartphone, smartwatch, MP3 player, gaming system, laptop, tablet, wireless, digital camera **Superlatives**: best, worst, generous, careful, thoughtful, peaceful	It's the most amazing smartphone. It's the most exciting laptop. Is this the best tablet?
7	56–63	**Weather:** windy, bright, wet, foggy, mild, chilly, freezing, icy **Nature:** trunk, branch, mud, puddle, wind	Why are you wearing a hat? Because it's chilly. Why did you stop? Because the wind took my hat!
8	64–71	**Air Travel 1:** suitcase, hand luggage, bag tag, ticket, check-in, airline, window seat, boarding pass **Air Travel 2:** gate, flight, aisle, flight attendant, emergency exit, seat belt	I'll buy the tickets. Will you sing for us today? Yes, we will. Will you dance for us today? No, we won't.

Extra Practice	Teamwork Activity
The Language Lodge: Pages 1–4 **Happy Campers app:** Unit 1	Circus Program 
The Language Lodge: Pages 5–8 **Happy Campers app:** Unit 2	Movie Storyboard 
The Language Lodge: Pages 9–12 **Happy Campers app:** Unit 3	Interview a Movie Star 
The Language Lodge: Pages 13–16 **Happy Campers app:** Unit 4	Movie Billboard 
The Language Lodge: Pages 17–20 **Happy Campers app:** Unit 5	The Solar System 
The Language Lodge: Pages 21–24 **Happy Campers app:** Unit 6	A New Gadget 
The Language Lodge: Pages 25–28 **Happy Campers app:** Unit 7	Weather Report 
The Language Lodge: Pages 29–32 **Happy Campers app:** Unit 8	Vacation Checklist 

Class-building activities allow students to participate equally.

Student Book lessons are organized around a **content centerpiece** used in different ways across **two** lessons, providing plenty of exposure and practice. A **musicalized echo** activity allows students to see, hear, and pronounce new vocabulary in a safe environment. The Grammar Pass provides examples of the new grammar. **Scaffolded activities** guide students to discover the grammar rules for themselves.

Lesson 1: Vocabulary

Lesson 2: Grammar

UNIT 4 Lesson 1

1 22 Listen. Then echo.

action movie
comedy
horror
drama
science fiction
western
documentary
musical

2 23 Listen and number.

Movie Fans

3 Page 13 The Language Lodge

32

Lesson 2

1 23 Sing: Movie Fans.

Who did you go with?
I went with my friend Sam!
We saw a lovely musical,
We watch them when
we can!

When did you go?
We went on Friday night,
We went to see a
horror film,
It gave us such a fright!

What did you see?
We saw a comedy,
We laughed a lot until
we cried,
It was funny to see!

Where did you go?
We went to Movie City,
A science fiction
movie played,
The actress was so pretty!

GRAMMAR PASS
Who did you go with?
When did you go?
What did you see?
Where did you go?

2 Look at the Grammar Pass. Complete.
1. ________ did you go? Movie City.
2. ________ did you eat? Pizza.
3. ________ did you go with? David.
4. ________ did you go? Yesterday.
5. We use Where, What, When, Who + ________ in questions about the past.

3 Ask and answer about the movies.

When did you go to the movies?
I went yesterday.

4 Page 14 The Language Lodge

33

Lesson 1: Vocabulary Practice

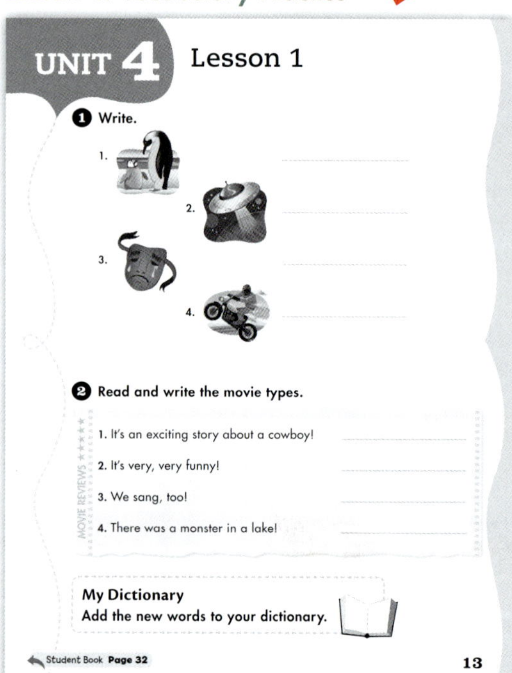
UNIT 4 Lesson 1

1 Write.
1. ________
2. ________
3. ________
4. ________

2 Read and write the movie types.

MOVIE REVIEWS
1. It's an exciting story about a cowboy! ________
2. It's very, very funny! ________
3. We sang, too! ________
4. There was a monster in a lake! ________

My Dictionary
Add the new words to your dictionary.

Student Book Page 32

13

Lesson 2: Grammar Practice

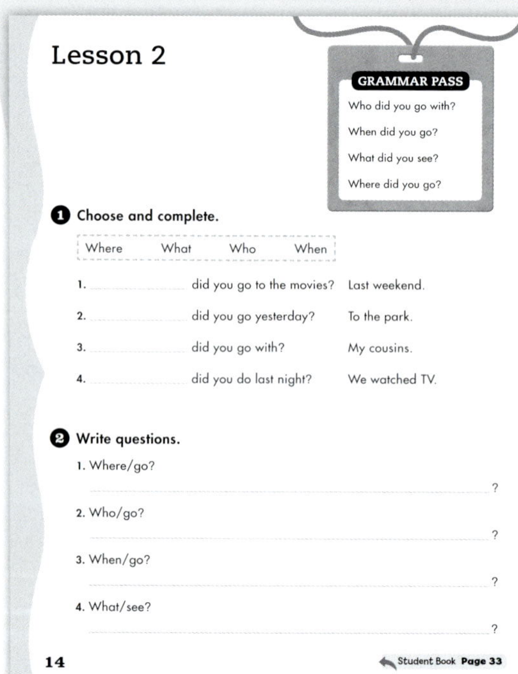
Lesson 2

GRAMMAR PASS
Who did you go with?
When did you go?
What did you see?
Where did you go?

1 Choose and complete.

Where What Who When

1. ________ did you go to the movies? Last weekend.
2. ________ did you go yesterday? To the park.
3. ________ did you go with? My cousins.
4. ________ did you do last night? We watched TV.

2 Write questions.
1. Where/go? ________?
2. Who/go? ________?
3. When/go? ________?
4. What/see? ________?

14

Student Book Page 33

Workbook-style pages in The Language Lodge provide **extensive practice** and review activities to help students **remember** and **assimilate** new language. My Dictionary has students create their own dictionaries to individualize how they learn.

Lesson 3: Vocabulary in Context

Lesson 4: Grammar in Context

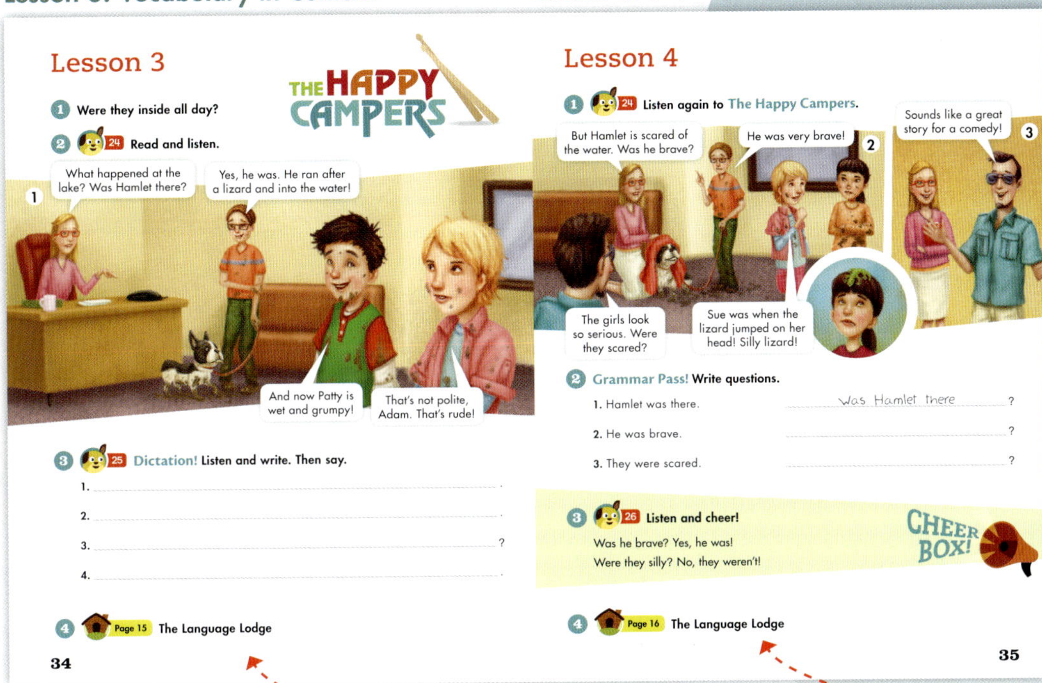

Lesson 3

THE HAPPY CAMPERS

1 Were they inside all day?

2 24 Read and listen.

3 25 Dictation! Listen and write. Then say.

1. .
2. .
3. ?
4. .

4 Page 15 The Language Lodge

34

Lesson 4

1 24 Listen again to The Happy Campers.

2 Grammar Pass! Write questions.

1. Hamlet was there. Was Hamlet there?
2. He was brave. ?
3. They were scared. ?

3 26 Listen and cheer!

Was he brave? Yes, he was!
Were they silly? No, they weren't!

CHEER BOX!

4 Page 16 The Language Lodge

35

"The Happy Campers" is an episodic comic strip story that follows the adventures of a group of children who make a movie. Students will develop reading and listening skills while they learn new vocabulary and grammar structures in context. **Sentence dictation** activities sharpen listening and writing skills. The **class-building grammar cheer** provides a memorable example of the new language.

The Language Lodge activities can be done in class or at home, and can be quickly checked using the **Presentation Kit**.

Lesson 3: Vocabulary Practice

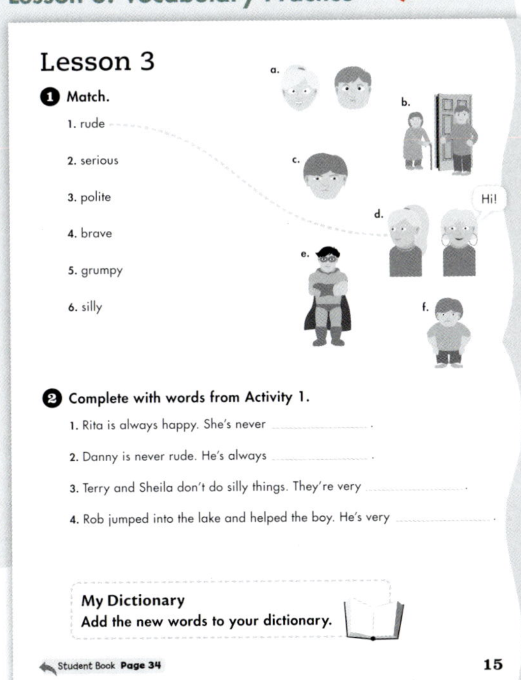

Lesson 3

1 Match.

1. rude
2. serious
3. polite
4. brave
5. grumpy
6. silly

2 Complete with words from Activity 1.

1. Rita is always happy. She's never .
2. Danny is never rude. He's always .
3. Terry and Sheila don't do silly things. They're very .
4. Rob jumped into the lake and helped the boy. He's very .

My Dictionary
Add the new words to your dictionary.

Student Book Page 34

15

Lesson 4: Grammar Practice

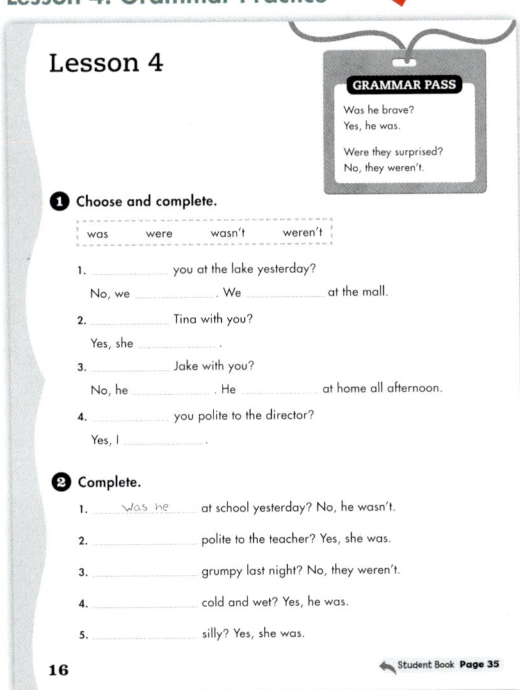

Lesson 4

GRAMMAR PASS
Was he brave?
Yes, he was.
Were they surprised?
No, they weren't.

1 Choose and complete.

was were wasn't weren't

1. you at the lake yesterday?
No, we . We at the mall.
2. Tina with you?
Yes, she .
3. Jake with you?
No, he . He at home all afternoon.
4. you polite to the director?
Yes, I .

2 Complete.

1. Was he at school yesterday? No, he wasn't.
2. polite to the teacher? Yes, she was.
3. grumpy last night? No, they weren't.
4. cold and wet? Yes, he was.
5. silly? Yes, she was.

16

Student Book Page 35

Synthesizing information develops **critical thinking skills**.

Lesson 5: Reading

Good **readers** make good **writers**!

A selection of **fiction** and **nonfiction** texts consolidates and reviews language while developing reading, listening, and fluency skills. Post-reading comprehension activities develop reading skills and comprehension strategies such as identifying details, sequencing events, identifying and describing characters and settings, drawing conclusions, and comparing and contrasting. Graphic organizers develop prewriting skills. These skills help students produce simple explanatory, narrative, and descriptive writing pieces.

Lesson 5

1 Who did Uncle Bob send a gift to?

Gary Mom frogs Andrea

2 27 Read and listen.

Uncle Bob's Jokes

Yesterday was Gary's birthday. He got a special gift from Uncle Bob. The gift box had a joke book, a water bottle, and a stone inside. It was an unusual gift, but jokes can be fun!

He opened the book and started reading a joke. It was called "How to Change Stones into Frogs!" It looked interesting. And Uncle Bob gave him all the things he needed to play the joke on his little sister, Andrea.

Gary and Andrea went into the yard. Gary put the stone in the gift box. Then he put the gift box next to the tree. He poured the water over the stone. "Close your eyes and count to 10, Andrea!" Gary said.

"OK!" Andrea said. She was very excited. She closed her eyes and counted to 10. Gary quietly took the stone out of the box, and put in a frog.

"Ready? OK, look!" Gary said. Andrea opened her eyes, and out jumped a big, fat frog. "Wow! A frog! That's amazing!" she said. "Now I'm going to try one of Uncle Bob's jokes!"

36

Lesson 5

1 Circle the circus performers from the photos.

trapeze artist juggler acrobat unicyclist

2 09 Read and listen.

Circus Arts

Circus arts started a long time ago. People went to the circus to watch performers do interesting things. Now there are a lot of famous circuses all over the world. Some travel the world to perform in different countries.

In the 1980s, a new type of circus started. There were a lot of people at every performance! People were excited about the new circuses, and they got bigger.

Today, circuses have amazing acrobats, dancers, trapeze artists, clowns, and interesting music. They are very talented and beautiful to watch.

Some circuses traveled to many places around the world. The shows were a success. People loved them! The performers were amazing and the costumes were beautiful! Now these shows are so popular that there are performances all over the world!

12

Lesson 5

1 What part of George Washington's body is the text about?

arms legs mouth feet hands tummy

Washington didn't want anyone to know about his bad teeth. He looked for a dentist to make a set of false teeth. John Greenwood was an important dentist in New York. Washington asked him to make false teeth for him. Greenwood made them from the teeth of a hippopotamus. They were strong and white. They were expensive, too.

George Washington wore his new false teeth for his official portrait. Look at his picture on the American dollar bill. Do you think he was wearing his false teeth for that picture, too?

"Walk the dogs," the robot repeated. Then the robot took Joshua's dogs, the small dog on the corner, the dog from the grocery store, and all of the dogs on the street out for a walk!

There were a lot of dogs in the yard, and a lot of angry people. "What did you do, Joshua?" Mom asked. "Oh, no, maybe this isn't the best robot!" Joshua said.

52

Lesson 6: Reading Comprehension / Writing

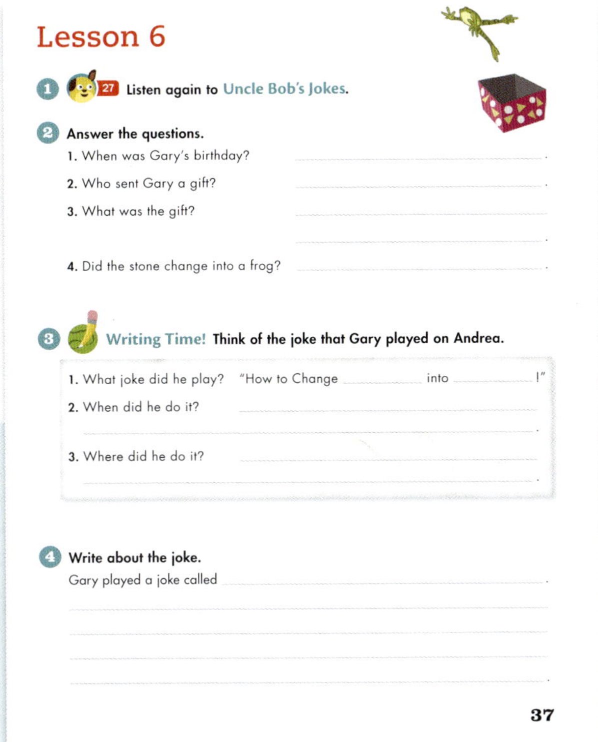

Lesson 6

1 27 Listen again to Uncle Bob's Jokes.

2 Answer the questions.

1. When was Gary's birthday? ________.
2. Who sent Gary a gift? ________.
3. What was the gift? ________.
4. Did the stone change into a frog? ________.

3 Writing Time! Think of the joke that Gary played on Andrea.

1. What joke did he play? "How to Change ________ into ________!"
2. When did he do it? ________.
3. Where did he do it? ________.

4 Write about the joke.

Gary played a joke called ________.

37

Think, create, communicate, and collaborate!

Lesson 7: Creative, Collaborative, and Critical Thinking Competencies

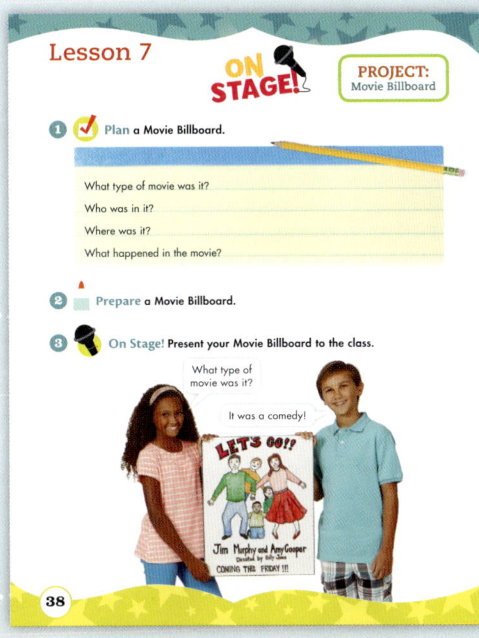

Lesson 7

ON STAGE!

PROJECT: Movie Billboard

1 Plan a Movie Billboard.

What type of movie was it?

Who was in it?

Where was it?

What happened in the movie?

2 Prepare a Movie Billboard.

3 On Stage! Present your Movie Billboard to the class.

38

"The Four Cs"—**critical thinking**, **communication**, **collaboration**, and **creativity**—are essential **21st century skills**. On Stage! lessons have students create, collaborate, and present a project using unit target language. Students put their creativity and communication skills on stage!

Lesson 8: Spelling and Review

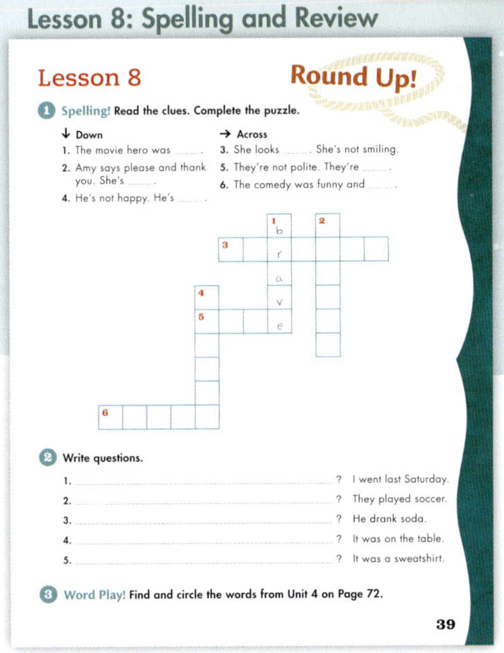

Lesson 8

Round Up!

1 Spelling! Read the clues. Complete the puzzle.

↓ Down

1. The movie hero was ________.
2. Amy says please and thank you. She's ________.
4. He's not happy. He's ________.

→ Across

3. She looks ________. She's not smiling.
5. They're not polite. They're ________.
6. The comedy was funny and ________.

2 Write questions.

1. ________? I went last Saturday.
2. ________? They played soccer.
3. ________? He drank soda.
4. ________? It was on the table.
5. ________? It was a sweatshirt.

3 Word Play! Find and circle the words from Unit 4 on Page 72.

39

Review and consolidation of new language are essential to learning. Seeing their own progress will make students **happy campers**!

Skills Book

The *Happy Campers* **Skills Book** is designed to support students in the development of limited, but specific, **speaking** and **listening**, **reading**, and **writing** skills.

Picture Talk lessons focus on developing simple visual literacy skills to practice vocabulary through speaking and listening.

UNIT 4 Picture Talk

1 Look at the pictures. Find and complete.

DKM Cinemas

western   action movie   musical   documentary   horror   science fiction

DKM Cinemas

1. Danny watched *Big Bats*. It was a documentary
2. Tim watched *Red Sun*. It was a
3. Lou watched *Lost in Time*. It was a ______ movie.
4. Claire watched *Jump Up*. It was an
5. Mo watched *Eyes at Night*. It was a ______ movie.
6. Karen watched *Sunny Sunday*. It was a

Ticket-000

2 Ask and answer.

22 23

Language practice through **skills** practice.

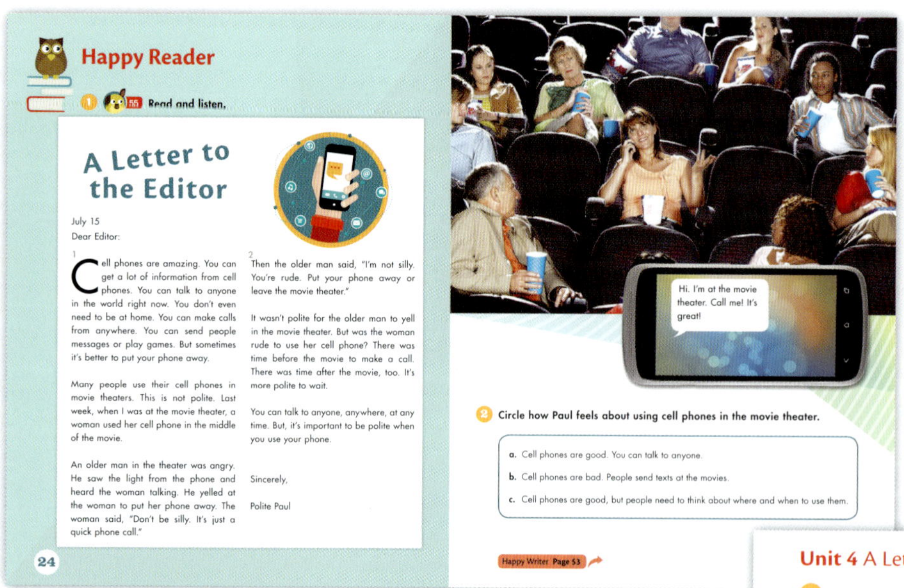
Happy Reader

1 55 Read and listen.

A Letter to the Editor

July 15

Dear Editor:

1 Cell phones are amazing. You can get a lot of information from cell phones. You can talk to anyone in the world right now. You don't even need to be at home. You can make calls from anywhere. You can send people messages or play games. But sometimes it's better to put your phone away.

Many people use their cell phones in movie theaters. This is not polite. Last week, when I was at the movie theater, a woman used her cell phone in the middle of the movie.

An older man in the theater was angry. He saw the light from the phone and heard the woman talking. He yelled at the woman to put her phone away. The woman said, "Don't be silly. It's just a quick phone call."

2 Then the older man said, "I'm not silly. You're rude. Put your phone away or leave the movie theater."

It wasn't polite for the older man to yell in the movie theater. But was the woman rude to use her cell phone? There was time before the movie to make a call. There was time after the movie, too. It's more polite to wait.

You can talk to anyone, anywhere, at any time. But, it's important to be polite when you use your phone.

Sincerely,

Polite Paul

2 Circle how Paul feels about using cell phones in the movie theater.

a. Cell phones are good. You can talk to anyone.
b. Cell phones are bad. People send texts at the movies.
c. Cell phones are good, but people need to think about where and when to use them.

24

Happy Writer Page 53

Happy Reader texts include fiction and nonfiction texts. Each reader is supported by a numbered reading guide and a dramatized reading on the **Class Audio CD**. The lesson includes a reading comprehension activity.

Happy Writer

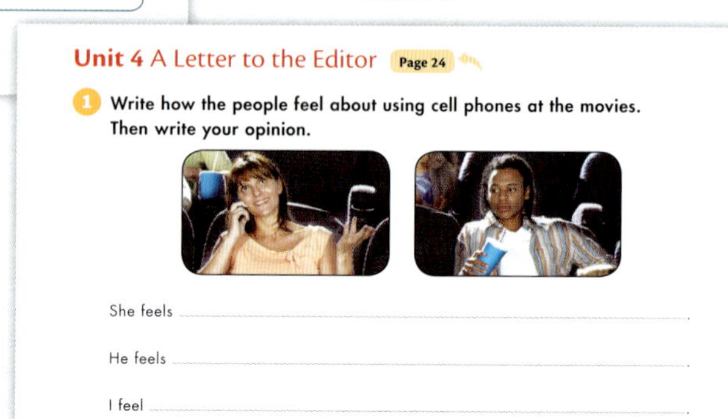
Unit 4 A Letter to the Editor Page 24

1 Write how the people feel about using cell phones at the movies. Then write your opinion.

She feels

He feels

I feel

The **Happy Writer** sections at the back of the Skills Book develop specific writing skills such as summarizing a text, writing a personal narrative, writing an opinion, comparing and contrasting, or retelling a story.

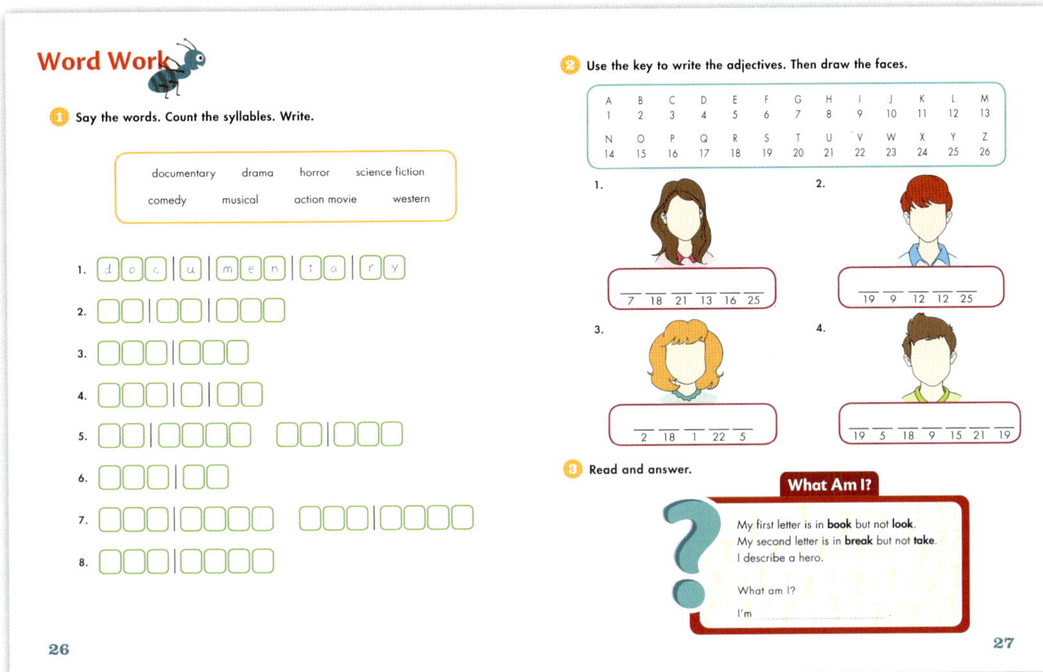
Word Work

1 Say the words. Count the syllables. Write.

documentary drama horror science fiction
comedy musical action movie western

1. d o c | u | m e n | t a | r y
2.
3.
4.
5.
6.
7.
8.

26

2 Use the key to write the adjectives. Then draw the faces.

A	B	C	D	E	F	G	H	I	J	K	L	M
1	2	3	4	5	6	7	8	9	10	11	12	13
N	O	P	Q	R	S	T	U	V	W	X	Y	Z
14	15	16	17	18	19	20	21	22	23	24	25	26

1. 7 18 21 13 16 25
2. 19 9 12 12 25
3. 2 18 1 22 5
4. 19 5 18 9 15 21 19

3 Read and answer.

What Am I?

My first letter is in **book** but not **look**.
My second letter is in **break** but not **take**.
I describe a hero.

What am I?

I'm ______.

27

Word Work

lessons provide spelling, reading, pronunciation, and thinking activities using the unit vocabulary. Students categorize words, find connections, identify spelling patterns, and syllabify words.

What Am I? practices reading comprehension skills and develops **critical thinking** skills such as analyzing information to correctly identify the answer to the riddle.

Happy Campers app

The **Happy Campers and The Inks 6** is available for download from the App Store℠ or Google Play™. It provides **game-based learning** to encourage students to practice unit vocabulary, so that learning continues seamlessly from school to home.

Download on the App Store

GET IT ON Google play

For more information, visit www.macmillanyounglearners.com/happycampers.

The *Happy Campers* **Teacher's Edition** is designed to help teachers **teach well** and create a **positive environment** in which their **students flourish**.

Each unit opens with a comprehensive overview of the language and skills objectives of the unit, allowing teachers to **prepare** for the lessons ahead.

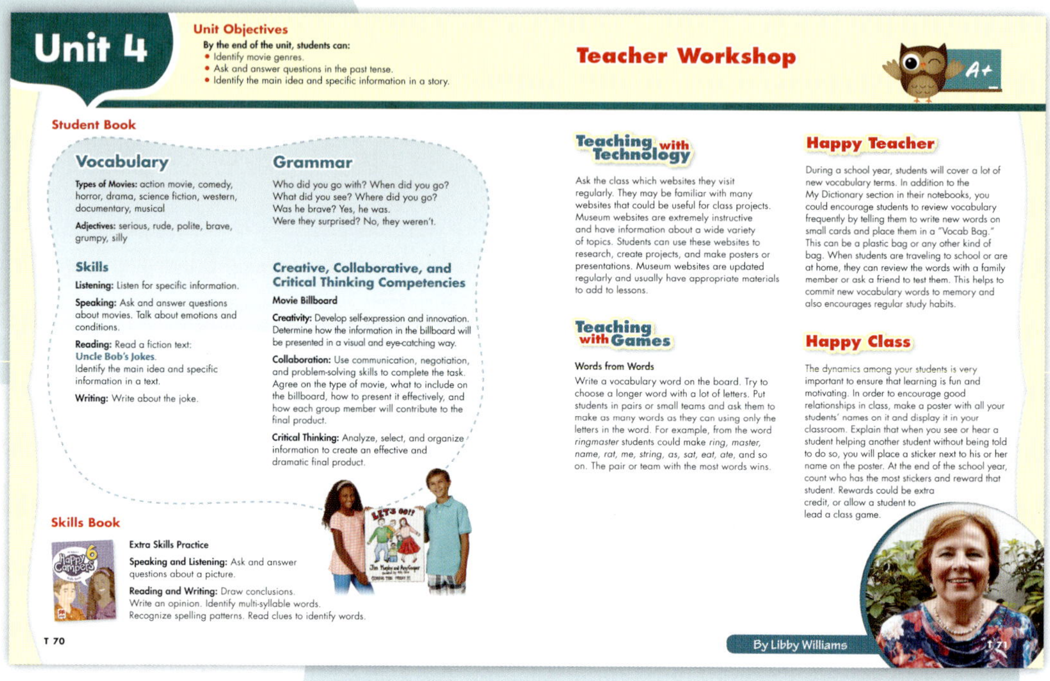

Unit 4

Unit Objectives

By the end of the unit, students can:

- Identify movie genres.
- Ask and answer questions in the past tense.
- Identify the main idea and specific information in a story.

Student Book

Vocabulary

Types of Movies: action movie, comedy, horror, drama, science fiction, western, documentary, musical

Adjectives: serious, rude, polite, brave, grumpy, silly

Grammar

Who did you go with? When did you go?
What did you see? Where did you go?
Was he brave? Yes, he was.
Were they surprised? No, they weren't.

Skills

Listening: Listen for specific information.

Speaking: Ask and answer questions about movies. Talk about emotions and conditions.

Reading: Read a fiction text: **Uncle Bob's Jokes**. Identify the main idea and specific information in a text.

Writing: Write about the joke.

Creative, Collaborative, and Critical Thinking Competencies

Movie Billboard

Creativity: Develop self-expression and innovation. Determine how the information in the billboard will be presented in a visual and eye-catching way.

Collaboration: Use communication, negotiation, and problem-solving skills to complete the task. Agree on the type of movie, what to include on the billboard, how to present it effectively, and how each group member will contribute to the final product.

Critical Thinking: Analyze, select, and organize information to create an effective and dramatic final product.

Skills Book

Extra Skills Practice

Speaking and Listening: Ask and answer questions about a picture.

Reading and Writing: Draw conclusions. Write an opinion. Identify multi-syllable words. Recognize spelling patterns. Read clues to identify words.

T 70

Teacher Workshop

Teaching with Technology

Ask the class which websites they visit regularly. They may be familiar with many websites that could be useful for class projects. Museum websites are extremely instructive and have information about a wide variety of topics. Students can use these websites to research, create projects, and make posters or presentations. Museum websites are updated regularly and usually have appropriate materials to add to lessons.

Teaching with Games

Words from Words

Write a vocabulary word on the board. Try to choose a longer word with a lot of letters. Put students in pairs or small teams and ask them to make as many words as they can using only the letters in the word. For example, from the word *ringmaster* students could make *ring, master, name, rat, me, string, as, sat, eat, ate*, and so on. The pair or team with the most words wins.

Happy Teacher

During a school year, students will cover a lot of new vocabulary terms. In addition to the My Dictionary section in their notebooks, you could encourage students to review vocabulary frequently by telling them to write new words on small cards and place them in a "Vocab Bag." This can be a plastic bag or any other kind of bag. When students are traveling to school or are at home, they can review the words with a family member or ask a friend to test them. This helps to commit new vocabulary words to memory and also encourages regular study habits.

Happy Class

The dynamics among your students is very important to ensure that learning is fun and motivating. In order to encourage good relationships in class, make a poster with all your students' names on it and display it in your classroom. Explain that when you see or hear a student helping another student without being told to do so, you will place a sticker next to his or her name on the poster. At the end of the school year, count who has the most stickers and reward that student. Rewards could be extra credit, or allow a student to lead a class game.

By Libby Williams

T 71

A unique program of ideas from **experienced teacher trainers** enhances the classroom experience. Workshops include ideas on how to use technology in the classroom, teaching with games, and classroom management tips to create a happy, learning-rich classroom environment.

Additional Resources

Presentation Kit icon

Happy Campers app icon

The Language Lodge icon

Skills Book icon

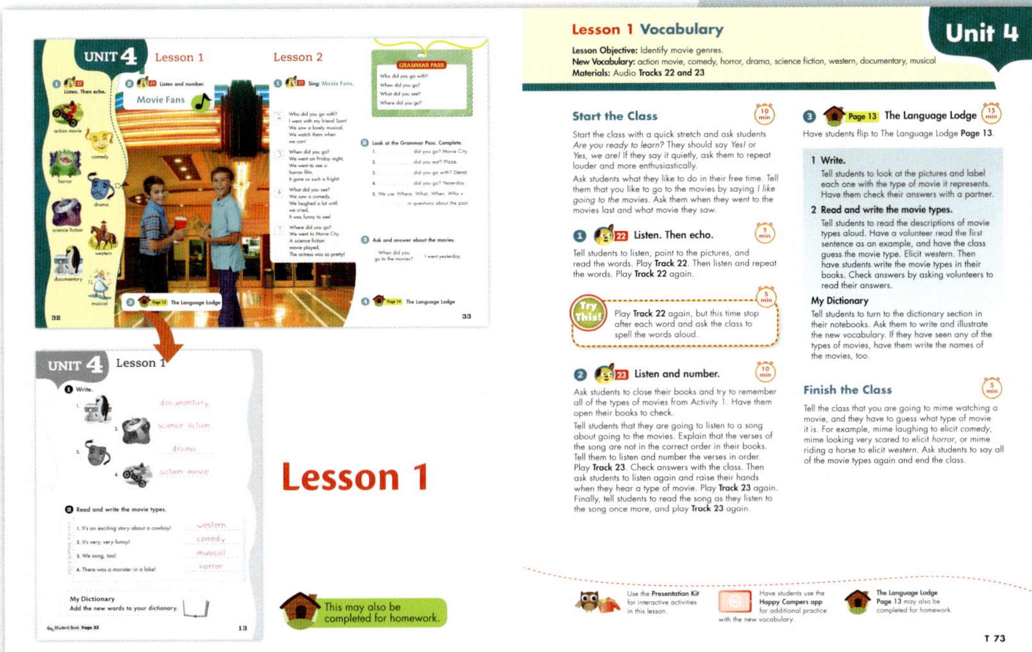

The lesson notes provide a step-by-step guide for teachers to deliver effective, time-efficient classes. Ideas to **start** and **finish** each class, and a **pacing guide** (5 min) are provided to support teachers in keeping students on track.

The interleaved pages provide the Student Book and corresponding pages from The Language Lodge.

Try This! Try This! sections in each lesson feature alternative activities to incorporate into everyday teaching practice.

Continuing professional development, **class by class**.

Class Audio CD

The **Class Audio CD** contains audio tracks for all listening activities across the Student Book and Skills Book. The *Happy Campers* **vibrant music and vocal program** includes echoes, songs, cheers, comic strip stories, and fiction and nonfiction reading and listening texts.

Teacher's Resource Center

The **Teacher's Resource Center** contains a range of downloadable software and materials to support teachers and enrich the *Happy Campers* program.

Assessment Pack

The **Assessment Pack** includes ready-made tests for each unit, as well as mid- and end-of-year tests. The **Test Generator** includes software for teachers to generate their own versions.

Students' native language is **digital**!

Presentation Kit

The **Presentation Kit** is a fully interactive presentation tool that can be used to project all Student Book and The Language Lodge pages. Language presentations are supported by lively **vocabulary echo** and **grammar cheer** videos, as well as **comic strip animations**. Interactive activities can be completed digitally or used to check answers as a whole class.

Visuals Pack

The Happy Campers **Visuals Pack** provides printable vocabulary flashcards and posters.

Happy Actors Pack

The **Happy Actors Pack** has plays, poems, and songs that can be used by students for open days and peer-to-peer performances.

Methodology Handbook

The **Methodology Handbook** is a printable e-book that provides a practical guide to the methodology and thinking behind the *Happy Campers* series.

Planners

Week-by-week **planners** help teachers organize their lessons and get maximum use out of the *Happy Campers* resources.

Creative teaching tools for today's classroom.

Unit 1

Unit Objectives

By the end of the unit, students can:

- Identify circus vocabulary.
- Talk about past experiences.
- Describe a circus.

Student Book

Vocabulary

Circus: circus, big top, ringmaster, parade, trapeze artist, tightrope walker, clown, unicyclist

Review: past tense irregular verb forms

Grammar

We were at the circus.
The big top was beautiful.
There was a circus.
There were tightrope walkers.

Skills

Listening: Listen for and identify circus vocabulary.

Speaking: Describe a circus in the past tense.
Use irregular past tense verbs.

Reading: Read a nonfiction text (social studies): **Circus Arts**.
Identify the main idea and specific information in the text.

Writing: Write about your circus visit.

Creative, Collaborative, and Critical Thinking Competencies

Circus Program

Creativity: Develop self-expression and innovation. Determine how the information in the Circus Program will be presented.

Collaboration: Use communication, negotiation, and problem-solving skills to complete tasks. Determine how each student will agree on the final product.

Critical Thinking: Identify the most important information. Analyze and organize information.

Skills Book

Extra Skills Practice

Speaking and Listening: Make statements about a picture and respond.

Reading and Writing: Recall details.
Summarize part of the text.
Recognize spelling patterns.
Read clues to identify words.
Compare and contrast verb forms.

Teacher Workshop

Teaching with Technology

The Internet is a wonderful resource for materials. Use Internet images to engage students, review new vocabulary, and extend activities. Have students label the images with the new vocabulary. You could use pairs of images and have students describe what is the same and what is different about them. Have students describe the image or use it to start a story.

Teaching with Games

Backs to the Board

Divide the class into teams. Each team chooses a team member, and those students stand with their backs to the board. Write one of the new vocabulary words on the board. Explain that each team can give clues to their team member at the board to help them guess the word. Tell students that they can describe the word, give other word clues, or act it out, but they can't say the word. The first student at the board to guess the word correctly wins a point for the team.

Happy Teacher

Managing classes can be challenging, especially if the classes are large. Setting up routines at the beginning of the year can help structure your lessons and manage students. Routines also help students focus during class, feel secure, and feel part of a community, creating a positive classroom environment. Try the following routine: nominate a class helper each class who writes the date on the board and helps you by handing out materials, reading directions, erasing the board, or setting up or operating technology such as a laptop or a CD player.

Happy Class

To re-energize students, try the following strategy: hold one hand in the air with five fingers up. Say *Five, four …* and put one finger down. Continue to count silently with the remaining fingers, and by the time you get to zero the class should be silent. If you get to zero and the class isn't silent you get a point. If they are silent before you finish counting, the class gets a point.

By Angela Llanas

UNIT 1

Lesson 1

1 04 Listen. Then echo.

circus
big top
ringmaster
parade
trapeze artist
tightrope walker
clown
unicyclist

2 05 Listen and complete.

At the Circus!

1. We were at the circus yesterday!
   The show was so much fun!
   The clowns were so funny!
   It was great for everyone!
2. We were at the circus yesterday!
   The parade was so much fun!
   The ringmaster was so talented!
   It was great for everyone!
3. We were at the circus yesterday!
   The trapeze artists were fun!
   The tightrope walker was amazing!
   It was great for everyone!
4. We were at the circus yesterday!
   The unicyclists were fun!
   The big top was so beautiful!
   It was great for everyone!

3 Page 1 The Language Lodge

8

Lesson 2

1 05 Sing: At the Circus!

GRAMMAR PASS

We were at the circus.

The big top was beautiful.

2 Look at the Grammar Pass. Circle.

1. *Were* talks about one person / more than one person.
2. *Was* talks about one thing / more than one thing.
3. The words *was* and *were* talk about the present / past.

3 Complete with *was* or *were*.

1. The big top ________ beautiful.
2. The tightrope walkers ________ talented.
3. The ringmaster's hat ________ black.
4. We ________ happy.

4 Page 2 The Language Lodge

9

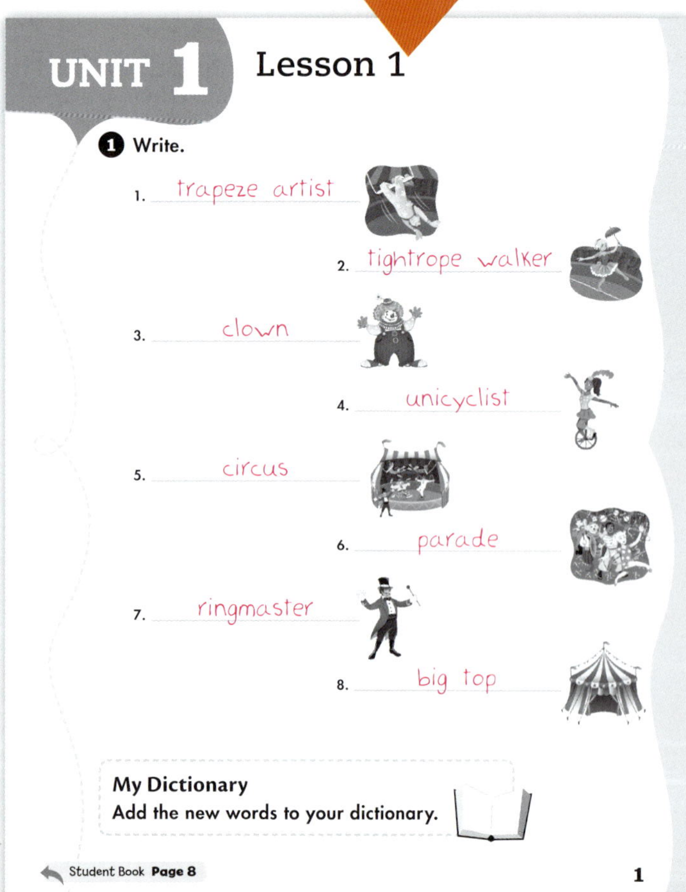

UNIT 1 Lesson 1

1 Write.

1. trapeze artist
2. tightrope walker
3. clown
4. unicyclist
5. circus
6. parade
7. ringmaster
8. big top

My Dictionary
Add the new words to your dictionary.

Student Book **Page 8**

1

Lesson 1

This may also be completed for homework.

Lesson 1 Vocabulary

Lesson Objective: Identify circus vocabulary.
New Vocabulary: circus, big top, ringmaster, parade, trapeze artist, tightrope walker, clown, unicyclist
Materials: Audio **Tracks 04 and 05**

Start the Class

5 min

Write *circus* on the board and ask students to suggest circus words they know. Students may respond in L1. Write the English words on the board.

1 04 Listen. Then echo.

5 min

Have students look at the pictures and identify the words in L1. Tell them to listen and point to the pictures as they hear the words. Play **Track 04**. Then play **Track 04** again and have students echo the words.

Try This! 5 min

Divide the class into two groups and have the groups take turns reading the vocabulary words and echoing them. Organize groups in categories such as boys and girls, students wearing glasses and students not wearing glasses, or students who like cats and students who like dogs. Or you may choose to have students decide how they will be grouped. Once the groups are organized, assign each group a role. Play **Track 04**. Then have the groups switch roles.

2 05 Listen and complete.

10 min

Tell students they are going to listen to a song about the circus. Tell them to read the lyrics in silence. Tell students to think about the words that will complete the sentences. Play **Track 05** once or twice and have students listen and complete the lyrics. Have students check their answers with a partner. Then play **Track 05** again for the class to check their answers. You may choose to pause the audio and have a volunteer say the word each time.

3 Page 1 The Language Lodge

20 min

Have students flip to The Language Lodge **Page 1**.

1 Write.

Draw a picture on the board of a big top. Then have a volunteer come to the board to write the word under or next to the picture. Explain to the class that they will work individually to write the word for each picture. Walk around the classroom to monitor students and provide help as needed. Have volunteers write the answers on the board.

My Dictionary

Explain to the class that they are going to be making their own dictionaries throughout the year. Tell them to keep a part of their notebooks for their dictionaries. Explain that they will be adding to it each time they have new vocabulary. Have students write the new words in their dictionary pages and draw a picture for each item to illustrate the meaning. When they have finished, tell them to learn the new spellings. Have volunteers write the new words on the board.

Finish the Class

5 min

Have the class stand up, shake their bodies, and stretch their arms up and then down while taking a deep breath. This will help them cool down toward the end of the lesson. Have volunteers mime one of the new words for the rest of the class to guess.

Use the **Presentation Kit** for interactive activities in this lesson.

Have students use the **Happy Campers app** for additional practice with the new vocabulary.

The Language Lodge Page 1 may also be completed for homework.

Lesson 2 Grammar

Lesson Objective: Describe a circus visit.
New Grammar: We were at the circus. The big top was beautiful.
Vocabulary Review: circus, big top, ringmaster, parade, trapeze artist, tightrope walker, clown, unicyclist
Materials: Audio **Track 05**, images of Lesson 1 vocabulary

Start the Class

5 min

Show the class images of the vocabulary words from Lesson 1 and have students identify them aloud. Repeat two or three times. Then change the order of the images and ask students to identify them.

1 05 Sing: At the Circus!

5 min

Tell students they are going to listen to "At the Circus!" again. Play **Track 05** and have students listen and read the lyrics. Play **Track 05** again and have the class sing along.

Try This!

5 min

Tell students they are going to sing the song again, and when they get to the last line in each verse, they will stand up, sing the line, and then sit down. You may choose to use other movements such as clapping, stomping feet, or raising arms. Play **Track 05**.

2 Look at the Grammar Pass. Circle.

10 min

Tell students to look at the song lyrics and find sentences with *was* or *were* in them. Have students read them aloud. After each sentence, ask *Is this sentence about one thing or more than one thing?* Then tell students to read the Grammar Pass and complete the activity by circling the correct answers. Read the first part of each sentence and have the class complete it together aloud. Finally, choose a few sentences from the song with *was* or *were* in them. Tell the class you are going to say a sentence. Explain that if the sentence is about one person or thing, they will sit. If the sentence is about two or more people or things, they will stand. When you have done this, you could vary the activity and provide more practice by nominating students to choose and say the sentences.

3 Complete with *was* or *were*.

5 min

Tell students to complete the sentences with *was* or *were*. Have students compare their answers with a partner, then have volunteers write the complete sentences on the board.

4 Page 2 The Language Lodge

15 min

Have students flip to The Language Lodge **Page 2**. Have a volunteer read the Grammar Pass aloud.

1 Complete with *was* or *were*.

Complete the first sentence aloud with the class. Then have students complete the sentences in their books. Tell them to compare answers with a partner. Then have volunteers read the completed sentences for the whole class to check.

2 Choose and complete.

Tell students to look at the words in the box and read the conversation. Have them work with a partner to choose the correct word from the box and write it in their books to complete the conversation. Walk around the classroom and help as needed. Then have volunteers share their answers aloud.

Finish the Class

5 min

Tell students to close their books. Write a location on the board, for example, *at the movies*. Put students into teams of three or four. Tell each team to write a complete sentence using the location on the board and *was* or *were* as quickly as possible. The first team to stand up and read a complete correct sentence scores a point. Repeat with other locations.

Use the **Presentation Kit** for interactive activities in this lesson.

The Language Lodge Page 2 may also be completed for homework.

For additional class time, use **Pages 4 and 5** of the Skills Book. Go to **Page 160** in the Happy Campers Teacher's Edition for teacher notes for this lesson. You may also choose to assign these pages as homework.

UNIT 1

Lesson 1

1 04 Listen. Then echo.

2 05 Listen and complete.

At the Circus!

1. We were at the circus yesterday!
The show was so much fun!
The ______ were so funny!
It was great for everyone!

2. We were at the circus yesterday!
The ______ was so much fun!
The ______ was so talented!
It was great for everyone!

3. We were at the circus yesterday!
The ______ were fun!
The ______ was amazing!
It was great for everyone!

4. We were at the circus yesterday!
The ______ were fun!
The ______ was so beautiful!
It was great for everyone!

3 Page 1 The Language Lodge

Lesson 2

1 05 Sing: At the Circus!

GRAMMAR PASS

We were at the circus.

The big top was beautiful.

2 Look at the Grammar Pass. Circle.

1. *Were* talks about
one person / (more than one person)
2. *Was* talks about
(one thing) / more than one thing.
3. The words *was* and *were* talk about
the present / (past.)

3 Complete with *was* or *were*.

1. The big top __was__ beautiful.
2. The tightrope walkers __were__ talented.
3. The ringmaster's hat __was__ black.
4. We __were__ happy.

4 Page 2 The Language Lodge

Lesson 2

This may also be completed for homework.

Lesson 2

GRAMMAR PASS

We were at the circus.

The big top was beautiful.

1 Complete with *was* or *were*.

1. We __were__ at the movie theater yesterday.
2. The movie __was__ good.
3. They __were__ at a party last weekend.
4. The game __was__ fun!
5. My brother and I __were__ at home last night.

2 Choose and complete.

were was

1. Julia: Where __were__ you yesterday?
2. Peter: We __were__ at a concert. It was fun!
3. Anna: Dan __was__ there.
And Jack and Carla __were__ there, too.
4. Julia: Where __was__ the concert?
5. Peter: It __was__ in the park.

Student Book Page 9

Lesson 3

THE HAPPY CAMPERS

1 What is in Jason's hand?

2 06 Read and listen.

3 07 **Dictation!** Listen and write. Then say.

1. We got tickets and went to the circus.
2. The acrobats did great tricks.
3. They wore wonderful costumes.
4. We sang and won the talent show.

4 Page 3 The Language Lodge

Lesson 4

1 06 Listen again to The Happy Campers.

2 **Grammar Pass!** Complete.

1. There ______ a tightrope walker.
2. The trapeze artists ______ wonderful costumes.
3. The clowns ______ great tricks!
4. Look what I ______ today!

3 08 Listen and cheer!

There was a circus. Fun, fun, fun!
There were trapeze artists. Hooray! Hooray!

CHEER BOX!

4 Page 4 The Language Lodge

Lesson 3

1 Find and circle six past tense verbs. Then write.

Z	Q	X	P	G	V	S
D	I	D	R	O	Y	A
W	O	N	Z	T	W	Z
X	S	A	N	G	O	O
W	E	N	T	V	R	G
Y	V	X	Z	Q	E	X
D	I	J	B	E	H	T

1. go went
2. wear wore
3. do did
4. get got
5. sing sang
6. win won

2 Complete with past tense verbs from the puzzle in Activity 1.

1. Yesterday I won first prize for my circus story at school.
2. We went to the park last weekend.
3. We sang songs in music class yesterday.
4. He did his homework last night.
5. She got a gift from her cousin last night.

My Dictionary
Add the new words to your dictionary.

Student Book Page 10

Lesson 3

This may also be completed for homework.

Lesson 3 Vocabulary in Context

Lesson Objective: Show understanding of irregular past tense verb forms.
New Vocabulary: irregular past tense verb forms
Vocabulary Review: circus, tightrope walker, trapeze artist
Materials: Audio **Tracks 06 and 07**, a ball

Start the Class

5 min

Play Backs to the Board (see **Page T 17**) with the new circus vocabulary. Play **Track 02** and have the class say the names of the characters aloud along with the audio.

1 What is in Jason's hand?

5 min

Have students look at the comic strip pictures. Ask *Where are the Happy Campers?* Direct students' attention to what Jason has in his hand and ask *What is in Jason's hand?* Elicit ideas and write them on the board.

2 06 Read and listen.

10 min

Tell students to read the comic strip as they listen. Play **Track 06**. Ask *What is in Jason's hand?* Elicit *a letter*. Play **Track 06** again and have students read and listen. Ask *What are the Happy Campers going to do?* Elicit *They're going to be in a movie*. Finally, have students read the comic strip independently and circle all the verbs in the past tense verb forms.

3 07 Dictation! Listen and write. Then say.

10 min

Tell students they will hear sentences and write what they hear. Play the first sentence of **Track 07** and pause the audio to allow students time to write. Repeat with the other sentences. Tell the class that they are going to hear the audio again and this time they will say the sentences after they hear them. Play **Track 07** again and monitor student pronunciation. Have volunteers write the sentences on the board for the class to check.

*Audio script **Track 07***
1. *We got tickets and went to the circus.*
2. *The acrobats did great tricks.*
3. *They wore wonderful costumes.*
4. *We sang and won the talent show.*

4 Page 3 The Language Lodge

15 min

Have students flip to The Language Lodge **Page 3**.

1 Find and circle six past tense verbs. Then write.

Explain that students have to find and circle six past tense verbs in the box and then write each one next to the correct present tense form of that verb. Check answers with the class.

2 Complete with past tense verbs from the puzzle in Activity 1.

Have a student read the first example sentence aloud. Then have students work in pairs to complete the other sentences using past tense verbs from Activity 1. Check answers with the class.

My Dictionary

Tell students to write the present and past tense verb forms in the dictionary section of their notebooks, along with a sentence for each form of the verb. Check that they have written the verbs and sentences correctly.

Finish the Class

5 min

Put the class into two teams. Have teams face each other, and give a ball to one student on Team A. Tell the student to say a present tense verb, for example, *win*, and toss the ball to a student on Team B. The student on Team B says the past tense form of the verb, for example, *won* and tosses the ball back to a different student on Team A, and so on. If a student cannot provide the past tense verb, the other team gets a point. Have the teams switch roles so that Team A gets practice using past tense verb forms.

Use the **Presentation Kit** for interactive activities in this lesson.

Have students use the **Happy Campers app** for additional practice with the new vocabulary.

The Language Lodge Page 3 may also be completed for homework.

Lesson 4 Grammar in Context

Lesson Objective: Talk about the circus using *There was/were.*
New Grammar: There was a circus. There were tightrope walkers.
Vocabulary Review: past tense irregular verb forms
Materials: Audio **Tracks 06 and 08**

Start the Class

5 min

Scramble the past tense verbs from Lesson 3 (*wore, went, did, sang, won, got*) and write them on the board (*rowe, tenw, idd, gans, onw, otg*). Put students into teams. Nominate one student to write for each team. Tell teams to unscramble the verbs. The first team to write all the verbs correctly wins.

1 06 Listen again to The Happy Campers.

5 min

Tell students to open their books, look at the pictures, and identify the characters. Ask students what they remember about the comic strip. Tell them to listen to the audio and read along again. Play **Track 06**. Then tell students to circle sentences with *There was* or *There were* in the comic strip. Play **Track 06** again.

Try This! 5 min

Divide the class into groups of four and assign one character from the comic strip to each group member. Give students time to rehearse their lines. Have groups stand at the board and read the comic strip. When a character speaks, a student takes a step forward. After reading, the student steps back.

2 Grammar Pass! Complete.

15 min

Have students look at the sentences they circled in Activity 1. Elicit when we use *There was* and when we use *There were* (to talk about one person or thing or to talk about more than one person or thing in the past). Elicit the circus performers from Lesson 1 and write them in a column on the right side of the board. Then write *There* on the left side of the board and *was* and *were* in a column in the center of the board. Have students work in pairs to make sentences using the words. Check that students are using a singular noun with *There was* and a plural noun with *There were*. Have pairs say one of their sentences. Write two or three sentences on the board. Leave them on the board for the Finish the Class activity. Have students read and complete the Grammar Pass activity in pairs. Then check answers with another pair.

3 08 Listen and cheer!

5 min

Tell students to read and listen to the cheer. Play **Track 08**. Then tell them to say the cheer, and play **Track 08** again.

4 Page 4 The Language Lodge

10 min

Have students flip to The Language Lodge **Page 4**. Have a volunteer read the Grammar Pass aloud.

1 Complete with *There was* or *There were*.

Have students complete the sentences in pairs. Tell pairs to share their answers.

2 Look and write.

Have students look at the pictures. Then have a student read the example sentence aloud. Have students work in pairs to write sentences about the other pictures using *There was* or *There were*. Have students share with the class.

Finish the Class

5 min

Have students study the sentences on the board for one minute. Tell them to close their eyes. Erase two words. Have students open their eyes and say the missing words. Continue until all words have been erased and students can say the sentences from memory.

Use the **Presentation Kit** for interactive activities in this lesson.

The Language Lodge Page 4 may also be completed for homework.

Lesson 3

1 What is in Jason's hand?

2 06 Read and listen.

3 07 **Dictation!** Listen and write. Then say.

1. ____________________.
2. ____________________.
3. ____________________.
4. ____________________.

4 Page 3 The Language Lodge

Lesson 4

1 06 Listen again to The Happy Campers.

2 **Grammar Pass!** Complete.

1. There __was__ a tightrope walker.
2. The trapeze artists __wore__ wonderful costumes.
3. The clowns __did__ great tricks!
4. Look what I __got__ today!

3 08 Listen and cheer!

There was a circus. Fun, fun, fun!
There were trapeze artists. Hooray! Hooray!

CHEER BOX!

4 Page 4 The Language Lodge

Lesson 4

This may also be completed for homework.

Lesson 4

GRAMMAR PASS

There was a circus.

There were tightrope walkers.

1 Complete with *There was* or *There were*.

1. __There were__ jugglers at the circus yesterday.
2. __There was__ a unicyclist.
3. __There was__ a clown.
4. __There were__ a lot of people.

2 Look and write.

1. There was a big top. 
2. __There were trapeze artists__. 
3. __There was a tightrope walker__. 
4. __There was a ringmaster__. 
5. __There were clowns__. 

Student Book Page 11

Lesson 5

Lesson 5

1 **Circle the circus performers from the photos.**

trapeze artist   juggler   acrobat   unicyclist

2 09 **Read and listen.**

Circus Arts

Circus arts started a long time ago. People went to the circus to watch performers do interesting things. Now there are a lot of famous circuses all over the world. Some travel the world to perform in different countries.

In the 1980s, a new type of circus started. There were a lot of people at every performance! People were excited about the new circuses, and they got bigger.

Today, circuses have amazing acrobats, dancers, trapeze artists, clowns, and interesting music. They are very talented and beautiful to watch.

Some circuses traveled to many places around the world. The shows were a success. People loved them! The performers were amazing and the costumes were beautiful! Now these shows are so popular that there are performances all over the world!

Lesson 5 Nonfiction Reading

Lesson Objective: Read a nonfiction text to practice unit language.
Vocabulary Review: trapeze artist, clown, ringmaster, acrobat, unicyclist
Grammar Review: *There was/were*
Materials: Audio **Track 09**

Start the Class

5 min

Ask students if they have been to a circus (or seen a circus on TV) and, if so, ask what they saw. Encourage them to use full sentences. If students have not been to or seen a circus, tell them to describe or invent their own circus experiences.

1 Circle the circus performers from the photos.

5 min

Tell students to open their books, look at the pictures, and say what they can see. Have a volunteer read the directions for Activity 1. Have students circle three performers they can see in the pictures. Check the answers with the class.

2 09 Read and listen.

20 min

Tell students to read the text as they listen to the audio. Play **Track 09**. Have students work in pairs to take turns reading alternate paragraphs of the text. Check comprehension by asking questions, for example, *Are there a lot of circuses? Do circuses today have acrobats? What started in the 1980s?*

Have pairs write one question about the text to ask another pair. Walk around the classroom and monitor the activity. Answer students' questions if they have any and correct if necessary.

Have one pair of students ask their question aloud. Tell the rest of the class to answer the question. Make sure each pair's questions are asked and answered.

Try This!

10 min

Explain to the class that you will point to one of the pictures and students will quickly read the text to find a sentence that is relevant to the picture. Tell them that several sentences in the text may be relevant. Point to one of the pictures and tell students to raise their hands when they have found a relevant sentence (or sentences). Accept all answers that relate to the picture you pointed to. You could also point to two of the pictures of performers to elicit the sentences *They are very talented and beautiful to watch* or *The performers were amazing and the costumes were beautiful!* The goal of the activity is to develop skimming skills and comprehension of the text. Conduct the activity at a fairly fast pace to add a competitive element and make it fun.

Finish the Class

10 min

Have students look at the pictures from the text for one minute and try to remember as much as they can. After a minute, tell students to close their books. Put students in teams. Ask questions about the pictures. Students have to answer as quickly as possible. For every correct answer, the team scores a point.

Use the **Presentation Kit** for interactive activities in this lesson.

Lesson 6 Reading Comprehension / Writing

Lesson Objectives: Identify the main idea and details in a nonfiction text. Write about a circus visit.
Vocabulary Review: trapeze artist, clown, ringmaster, acrobat, unicyclist, circus
Grammar Review: There were many people. The show was a success.
Materials: Audio **Track 09**

Start the Class

5 min

Review vocabulary from Lesson 1 by playing the Shark Game. Draw steps leading to water with a shark in it. Draw a stick figure on the top step. Think of one of the words and write the relevant number of blank spaces on the board. Tell students to guess letters. If the letter is in the word, write it in the appropriate blank space. If the letter isn't in the word, move the stick figure down a step. Tell students they have to guess the word before the shark eats the person. You could play the game as a class or have students play in groups.

1 09 Listen again to Circus Arts.

10 min

Tell students they are going to listen to "Circus Arts" again. Make sure that they follow the text in their books as they listen. Play **Track 09**. Then play **Track 09** again and stop the audio at regular intervals. Ask students to tell you what they remember.

2 Circle *True* or *False*.

5 min

Tell students to read the text, but this time have them read the text individually. Then put students into pairs. Have them read the statements and refer back to the text to decide if the statements are true or false. Have them circle the correct answer in their books for each statement. Once everyone has finished, have students share their answers with the class. Tell students to give evidence from the text to justify their answers.

Try This!

5 min

When you are moving from reading to writing, oral work can bridge and support these two skills. Put students into pairs and have them ask and answer the questions in Activity 3 orally. You may want to ask them to find similarities and differences in the answers. Monitor and help as necessary. Encourage students to speak in full sentences and help them with vocabulary. Have volunteers demonstrate for the class.

3 Writing Time! Answer the questions.

10 min

Have students work individually to write their answers to the questions. Tell students they can invent a circus if they haven't seen one. Tell students to compare their answers with a partner. Have as many students as possible share their answers with the class.

4 Write about your visit to the circus.

10 min

Explain that students will use their answers from Activity 3 to write a paragraph about their circus visits. Read *The last time I went to the circus …* and have students complete the sentence aloud. Then have students work individually to write a paragraph. Walk around the classroom to monitor students' work. Check that they are using past tense verbs correctly. Encourage them to read their work when they have finished to correct any mistakes and, if necessary, write a clean, corrected version. Have volunteers share their paragraphs with the class. Encourage positive feedback.

Finish the Class

5 min

Have students read each other's paragraph about their circus visits. Then ask and answer questions about it.

Use the **Presentation Kit** for interactive activities in this lesson.

For additional class time, use **Pages 6 and 7** of the Skills Book. Go to **Page 161** in the Happy Campers Teacher's Edition for teacher notes for this lesson. You may also choose to assign these pages as homework.

Lesson 6

Lesson 6

1 09 Listen again to Circus Arts.

2 Circle *True* or *False*.

1. Circus arts are not famous all over the world. True **False** (circled)
2. There were a lot of people at every performance. **True** (circled) False
3. People were excited about the new circuses. **True** (circled) False
4. The shows were a success. **True** (circled) False

3 Writing Time! Answer the questions.

1. When was the last time you went to the circus?
(Students' own answers) .
2. Where was the circus?
(Students' own answers) .
3. What acts were there?
(Students' own answers) .
4. Which was your favorite act?
(Students' own answers) .

4 Write about your visit to the circus.

The last time I went to the circus ______.

(Students' own answers)

______.

Lesson 7

Lesson 7

ON STAGE!

PROJECT: Circus Program

1 **Plan** your Circus Program. Choose a name. Write about your circus artists.

Name of Circus: (Students'

Location: own

Ticket Price: answers.)

Artists:

2 **Prepare** your Circus Program.

3 **On Stage!** Tell the class about your Circus Program.

We went to the Sunshine Circus.

There was a clown. He was cool!

Lesson 7 Creative, Collaborative, and Critical Thinking Activity

Lesson Objective: Plan, create, and present a Circus Program.
Vocabulary Review: circus, big top, ringmaster, parade, trapeze artist, tightrope walker, clown, unicyclist
Grammar Review: past tense irregular verb forms, *there was/were*
Materials: construction paper, glue, scissors, markers

Start the Class

5 min

Show students an example of a circus program. You can find examples by typing in "circus program" in a search engine, or you can use the information you find to create your own example program. Put students into pairs to look at the program and identify (1) what information it contains, (2) how the information is presented, and (3) how pictures enhance the information.

Bring the class back together to share the information they found in the circus program. A good example of a program should contain the circus name, location, ticket price, and a list of circus artists. Guide the class to categorize the information in this way, as it will help them with Activities 1 and 2.

1 Plan your Circus Program. Choose a name. Write about your circus artists.

10 min

Have a volunteer read the directions for Activity 1. Tell the class that they will create a circus program in pairs. Put students in pairs and tell them to read and complete the chart. Encourage them to be imaginative and to come up with funny, unusual, and/or interesting information about the circus and artists. For example, the circus could be located on the moon, or all the performers could be children. Monitor to make sure that both students are contributing equally in each pair and provide help as needed.

2 Prepare your Circus Program.

15 min

Distribute materials to each pair. Tell students that they will create their own Circus Programs. Have them look at the program the two girls are holding in the photo as an example. Tell students to use the information they planned in Activity 1 to prepare their programs, and to decorate their programs with images and drawings.

Encourage pairs to discuss and agree on the design and layout of the program and what each partner will do to create the program. Walk around the classroom to encourage and help as necessary.

3 On Stage! Tell the class about your Circus Program.

10 min

Tell students to imagine they have been to the circus they created, and they are going to tell their friends about it. Tell them to look at the photo. Ask students what the girls in the photo are talking about (*the circus*), what they did (*They went to the circus*), and what they saw (*There were acrobats, There was a unicyclist*, etc.). Model the example dialogue with a confident student. Put each pair together with another pair and have them take turns to present their Circus Programs. If there is time, ask pairs to present their programs to the whole class.

Try This!

5 min

Before students present to the class, hold a quick discussion about what makes a good presentation, such as speaking clearly, using their programs as visual aids, pointing to information or pictures while speaking, smiling and looking at the audience, and thanking the audience at the end. Make a brief list of ideas on the board. Encourage students to remember these tips when they give their presentations.

Finish the Class

5 min

Display all the Circus Programs around the classroom. Give students a little time to look at them all, and then take a class vote on the best Circus Program.

Use the **Presentation Kit** for interactive activities in this lesson.

Lesson 8 Review

Lesson Objective: Review language from Unit 1.
Vocabulary Review: circus, big top, ringmaster, parade, trapeze artist, tightrope walker, clown, unicyclist, past tense irregular verb forms
Grammar Review: We were at the circus. The big top was beautiful. There was a circus. There were tightrope walkers.

Start the Class

10 min

Put students in groups of six to eight. Give each student a sheet of paper. Have each student write his or her favorite circus word on the paper. Then have the teams pool their words together, and write one sentence using for each word on their sheets of paper. They can add any words they need to make their sentence grammatically correct. Have each team read their sentence to the rest of the class.

1 Spelling! Write.

5 min

Tell students to look at the pictures, then label them on the lines with the correct word. Have them work individually, and tell them to try not to look in their books or notebooks, but to try to remember how to spell the words on their own. Monitor and provide help as needed. Have students compare their answers in pairs. Then check answers with the whole class.

2 Choose and complete with the past tense verbs.

5 min

Have a volunteer read the directions. Put students into pairs. Tell them to look at the verbs in the box, read the text, and choose verbs from the box to complete the text. Walk around the classroom to monitor and help if necessary. Check answers with the class.

Try This!

10 min

Write half of each vocabulary word from Unit 1 on pieces of paper, for example, cir/cus. Give each student a piece of paper. Make sure that you distribute matching pairs, so that every student can find the other half of his or her vocabulary item. Shuffle the papers before handing them out so that the word halves are not given to neighboring students. Tell students to hold their pieces of paper up in front of them and walk around the classroom to find the other halves of their vocabulary items as quickly as they can.

3 Word Play! Find and circle the words from Unit 1 on Page 72.

10 min

Have students turn to **Page 72** and tell them to find and circle the circus and past tense verb vocabulary words from Unit 1. Then have students check the words they found with a partner.

Finish the Class

10 min

Tell students to go to the dictionary section in their notebooks and check that all the words they have circled in Activity 3 are in their dictionaries. Give them time to add words if necessary.

Finish the class by reflecting with students about what they can now do, for example, use *There was* and *There were*, name circus artists, describe a circus using past tense verbs.

Use the **Presentation Kit** for interactive activities in this lesson.

For additional class time, use **Pages 8 and 9** of the Skills Book. Go to **Page 162** in the Happy Campers Teacher's Edition for teacher notes for this lesson. You may also choose to assign these pages as homework.

Lesson 8

Lesson 8

Round Up!

1 Spelling! Write.

1. parade

2. trapeze artist

3. circus

4. tightrope walker

5. unicyclist

2 Choose and complete with the past tense verbs.

sang   wore   were   went   was

We went to the circus yesterday. There were acrobats, unicyclists, and dancers. They wore beautiful costumes. There was a singer, too. She sang a lot of songs. The acrobats were great! It was a great evening!

3 Word Play! Find and circle the words from Unit 1 on Page 72.

Unit 2

Unit Objectives

By the end of the unit, students can:

- Identify movie vocabulary.
- Talk about past events.
- Sequence information in a reading text.

Student Book

Vocabulary

Movies 1: movie studio, director, cameraman, scene, cartoon, producer, movie star, script

Movies 2: personal assistant, makeup artist, sound engineer, "Positions, please," "Action," "Cut"

Grammar

I talked to a movie star.
The director wave at me!
She sat in the office. They ate pizza.

Skills

Listening: Listen for and identify people and elements involved in making movies.

Speaking: Ask and answer questions about making movies.
Talk about past events.

Reading: Read a fiction text: **Ivan's Movie**.
Identify the main idea and specific information in the text.

Writing: Sequence events.
Write about your movie.

Creative, Collaborative, and Critical Thinking Competencies

Movie Storyboard

Creativity: Develop self-expression and innovation. Determine the information and scenes to be included in the Movie Storyboard.

Collaboration: Use communication, negotiation, and problem-solving skills to reach decisions and complete tasks. Discuss and agree on how each student will contribute to the final product.

Critical Thinking: Identify key elements in the chosen movie. Analyze and organize associated pictures and words to create the movie storyboard.

Skills Book

Extra Skills Practice

Speaking and Listening: Describe two pictures by finding differences between them.

Reading and Writing: Identify the sequence of events. Recall details.

Teacher Workshop

Teaching with Technology

There are free websites that allow students to create their own movies using cell phone photos or videos. Using these websites, students can create a movie. They can select photos, upload them, and write a sentence in English for each photo and show their movies in class.

Teaching with Games

Snap!

Materials: card stock, scissors

Make pairs of cards, such as pairs with matching words and pictures, to practice new vocabulary items. Shuffle the cards together to make one set. Students place the cards face down and take turns turning over two cards at a time. The goal of the game is to find matching pairs. When a student finds a matching pair, he or she says *Snap!* The student with the most pairs is the winner.

Happy Teacher

It is important to organize students in groups quickly to maximize valuable class time. If students are sitting in rows, the quickest way is to have pairs of students turn around and face the pair behind them to make a group of four. If you want to mix students, you can give each student a number: one, two, three, or four. Tell all number fours to go to one corner, all the threes to go to another corner, and so on.

For project work, put students in set groups that they will always be in for project lessons. Have these groups sit in the same place in the classroom each time.

Happy Class

Explain to students that they should not make a lot of noise in class. A fun way to demonstrate without being noisy is to whisper a number from one to five to each student. Tell students they have to find other students with the same number without talking. They can gesture, point, or draw something on a piece of paper.

Tell students if they are making too much noise, you will indicate this with a special signal, such as raising your hand. When students see this, they must stop talking for a moment, and then they can resume talking quietly.

By Gabriel Diaz Maggioli

UNIT 2

Lesson 1

1 [10] Listen. Then echo.

2 [11] Listen and circle.

Making Movies

3 Page 5 The Language Lodge

Lesson 2

1 [11] Sing: Making Movies.

I like the theater! I also like TV!
But movies on the big screen
Are what I like to see!

1. I visited a studio / theater.
It was great to see!
I talked to a movie star / producer,
The director waved at me!

2. I read a movie script / cartoon,
There were exciting scenes!
The cameraman / director
filmed me,
For the big screen!

GRAMMAR PASS

I talked to a movie star.

The director waved at me!

2 Look at the Grammar Pass. Complete.

1. I ________ to a movie star. (talk)
2. He ________ me a scene. (show)
3. I ________ a movie studio. (visit)
4. Regular verbs add ________ to talk about the past.

3 Unscramble.

1. the / talked / cameraman / They / to
They talked to the cameraman.
2. movie / I / the / watched
________.
3. a / filmed / He / scene
________.

4 Page 6 The Language Lodge

UNIT 2 Lesson 1

1 Write. Then find and circle the movie words.

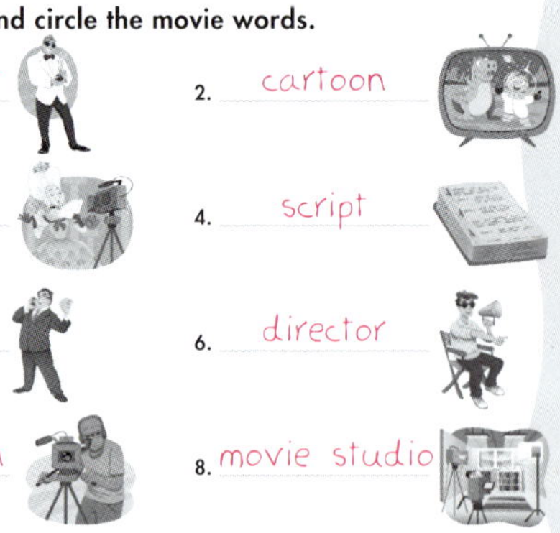

1. movie star
2. cartoon
3. scene
4. script
5. producer
6. director
7. cameraman
8. movie studio

S	R	M	O	V	I	E	S	T	U	D	I	O	L	D	S
T	C	A	R	M	D	D	I	R	E	C	T	O	R	E	C
E	O	E	M	N	T	I	N	O	R	L	O	V	I	C	R
R	S	N	N	I	Y	S	E	C	A	R	T	O	O	N	I
N	P	I	S	E	R	M	P	R	O	D	U	C	E	R	P
C	A	M	E	R	A	M	A	N	R	C	T	Q	R	U	T
P	Y	W	V	B	N	M	O	V	I	E	S	T	A	R	Z

My Dictionary
Add the new words to your dictionary.

Student Book Page 16

Lesson 1

This may also be completed for homework.

Lesson 1 Vocabulary

Lesson Objective: Identify people and processes involved in making movies.
New Vocabulary: movie studio, director, cameraman, scene, cartoon, producer, movie star, script
Materials: Audio **Tracks 10 and 11**

Start the Class

5 min

Play the Shark Game (see **Page T 29**) with the names of a few famous movies, movie characters, or movie stars, for example, *Harry Potter and the Chamber of Secrets*, *Shrek*, *Emma Watson*, *Nemo*, etc.

1 10 Listen. Then echo.

15 min

Have students look at the pictures. Then have them identify the pictures in L1. Make sure students understand exactly what each picture represents. You may need to explain the difference between a director and a producer.

Tell students to listen to the words and read them at the same time. Play **Track 10**. Then tell students to repeat the words; play **Track 10** again.

Divide the class into rows. Say one of the new words and have a row repeat the word, then the next row, and so on. This should mimic a real echo. Continue with all of the new vocabulary items.

2 11 Listen and circle.

10 min

To prepare students for the listening activity, have them look at the photo on **Pages 16 and 17** for a while. Tell them to point to the picture and say any of the new words they can remember.

Tell students they are going to listen to a song about making movies. Have them listen and follow the song lyrics in their books. Play **Track 11**. Tell students that you are going to play the audio again, and this time they should listen and circle the correct words in lines 4, 6, 8, and 10.

Review the answers by playing **Track 11** again with pauses for students to check that they have circled the correct words.

3 Page 5 The Language Lodge

10 min

Have students flip to The Language Lodge **Page 5**.

1 Write. Then find and circle the movie words.

Have students look at the pictures and label them. Check answers with the class.

Tell students to work in pairs to find and circle the new words in the word puzzle. Check answers by having volunteers point to and say one of the words in the puzzle.

My Dictionary

Tell students to turn to the dictionary section in their notebooks. Have them write the new words and draw a picture or write a description for each one to help them remember what the words mean.

Try This!

5 min

Tell pairs to choose four words from the word puzzle and write a correct sentence using those words. They can add any other words they need. Have pairs read their sentences aloud. Ask the rest of the class if the sentence is correct, and if not, to correct it.

Finish the Class

5 min

Write these scrambled words on the board: *mesiavtor*, *cmanraeam*. Have students race to unscramble the words (*movie star*, *cameraman*). Then ask the class whether they would rather be movie stars or cameramen. Ask volunteers to give reasons.

Use the **Presentation Kit** for interactive activities in this lesson.

Have students use the **Happy Campers app** for additional practice with the new vocabulary.

The Language Lodge Page 5 may also be completed for homework.

Lesson 2 Grammar

Lesson Objective: Talk about making movies using past tense verbs.
New Grammar: I talked to a movie star. The director waved at me!
Vocabulary Review: movie studio, director, cameraman, scene, cartoon, producer, movie star, script
Materials: Audio **Track 11**

Start the Class

5 min

Ask the class if they like movies, what their favorite movies are, and to name their favorite actors.

1 11 Sing: Making Movies.

10 min

Tell students they are going to sing the song from Lesson 1. Play **Track 11** and have them follow in their books and sing along. Encourage them to copy intonation and stress as they sing. Play the song again and have students sing with expression.

Try This! 5 min

If students have difficulty repeating the lyrics of the song, choose a line and say the last word in the line. Have the class repeat. Then say the second to last word and the last word for the class to repeat. Continue until you have said all the words in the line, for example, *TV! like TV! also like TV! I also like TV!*

2 Look at the Grammar Pass. Complete.

10 min

Ask students if the song is mostly about the present, the future, or the past. Elicit *the past*. Refer students to the Grammar Pass and have two volunteers read the sentences aloud. Have students discover how we make regular past verbs (*add* -ed *at the end of the main verb*).

Have students work in pairs to complete the sentences using the past tense verbs in parentheses in Items 1 to 3. Have them write the correct answer in Item 4. Check answers with the class.

While checking, review pronunciation of *-ed* endings. Write these sounds as headings on the board and one example under each heading:

/d/	/t/	/id/
climbed	*watched*	*visited*

Say other regular past tense verbs students know. Ask them to repeat and say which column on the board they belong to, for example, *liked, played, started, walked*.

3 Unscramble.

5 min

Tell students to look at Item 1. Have a student to read the example answer. Then have students work in pairs to unscramble the other sentences. Check answers with the class.

4 Page 6 The Language Lodge

10 min

Have students flip to The Language Lodge **Page 6**. Have a volunteer read the Grammar Pass aloud.

1 Choose and complete with past tense verbs.

Tell students to read the verbs in the box. Have students work in pairs to choose the correct verb from the box and write the past tense verb to complete the sentences.

2 Write the past tense verbs.

Tell students to work independently to write the past tense of the verbs. Check answers with the class.

Finish the Class

5 min

Play a game of True or False with the song lyrics. Say true and false lyrics, for example, *I visited a studio. True! I read a book. False!* Have the class repeat the true lyrics. Any student who answers incorrectly is out of the game.

Use the **Presentation Kit** for interactive activities in this lesson.

The Language Lodge Page 6 may also be completed for homework.

For additional class time, use **Pages 10 and 11** of the Skills Book. Go to **Page 163** in the Happy Campers Teacher's Edition for teacher notes for this lesson. You may also choose to assign these pages as homework.

UNIT 2

Lesson 1

1 10 Listen. Then echo.

2 11 Listen and circle.

Making Movies

3 Page 5 The Language Lodge

Lesson 2

1 11 Sing: Making Movies.

I like the theater! I also like TV!
But movies on the big screen
Are what I like to see!

1. I visited a studio / theater.
It was great to see!
I talked to a movie star / producer,
The director waved at me!

2. I read a movie script / cartoon,
There were exciting scenes!
The cameraman / director
filmed me,
For the big screen!

GRAMMAR PASS

I talked to a movie star.

The director waved at me!

2 Look at the Grammar Pass. Complete.

1. I talked to a movie star. (talk)
2. He showed me a scene. (show)
3. I visited a movie studio. (visit)
4. Regular verbs add -ed to talk about the past.

3 Unscramble.

1. the / talked / cameraman / They / to
They talked to the cameraman.
2. movie / I / the / watched
I watched the movie.
3. a / filmed / He / scene
He filmed a scene.

4 Page 6 The Language Lodge

Lesson 2

This may also be completed for homework.

Lesson 2

GRAMMAR PASS

I visited a movie studio.

The director waved at me!

1 Choose and complete with past tense verbs.

listen walk play watch

1. We walked in the park yesterday.
2. I listened to the director's instructions carefully.
3. We watched a soccer game on TV.
4. They played volleyball on Saturday.

2 Write the past tense verbs.

1. visit visited
2. like liked
3. talk talked
4. walk walked

Student Book Page 17

Lesson 3

THE HAPPY CAMPERS

1 Why did Patty and Adam feel sick?

2 12 Read and listen.

3 13 Dictation! Listen and write. Then say.

1. Where's the makeup artist?
2. The director says, "Positions, please," "Action," and "Cut"
3. The sound engineer has a microphone.
4. She is his personal assistant.

4 Page 7 The Language Lodge

Lesson 4

1 12 Listen again to The Happy Campers.

2 Grammar Pass! Write past tense verbs.

1. meet ______	2. do ______
3. sit ______	4. eat ______
5. drink ______	6. feel ______
7. take ______	

3 14 Listen and cheer!

We ate, we drank! We felt fine!
We took a trip and had a good time!

CHEER BOX!

4 Page 8 The Language Lodge

Lesson 3

1 Complete the speech bubbles.

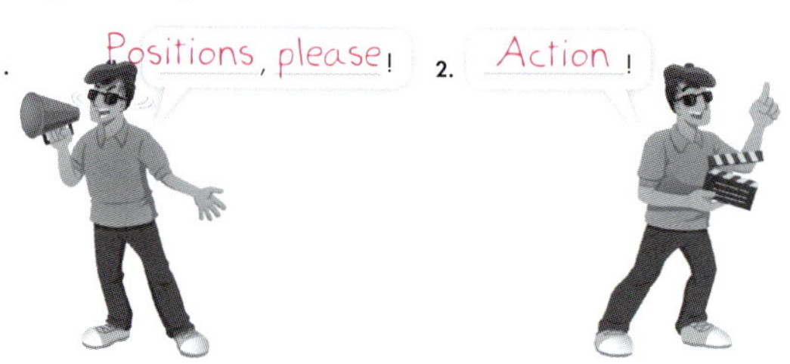

2 Answer the questions. Then match.

1. Who helps a director?
personal assistant
2. Who works with microphones?
sound engineer
3. Who puts makeup on the actors?
makeup artist
4. Who says "Action!"?
director

My Dictionary
Add the new words to your dictionary.

Student Book **Page 18**

Lesson 3

This may also be completed for homework.

Lesson 3 Vocabulary in Context

Lesson Objective: Identify more movie-related vocabulary.
New Vocabulary: personal assistant, makeup artist, sound engineer, "Positions, please," "Action," "Cut"
Vocabulary Review: director, script, microphone, scene
Materials: Audio **Tracks 12 and 13**, a set of Snap! cards for each group

Start the Class

5 min

Point to each character and have students identify them (*Zac, the director; Madison, his assistant; Hamlet, Madison's dog; Jason; Sue; Patty; Adam*).

1 Why did Patty and Adam feel sick?

5 min

Tell students to look at the pictures in the comic strip and ask them why they think Patty and Adam feel sick. Accept students' ideas and tell them they are going to discover the answer in the next activity.

2 12 Read and listen.

10 min

Tell students to read the comic strip as they listen to the track. Play **Track 12**. Elicit the answer to the question in Activity 1 *Patty ate six pancakes and Adam drank three smoothies.* Play **Track 12** again while students read along.

Ask *Whose job is to help the director?* Elicit *Madison.* Ask *What does a makeup artist do?* Elicit *Put makeup on actors.* Ask *What does the director say when he wants filming to stop?* Elicit *Cut.* Write the new vocabulary on the board and drill pronunciation.

3 13 Dictation! Listen and write. Then say.

10 min

Tell students they will hear sentences and will write what they hear. Play **Track 13**. Play **Track 13** again for students to complete the sentences. Tell the class that they are going to hear the audio again and will repeat the sentences. Play **Track 13** again and monitor students' pronunciation. Have volunteers write the sentences on the board for the class to check.

Audio script ***Track 13***
1. Where's the makeup artist? 2. The director says, "Positions, please," "Action," and "Cut."
3. The sound engineer has a microphone.
4. She is his personal assistant.

Try This!

5 min

Have students work in pairs. Students select their three favorite new words from the lesson and dictate them to their partners. They then check each other's spelling in their books.

4 Page 7 The Language Lodge

10 min

Have students flip to The Language Lodge **Page 7**.

1 Complete the speech bubbles.
Have a volunteer read the directions. Then have students complete the speech bubbles individually. Check answers with the class.

2 Answer the questions. Then match.
Tell students to answer the questions, then look at the pictures, and match them with the correct answer. Have volunteers share their answers with the class.

My Dictionary
Have students turn to the dictionary section in their notebooks. Have them write the new vocabulary and a sentence using each new word.

Finish the Class

5 min

Prepare a set of Snap! cards (see **Page T 25**) for each group with illustrations of the following: a personal assistant, a makeup artist, a sound engineer, a megaphone and the word *Action!*, a microphone, a notepad, and a makeup brush. To keep a pair they turn over, students have to say a correct sentence, for example, *A makeup artist uses a brush.*

Use the **Presentation Kit** for interactive activities in this lesson.

Have students use the **Happy Campers app** for additional practice with the new vocabulary.

The Language Lodge Page 7 may also be completed for homework.

Lesson 4 Grammar in Context

Lesson Objective: Talk about the past using irregular verbs.
New Grammar: She sat in the office. They ate pizza.
Vocabulary Review: director, script, makeup artist, sound engineer, personal assistant, sound engineer
Materials: Audio **Tracks 12 and 14**

Start the Class

5 min

Tell students you are going to talk about "The Happy Campers" comic strip and they have to correct you if you make any mistakes. When they hear incorrect information, they should raise their hands. You will then ask them to give the correct information.

Say *The Happy Campers were in a movie theater. They were with the director and Madison, the movie star. They needed a microphone, so they called the makeup artist. Jason and Sue ate pancakes.*

1 12 Listen again to The Happy Campers.

5 min

Tell students they are going to listen again to the "The Happy Campers" comic strip. Tell them to read along as they listen. Play **Track 12**. Then play **Track 12** again and have students listen and underline all the past tense verbs in the comic strip.

Try This! 10 min

Ask students to select a sentence from the story. Give them time to practice. Go around the class helping with pronunciation. Then students take turns saying their sentences and the class has to say which character said it, for example, *Yummy, pancakes! Patty!*

2 Grammar Pass! Write past tense verbs.

10 min

Have students look at the verbs they underlined in frame 5 of the comic strip. Ask if the verbs are in the past or present tense (*past*). Remind students that in English there are regular and irregular verbs. Elicit the rule for making regular past tense verbs (*add -ed*). Ask whether the verbs in frame 5 are regular or irregular (*irregular*).

Tell students to look at the present tense verbs in Activity 2 and write the past tense form. Have students give their answers for the class to check.

3 14 Listen and cheer!

5 min

Tell the class to listen to and read the cheer. Play **Track 14**. Play **Track 14** again and have students say the cheer. Divide the class in sections or rows. Have each section or row do an action as they are saying the cheer, for example, row 1 stands up and sits down, row 2 turns around, and row 3 claps to the rhythm.

4 Page 8 The Language Lodge

10 min

Have students flip to The Language Lodge **Page 8**. Have a volunteer read the Grammar Pass aloud.

1 Find and circle six past tense verbs. Then write.

Have students work in pairs to find and circle the past tense verbs in the word puzzle. Then have them write the verbs in their books. Tell students to point to the verbs in the puzzle, then write the verbs on the board for the class to check.

2 Use the words from Activity 1 to complete the sentences.

Tell students to look at the list of verbs they wrote in Activity 1, then choose the correct verbs to complete the sentences. Have them compare their answers with a partner. Then check answers with the class.

Finish the Class

5 min

Ask students to use one of the new irregular past tense verbs and say a sentence about something they did yesterday. Ask volunteers to say their sentences aloud.

Use the **Presentation Kit** for interactive activities in this lesson.

The Language Lodge Page 8 may also be completed for homework.

Lesson 3

THE HAPPY CAMPERS

1 Why did Patty and Adam feel sick?

2 12 Read and listen.

3 13 Dictation! Listen and write. Then say.

1. ____________________________?
2. ____________________________.
3. ____________________________.
4. ____________________________.

4 Page 7 The Language Lodge

Lesson 4

1 12 Listen again to The Happy Campers.

2 Grammar Pass! Write past tense verbs.

1. meet met
2. do did
3. sit sat
4. eat ate
5. drink drank
6. feel felt
7. take took

3 14 Listen and cheer!

We ate, we drank! We felt fine!
We took a trip and had a good time!

CHEER BOX!

4 Page 8 The Language Lodge

Lesson 4

This may also be completed for homework.

Lesson 4

GRAMMAR PASS

She sat in the office.

They ate pizza.

1 Find and circle six past tense verbs. Then write.

M	Z	X	S	A	T	W
E	Q	A	T	E	J	R
T	D	R	A	N	K	Q
H	W	F	E	L	T	A
T	O	O	K	F	G	D
K	Z	J	D	G	D	X

1. sit sat
2. eat ate
3. meet met
4. drink drank
5. feel felt
6. take took

2 Use the words from Activity 1 to complete the sentences.

1. The director sat in his chair and shouted, "Action!"
2. We met the actors in the show.
3. He ate a sandwich and drank a smoothie for lunch.
4. I took my dog for a walk.
5. She felt sick.

Student Book Page 19

Lesson 5

Lesson 5

1 **What does Ivan need to make his movie?**

(actors) (a script) a movie camera a movie studio (a cell phone)

2 15 **Read and listen.**

Ivan's Movie

Ivan really loved movies. He liked watching them, and he wanted to be a director and a cameraman someday. He secretly liked the idea of being a famous actor, too. He made a lot of funny and interesting videos of his family and his friends at school. One day, his teacher gave the class a project: Teach the class how to do something new.

That evening, Ivan sat in his room for a long time thinking about his project. He watched movies and read some books to get ideas. He got his notebook and pens. He walked around. Then, he had an idea! He was an expert cell phone movie director! "I can teach everyone how to make a movie — with a cell phone!" Ivan said.

"First, think of an idea for your movie. Then, write the script. Think about where you want to film, and what actors and costumes you need. Then film your movie. Finally, edit the movie on your computer. Cut!"

Ivan's movie was a great success. He was the cameraman, the director, and the star of his own movie!

Lesson 5 Fiction Reading

Lesson Objective: Read a fiction text to practice unit language.
Vocabulary Review: movie, actor, cameraman, studio, director, producer, cell phone
Grammar Review: past tense verbs
Materials: Audio **Track 15**

Start the Class

5 min

Review vocabulary from Lessons 1 and 3. Give a time limit of two minutes. Ask students to remember as many words as they can about making movies and write a list in their notebooks. After two minutes, ask them to count how many words they have. Choose the student with the most words to read his or her list slowly.

1 What does Ivan need to make his movie?

5 min

Tell the class they are going to read a text about a boy named Ivan and a movie that he makes. Have them read the list of possible things Ivan needs to make his movie. In pairs, have students discuss and circle the things they think Ivan needs. Discuss answers with the class. Ask if students can think of any other things needed to make a home movie. Elicit or suggest *costumes* and *computer*. Say that there are several ways of making movies, and students will discover how Ivan made his movie in Activity 2.

2 15 Read and listen.

20 min

Tell students to read along with the text as they listen. Play **Track 15**. Ask students to listen for what Ivan needed to make his movie (*cell phone, script, actors, costumes, computer*), and play **Track 15** again.

Play **Track 15** again, then ask questions to check understanding, such as *Did Ivan want to be a producer? What project did Ivan's teacher give the class? Who starred in Ivan's movie?*

Put students in groups of three. Assign a paragraph of the text to each student, and have them read the text in their groups. Walk around the classroom to check pronunciation and help as needed.

Try This!

10 min

Write the following descriptions of what people do on a movie set on the left-hand side of the board:

Read, memorize, and act out the script.
Tell the actors what to do.
Look after costs and find the director.
Put the microphones in the correct place.
Help the director.
Paint the actors' faces.
Film the scenes.

Say each function and then ask students to say who does this (*actor/movie star, director, producer, sound engineer, personal assistant, makeup artist, cameraman*). Each time, ask a volunteer to come to the board and write the name of the job next to the description.

Finish the Class

10 min

Have students look at the text again and choose one sentence they like. Tell students to memorize the sentences they chose. Put students in groups of four to six. Have each student tell the rest of the group his or her sentence. Then ask students to race to stand in line in the order in which the sentences appear in the story. If two students have chosen the same sentence, they should stand next to one another instead of in line. Ask the first group to say their sentences in order, and ask the rest of the class to check that the order is correct. If they are not correct, ask the next group to say their sentences.

Use the **Presentation Kit** for interactive activities in this lesson.

Lesson 6 Reading Comprehension / Writing

Lesson Objectives: Read for specific information and sequence events. Write about a movie.
Vocabulary Review: cameraman, director, script, "Cut"
Grammar Review: She sat in the office. I talked to a movie star.
Materials: Audio **Track 15**

Start the Class

5 min

Review the text from Lesson 5 by making true and false statements about it and having students say *True!* or *False!* Ask students to correct the false statements, for example, *Ivan secretly liked the idea of being a sound engineer. False! Ivan secretly liked the idea of being a famous actor.*

1 15 Listen again to Ivan's Movie.

5 min

Tell students they are going to listen to "Ivan's Movie" again. Ask them to listen for what Ivan did when he was thinking about how to make his movie (*sat in his room, watched movies, read a book, got his notebook and pens, walked around*). Play **Track 15**.

Try This!

5 min

Have students work in groups. Tell the groups to prepare a list of their three favorite movies. Have each group share their list with the rest of the class. Write all the movies students suggest on the board. Take a vote to discover the class's favorite movie.

2 Put the steps to make a movie in order.

5 min

Ask a volunteer to read the directions. Have students read the steps in the box. Then have them work in pairs to write the steps in the correct order. Ask students to say the steps in order. Ask the rest of the class if they agree.

3 Writing Time! Complete the chart about your movie.

10 min

Tell students they are going to think about a movie they want to make and to write notes in the chart about it. Have them look at the chart and make sure they understand what information they need to provide.

Have students work individually. Give them some time to think about and make notes about their movies. Walk around the classroom to monitor and help as much as necessary. Encourage students who find it difficult to come up with ideas by making suggestions and providing guidance.

4 Write about your movie.

15 min

Tell students they are going to write a paragraph about their movies using their information in the chart from Activity 3. Give students time to write their paragraphs. Encourage them to read their work when they have finished and correct any mistakes they find. Then have students work in pairs. Have them read each other's paragraphs. Ask students to check for errors and provide their partner with two opinions: something they really like about the movie, and an idea to make the movie more interesting. Allow time for students to revise their paragraphs if they want to. Have as many students as possible read their paragraphs to the class.

Finish the Class

5 min

Discuss the class's favorite movie. Ask students to tell the class anything they know about the movie, such as the story, where it is set, who the director is, and the names of characters or actors in the movie. Ask students to find out more information about the movie or similar information about their own favorite movies for homework.

Use the **Presentation Kit** for interactive activities in this lesson.

For additional class time, use **Pages 12 and 13** of the Skills Book. Go to **Page 164** in the Happy Campers Teacher's Edition for teacher notes for this lesson. You may also choose to assign these pages as homework.

Lesson 6

Lesson 6

1 (15) Listen again to **Ivan's Movie**.

2 **Put the steps to make a movie in order.**

edit the movie	write the script	think of an idea
film the movie	choose the place	choose the actors

1. think of an idea
2. write the script
3. choose the place
4. choose the actors
5. film the movie
6. edit the movie

3 **Writing Time!** **Complete the chart about your movie.**

My Movie

Idea: (Students' own answers.)

Characters: ______

Where: ______

What happens: ______

4 **Write about your movie.**

My movie is about (Students' own answers) .

______

______

______ .

Lesson 7

Lesson 7

ON STAGE!

PROJECT:
Movie Storyboard

1 **Plan your Movie Storyboard. Write your ideas.**

Choose a story you know.
Who are the characters?
Where are they?
What are they doing?

(Students' own answers.)

2 **Prepare your Movie Storyboard. Draw and write your story scenes.**

3 **On Stage! Share your Movie Storyboard with the class.**

Lesson 7 Creative, Collaborative, and Critical Thinking Activity

Lesson Objective: Plan, create, and present a Movie Storyboard.
Vocabulary Review: scene, movie star
Grammar Review: past tense verbs
Materials: index cards or sheets of paper; glue; poster board; markers, colored pencils, or crayons; a red and a green sticker or sticky note for each student

Start the Class

5 min

Start the class by reviewing students' movie research. Have several students stand up and share what they have discovered about the movie of their choice.

Try This! 5 min

If the movie that the class elected as their favorite movie is suitable to be shown in class, arrange for students to watch it in a future class. You may want to create some activities to accompany the viewing of the movie, such as filling in blanks about the story, matching characters with descriptions, ordering the main events in the plot, and so on. If subtitles are used in the movie, make sure they are in English.

1 Plan your Movie Storyboard. Write your ideas.

10 min

Ask a volunteer to read the directions and the categories in the chart. Explain that a movie storyboard consists of the main scenes in a movie placed in the order in which they happen. Have students get into their project groups. Tell the groups to discuss and choose a story that they know well (it doesn't have to be a movie—it could be a book, for example). When they have chosen their story, have them make notes about the main characters, where the story takes place, and what the characters are doing. Walk around the classroom and monitor.

2 Prepare your Movie Storyboard. Draw and write your story scenes.

15 min

Hand out the materials. Refer students to the storyboard in the photo to give them an idea of what a completed storyboard will look like. Tell groups to discuss what scenes they are going to show in their Movie Storyboards. They should use the information from Activity 1. Tell them they can draw and color the scenes in the storyboards on index cards or sheets of paper, then glue them onto the poster board to make their final Movie Storyboards. Have groups decide how each member of the group is going to contribute to creating their storyboards. As they work, walk around the classroom to help and encourage as necessary. Make sure all students in the group are contributing.

3 On Stage! Share your Movie Storyboard with the class.

10 min

Have students look again at the photo of the two girls presenting their storyboard. Have a student read the speech bubble. Remind students to speak clearly, be enthusiastic, and look at their audience as they are making their presentations.

Have each group take turns to come to the board, and present their Movie Storyboard. Make sure every group receives applause after their presentation.

Finish the Class

5 min

Display the Movie Storyboards around the classroom. Give each student a red and a green sticker or sticky note. Tell them to walk around the classroom and look at all the storyboards, and to put a green sticker next to their favorite story and a red sticker next to the best illustrated storyboard.

When they have done this, have students help you count the stickers. Announce the winning storyboard in each category. Praise all the groups for creating such great Movie Storyboards.

Use the **Presentation Kit** for interactive activities in this lesson.

Lesson 8 Review

Lesson Objective: Review language from Unit 2.
Vocabulary Review: movie studio, director, cameraman, scene, cartoon, producer, movie star, script, personal assistant, makeup artist, sound engineer, "Positions, please," "Action," "Cut"
Grammar Review: I talked to a movie star. The director waved at me! She sat in the office. They ate pizza.
Materials: Audio **Track 11**

Start the Class

10 min

Tell students to take turns coming to the board and writing one thing they learned in this unit (it can be a vocabulary term, information about making movies, or something they remember from a text). Encourage students to do this without looking at their books or notebooks. Continue until the board is full. Congratulate the class on learning so much in this unit!

1 Spelling! Write.

10 min

Tell students to look at the pictures. Then have them write the correct vocabulary word for each item. Have students compare their answers with a partner. Then tell students to write the words on the board. Ask the class to say if the words are spelled correctly each time.

2 Choose and complete with the past tense verbs.

10 min

Put students in pairs. Have them take turns saying one of the verbs in the box for their partners to say the same verb in the past tense.

Then have students work individually to read the sentences and complete them with one of the past tense verbs in the box. Have students compare their answers with a partner, then check answers with the class.

3 Word Play! Find and circle the words from Unit 2 on Page 72.

5 min

Have students turn to **Page 72** and tell them to find and circle the movie vocabulary words from Unit 2. Then have students check the words they found with a partner.

Try This! 5 min

Have students work in pairs. Each student chooses five new words from the unit. They take turns acting out the words for their partners. Have a few pairs of students demonstrate for the rest of the class.

Finish the Class

10 min

Play **Track 11** (the "Making Movies" song) and have students sing along. Ask students to work in pairs and write a new verse for the song. Ask pairs to sing or read their new verse to the class.

Use the **Presentation Kit** for interactive activities in this lesson.

For additional class time, use **Pages 14 and 15** of the Skills Book. Go to **Page 165** in the Happy Campers Teacher's Edition for teacher notes for this lesson. You may also choose to assign these pages as homework.

Lesson 8

Lesson 8

Round Up!

1 Spelling! Write.

1. cameraman

2. producer

3. script

4. movie studio

5. director

6. cartoon

2 Choose and complete with the past tense verbs.

listen	drink	sit	meet	take

1. They sat under a tree and ate their sandwiches.
2. We listened to the director and followed his instructions.
3. The cameraman drank water in the studio.
4. We took the dog for a walk.
5. He met the producer at the studio.

3 Word Play! Find and circle the words from Unit 2 on Page 72.

Unit 3

Unit Objectives

By the end of the unit, students can:

- Identify clothing.
- Understand commands.
- Use negative sentences and ask and answer questions in the past tense.

Student Book

Vocabulary

Clothes: sweatshirt, sweatpants, cardigan, vest, leggings, tights, hoodie, dress

Commands: pay attention, go to bed, waste (your) time, rehearse a scene, be on time, learn your lines

Grammar

I didn't want to be late. I didn't have any money.
Did you stay up late last night? Yes, I did.
Did he learn his lines? No, he didn't.

Skills

Listening: Listen for specific information.

Speaking: Talk about clothing. Talk about what people didn't have or do. Narrate and describe past events.

Reading: Read a nonfiction text (science): **The Story of Velcro**. Identify the main idea and specific information.

Writing: Write about your clothing invention.

Creative, Collaborative, and Critical Thinking Competencies

Interview a Movie Star

Creativity: Develop self-expression and innovation to act out the interview.

Collaboration: Use communication, negotiation, and problem-solving skills to make decisions about what movie star to choose, the roles in the interview, and how to present the interview.

Critical Thinking: Use analytical and prioritizing skills to identify the most important information and what questions to ask.

Skills Book

Extra Skills Practice

Speaking and Listening: Make statements about a picture and respond.

Reading and Writing: Recall details. Recognize spelling patterns. Read clues to identify words.

Teacher Workshop

Teaching with Technology

Help students prepare for class by having them find information about the content of the lesson on the Internet, especially for Lesson 7. There are many websites devoted to movie stars that are suitable for young learners, containing biographies, photos, lists of movies, and trivia information. Encourage students to use websites that are in English.

Teaching with Games

Chain Memory Game

This is a great game to help students remember vocabulary. Have students work in groups of six to eight and sit in a circle. One student starts by saying, for example, *I went to the mall and I bought a dress.* The student on his or her right repeats the sentence and adds another item, for example, *I went to the mall and I bought a dress and a sweatshirt.* The game continues in this way around the whole group. If a student gets the list wrong, have the other students in the group correct the list.

Happy Teacher

Before a reading or listening activity, prepare students by activating their background knowledge and asking them to do the following: looking at illustrations or the title of the text and predict what the text is going to be about; writing some student predictions on the board; using words from the text that you give them and saying a sentence about what they think the text will be about.

When students read the text, ask them to check their predictions.

Happy Class

When students are presenting to the class, promote active listening for the rest of the class. Students can actively listen by doing any of the following: writing a check mark next to the same ideas in their work; writing down new ideas they hear their classmates say; knowing they must answer questions about the presentation afterward; saying the most interesting or funny thing they found out in the presentation; saying their opinions.

Always try to give students a reason to listen.

By Lesley Painter-Farrell

UNIT 3

Lesson 1

1 (16) Listen. Then echo.

sweatshirt
sweatpants
cardigan
vest
leggings
tights
hoodie
dress

2 (17) Listen and circle.

Window Shopping

3 Page 9 The Language Lodge

Lesson 2

1 (17) Sing: Window Shopping.

Window shopping before I go to school.
Window shopping is very, very cool!

1. The hoodie / dress in the store
Was very, very fine.
I wanted that hoodie
I wished that it was mine!
But it wasn't!
I didn't have my money!
It really was a bore,
So I left the hoodie
There in the store!

2. The leggings / vest in the store
Were very, very fine.
I wanted those leggings
I wished that they were mine!
But they weren't!
I didn't take my wallet!
It really was a bore,
So I left those leggings
There in the store!

3. The sweatpants / tights in the store
Were very, very fine.
I wanted those sweatpants
And wished that they were mine!
But they weren't!
I didn't want to be late!
It really was a bore,
So I left those sweatpants
There in the store!

GRAMMAR PASS

I didn't want to be late.

I didn't take my wallet.

2 Look at the Grammar Pass. Circle.

1. I didn't have / had my books at school.
2. She didn't watched / watch the movie.
3. He didn't listen / listened to the song.
4. Use *didn't* + infinitive to talk about affirmative / negative sentences in the past.

3 Write negative sentences.

1. He didn't buy the sweatpants at the store.
2. She ________ to the circus.
3. I ________ basketball.
4. They ________ pizza.

4 Page 10 The Language Lodge

UNIT 3 Lesson 1

1 Read the clues. Complete the puzzle.

→ Across

1. A girl wears this to go to a party
5. Girls wear them on their legs
6. You wear these pants to exercise
7. This is a sweater that opens in the front

↓ Down

2. You wear this to exercise, but it doesn't have a hood
3. It is a sweater with no arms
4. Girls wear this to cover their feet and legs

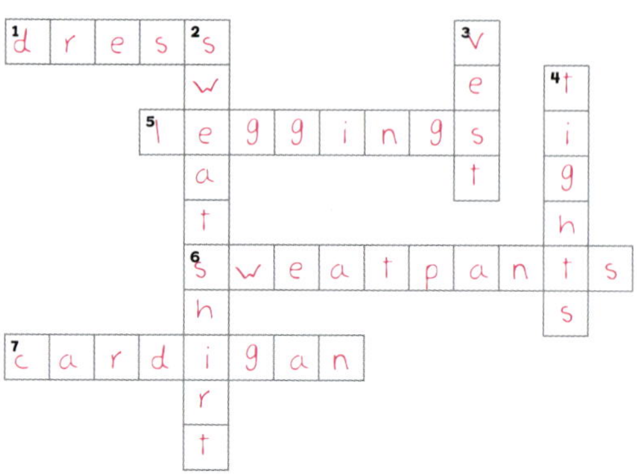

My Dictionary
Add the new words to your dictionary.

Student Book Page 24

Lesson 1

This may also be completed for homework.

Lesson 1 Vocabulary

Lesson Objective: Identify clothing.
New Vocabulary: sweatshirt, sweatpants, cardigan, vest, leggings, tights, hoodie, dress
Materials: Audio **Tracks 16 and 17**

Start the Class

5 min

Brainstorm the names of clothes that students already know. Write them on the board. Then write the following column headings on the board: *Birthday Party* and *School*. Discuss with the class what clothes they would wear at each of these places. Have students write the clothes under the correct headings on the board.

1 16 Listen. Then echo.

5 min

Tell students to listen, point to the pictures, and read the words. Play **Track 16**. Then tell students to repeat the words. Play **Track 16** again.

Try This! 5 min

Explain to students that they are going to listen and repeat the words again. But this time have girls repeat the word if the clothing is worn mostly by girls, for example, *tights*. Have boys repeat the word if the clothing is worn mostly by boys, for example, *hoodie*. All students repeat if the clothing is worn by girls and boys. Play **Track 16**. Switch roles to give students a chance to repeat the words.

2 17 Listen and circle.

10 min

Ask students to cover the vocabulary sidebar and look at the photo. Have them work in pairs and take turns naming clothes in the picture.

Start by asking students how they buy clothes. *Where do you go? Who do you go with? How do you choose your clothes?* Elicit or explain the meaning of *window shopping*.

Tell students to listen and follow the song in their books. Play **Track 17**. Then tell students to listen again and circle the correct item of clothing from the pairs of options in the lyrics *(hoodie, leggings, sweatpants)*.

Play **Track 17** again. Have students compare their answers with a partner, then check answers with the class.

Tell students to say a true sentence about themselves using the new clothing vocabulary, for example, *I wore a dress to a birthday party.*

3 Page 9 The Language Lodge

15 min

Have students flip to The Language Lodge **Page 9**.

1 Read the clues. Complete the puzzle.

Have students work in pairs. Tell them to read the clues and solve them by writing the correct word in the puzzle grid. Walk around the classroom to monitor and help as necessary. Have pairs check their answers with another pair, and then check answers with the class.

My Dictionary

Ask students to turn to the dictionary section in their notebooks. Have them write the new words and draw a picture to illustrate each one.

Finish the Class

10 min

Draw a large Venn diagram (two intersecting circles) on the board. Label the left-hand section *Boys*, the center section *Boys and Girls*, and the right-hand section *Girls*. Ask students to come to the board and write the names of items of clothing they know in the appropriate section. Then have students copy the Venn diagram in their My Dictionary pages.

Use the **Presentation Kit** for interactive activities in this lesson.

Have students use the **Happy Campers app** for additional practice with the new vocabulary.

The Language Lodge Page 9 may also be completed for homework.

Lesson 2 Grammar

Lesson Objective: Respond to statements using the past tense.
New Grammar: I didn't want to be late. I didn't take my wallet.
Vocabulary Review: sweatshirt, sweatpants, cardigan, vest, leggings, tights, hoodie, dress
Materials: Audio **Track 17**

Start the Class

10 min

Ask students to make a list of five of their favorite clothes. Then have them work in groups. Students share their lists and create one group list. Have each group take turns reading their group list to the class. Write all the different items of clothing on the board and keep count by putting a check mark next to them each time they are mentioned. Then ask the class to count the check marks to find the class's favorite items of clothing.

1 17 Sing: Window Shopping.

5 min

Tell students they are going to sing the song from Lesson 1. Play **Track 17** and have them follow in their books and sing along. Then tell them to clap along with the rhythm while they sing the song again. Play **Track 17** again.

Try This! 5 min

Have students work in groups to write a new verse for the song using a different item of clothing. Play **Track 17** again and ask groups to take turns to sing their new verse.

2 Look at the Grammar Pass. Circle.

10 min

Tell students this anecdote about a shopping trip and ask them to listen for what you wanted to buy and whether you bought it: *I went to the mall. I wanted to buy a hoodie with the name of our city on it. I saw three hoodies: one said "Madrid," the other one said "Shanghai," and the third one said "Santiago"* (or any combination of cities that does not include the one you live in). Ask *Did I buy a hoodie?* Elicit *No, you didn't buy a hoodie.*

Direct students' attention to the Grammar Pass and ask a volunteer to read the sentence. Have students read the sentences and circle the correct answers. Check answers with the class. Write *didn't + verb to talk about negative sentences in the past.* Have students copy this into their notebooks.

3 Write negative sentences.

5 min

Have a student say the example sentence. Then have students work individually to complete the other sentences using a negative past tense verb. Have students check answers with a partner, then have students read the sentences for the class to check.

4 Page 10 The Language Lodge

10 min

Have students flip to The Language Lodge **Page 10**. Have a volunteer read the Grammar Pass aloud.

1 Complete.

Read the first sentence aloud for the class. Then have students work individually to complete the other sentences. Check answers with the class.

2. Choose and complete with past tense verbs.

Have students read the verbs in the box and look at the pictures. Read the first sentence aloud with the class. Then have students work in pairs to complete the other sentences. Check answers with the class.

Finish the Class

5 min

Have students use two of the verbs from The Language Lodge Activity 2 to write a true sentence and a false sentence about themselves using the past tense. Then have them share their sentences for the class to guess which sentence is true.

Use the **Presentation Kit** for interactive activities in this lesson.

The Language Lodge Page 10 may also be completed for homework.

For additional class time, use **Pages 16 and 17** of the Skills Book. Go to **Page 166** in the Happy Campers Teacher's Edition for teacher notes for this lesson. You may also choose to assign these pages as homework.

UNIT 3

Lesson 1

1 (16) Listen. Then echo.

2 (17) Listen and circle.

Window Shopping

3 Page 9 The Language Lodge

Lesson 2

1 (17) Sing: Window Shopping.

Window shopping before I go to school.
Window shopping is very, very cool!

1. The hoodie / dress in the store
Was very, very fine.
I wanted that hoodie
I wished that it was mine!
But it wasn't!
I didn't have my money!
It really was a bore,
So I left the hoodie
There in the store!

2. The leggings / vest in the store
Were very, very fine.
I wanted those leggings
I wished that they were mine!
But they weren't!
I didn't take my wallet!
It really was a bore,
So I left those leggings
There in the store!

3. The sweatpants / tights in the store
Were very, very fine.
I wanted those sweatpants
And wished that they were mine!
But they weren't!
I didn't want to be late!
It really was a bore,
So I left those sweatpants
There in the store!

GRAMMAR PASS

I didn't want to be late.

I didn't take my wallet.

2 Look at the Grammar Pass. Circle.

1. I didn't (have) / had my books at school.
2. She didn't watched / (watch) the movie.
3. He didn't (listen) / listened to the song.
4. Use *didn't* + infinitive to talk about affirmative / (negative) sentences in the past.

3 Write negative sentences.

1. He didn't buy the sweatpants at the store.
2. She didn't go to the circus.
3. I didn't play basketball.
4. They didn't eat pizza.

4 Page 10 The Language Lodge

Lesson 2

GRAMMAR PASS

I didn't want to be late.

I didn't take my wallet.

1 Complete.

1. He didn't wear a sweatshirt. He wore a hoodie.
2. We didn't watch the soccer game. We watched a movie.
3. They didn't go to the movies. They went to the concert.
4. He didn't like the cardigan. He liked the vest.

2 Choose and complete with past tense verbs.

win	eat	wear	drink

1. She ate popcorn.

2. He drank water.

3. They won the game.

4. I wore a hoodie.

Student Book Page 25

Lesson 2

This may also be completed for homework.

Lesson 3

THE HAPPY CAMPERS

1 How's the weather at the end of the story?

2 18 Read and listen.

3 19 Dictation! Listen and write. Then say.

1. Please be on time.
2. Did you learn you lines?
3. Pay attention and don't waste time.
4. It's important to rehearse the scene.

4 Page 11 The Language Lodge

Lesson 4

1 18 Listen again to The Happy Campers.

2 Grammar Pass! Read and circle.

1. Did you stay up late last night? Yes, I did. No, I didn't.
2. Did you waste time? Yes, I did. No, I didn't.
3. Did you learn your lines? Yes, I did. No, I didn't.

3 20 Listen and cheer!

Did you go to the party? Yes, I did! Yes, I did!
Did you have breakfast? No, I didn't! No, I didn't!

CHEER BOX!

4 Page 12 The Language Lodge

Lesson 3

1 Find and circle six verbs in the puzzle. Complete the sentences.

V	G	O	P	A	Y	Y	L
R	E	H	E	A	R	S	E
Q	W	K	Z	J	X	T	A
W	A	S	T	E	X	A	R
Z	W	L	B	E	K	Y	N

1. Go to bed early!
2. Don't waste your time!
3. Be on time!
4. Pay attention!
5. Learn your lines!
6. Rehearse the scene!

2 Choose and complete.

Pay attention Go to bed Learn your lines

1. One thing a teacher says: Pay attention.
2. One thing parents say: Go to bed.
3. One thing a director says: Learn your lines.

My Dictionary
Add the new words to your dictionary.

Student Book Page 26

Lesson 3

This may also be completed for homework.

Lesson 3 Vocabulary in Context

Lesson Objective: Recognize and understand commands.
New Vocabulary: pay attention, go to bed, waste (your) time, rehearse a scene, be on time, learn your lines
Vocabulary Review: leggings
Materials: Audio **Tracks 18 and 19**

Start the Class

5 min

Ask students to look at the pictures in the comic strip and describe the clothes the characters are wearing and to predict what the comic strip may be about.

1 How's the weather at the end of the story?

5 min

Have students work with a partner to look at the pictures and answer the question. Have volunteers share their ideas with the class. Encourage them to explain their answers.

2 18 Read and listen.

10 min

Tell students to read the comic strip as they listen to the audio. Play **Track 18**. Ask questions to check understanding, for example, *Did the story take place over one day or two days? What do you think The Happy Campers are rehearsing for? Did Sue learn her lines? Do you think Patty learned her lines? Why or why not?*

Put students in groups of four. Assign each student a character. Have the groups read the comic strip aloud.

3 19 Dictation! Listen and write. Then say.

10 min

Tell students they will hear sentences and write what they hear. Tell students to listen to the first sentence and then write it. Play **Track 19** and pause after each sentence to allow students time to write. Play **Track 19** again and have students say the words along with the audio. Then have volunteers write the sentences on the board for the class to check.

*Audio script **Track 19***
1. Please be on time. 2. Did you learn your lines?
3. Pay attention and don't waste time.
4. It's important to rehearse the scene.

Try This! 5 min

Have students work in pairs. Each student selects his or her favorite sentence from the comic strip and dictates it to his or her partner. They will then check each other's sentence against the text.

4 Page 11 The Language Lodge

10 min

Have students flip to The Language Lodge **Page 11**.

1 Find and circle six verbs in the puzzle. Complete the sentences.

Have a volunteer read the directions. Tell students to work independently to complete the activity and then compare their answers with a partner. Have volunteers read their completed sentences.

2 Choose and complete.

Have the class read the directions and the commands in the box aloud. Then have volunteers read the completed sentences to the class.

My Dictionary

Ask students to turn to the dictionary section of their notebooks. Have them write the new words and draw a picture to illustrate each one.

Finish the Class

5 min

Explain to the class that you will say a word and they will say a command using the word. Say, for example, *bed!* Elicit *Go to bed!* Continue with these other prompts: *lines, attention, on time, scene, (your) time.*

Use the **Presentation Kit** for interactive activities in this lesson.

Have students use the **Happy Campers app** for additional practice with the new vocabulary.

The Language Lodge Page 11 may also be completed for homework.

Lesson 4 Grammar in Context

Lesson Objective: Ask and answer questions in the past tense.
New Grammar: Did you stay up late last night? Yes, I did. Did he learn his lines? No, he didn't.
Vocabulary Review: pay attention, go to bed, waste (your) time, rehearse a scene, be on time, learn your lines
Materials: Audio **Tracks 18 and 20**

Start the Class

5 min

With books closed, write on the board: ____ *didn't go to bed early last night.* ____ *didn't waste time last night.* ____ *learned her lines.* Then ask students to complete the sentences with one of The Happy Campers' names (*Jason, Patty, Sue*).

1 18 Listen again to The Happy Campers.

5 min

Tell students that they are going to listen to and read the comic strip again. Play **Track 18**. Have them underline all the questions in the comic strip in one color and all the answers in another color, and play **Track 18** again.

2 Grammar Pass! Read and circle.

5 min

Write *Did you learn your lines? Yes, I did. / No, I didn't* on the board. Have students notice the word order of the question (*Did + subject + verb + object*). Point out that the short answers do not repeat the main verb.

Tell students to look at the small pictures of the characters. Have them refer back to the comic strip in order to circle the correct answer for each question. Check answers with the class.

Try This!

5 min

Have students ask questions about the comic strip. Write a few of their questions on the board. Have students read the questions orally. Then ask students to close their eyes. Erase all the verbs in the questions. Ask students to open their eyes and say the complete questions, including the missing verbs.

3 20 Listen and cheer!

5 min

Tell students to listen to and read the cheer. Play **Track 20**. Then play **Track 20** again and have students say the cheer.

4 Page 12 The Language Lodge

15 min

Have students flip to The Language Lodge **Page 12**. Have a volunteer read the Grammar Pass aloud.

1 Unscramble.

Write on the board: *party / go / you / to / Did / the / ?* Elicit the unscrambled question (*Did you go to the party?*) and have a student write it on the board. Have students unscramble the questions in their books. Check answers with the class.

2 Complete the questions. Then write the answers.

Read the first question and answer aloud with the class. Point out the check mark, indicating that the answer should be positive. Explain the cross indicates a negative answer.

Have students complete the other questions and answers. Check answers with the class.

Finish the Class

10 min

Play a game. Tell students to think of something they did yesterday, such as learned English, ate breakfast, got dressed, and so on. Have them mingle, asking questions in order to find other students who did the same thing, for example, *Did you learn English yesterday? Yes, I did. / No, I didn't.* Students who did the same thing stand together. After a few minutes, have students say what they did yesterday.

Use the **Presentation Kit** for interactive activities in this lesson.

The Language Lodge Page 12 may also be completed for homework.

Lesson 3

1 How's the weather at the end of the story?

2 18 Read and listen.

THE HAPPY CAMPERS

3 19 **Dictation!** Listen and write. Then say.

1. ______________________________.
2. ______________________________?
3. ______________________________.
4. ______________________________.

4 Page 11 The Language Lodge

Lesson 4

1 18 Listen again to The Happy Campers.

2 **Grammar Pass!** Read and circle.

1. Did you stay up late last night? (Yes, I did.) No, I didn't.
2. Did you waste time? Yes, I did. (No, I didn't.)
3. Did you learn your lines? (Yes, I did.) No, I didn't.

3 20 Listen and cheer!

Did you go to the party? Yes, I did! Yes, I did!
Did you have breakfast? No, I didn't! No, I didn't!

CHEER BOX!

4 Page 12 The Language Lodge

Lesson 4

GRAMMAR PASS

Did you stay up late last night?
Yes, I did.

Did he learn his lines?
No, he didn't.

1 **Unscramble.**

1. the / they / watch / Did / movie
Did they watch the movie?
2. school / Did / walk / to / she
Did she walk to school?
3. umbrella / bring / we / Did / an
Did we bring an umbrella?
4. time / waste / he / Did / his
Did he waste his time?

2 **Complete the questions. Then write the answers.**

1. Did Sally have a good time yesterday? (have)
✔ Yes, she did.
2. Did they get up early this morning? (get)
✘ No, they didn't.
3. Did he learn his lines last night? (learn)
✔ Yes, he did.
4. Did they pay attention yesterday? (pay)
✘ No, they didn't.

Student Book Page 27

Lesson 4

This may also be completed for homework.

Lesson 5

1 **What did George de Mestral see on his walk?**

a house   clothes   (a plant)   an animal   an astronaut

2 21 **Read and listen.**

The Story of Velcro

There was an engineer in Switzerland. His name was George de Mestral. One day in 1948, de Mestral and his dog went for a walk. When they arrived home, he noticed that parts of a plant were stuck, like stickers, on his pants and his dog's fur.

De Mestral looked at the small balls from the plant. He saw something very interesting. They had little "teeth" on them! He didn't stop thinking about the plants. He wanted to make something useful with that idea.

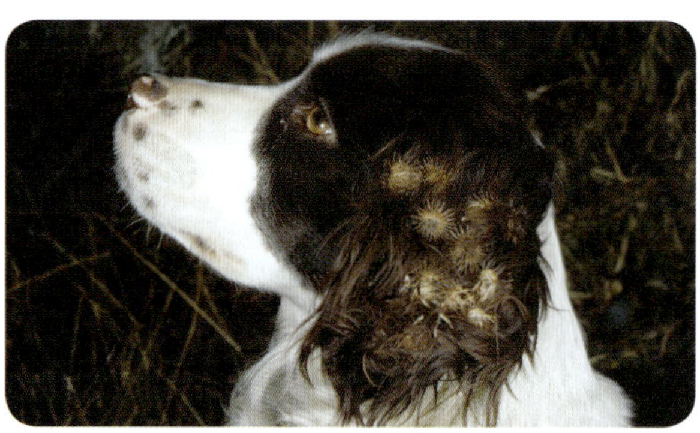

He invented a material with little "teeth" like the plant he saw. It was very easy to open and close. He called his new idea Velcro. NASA used Velcro on their clothes for astronauts, and they loved it.

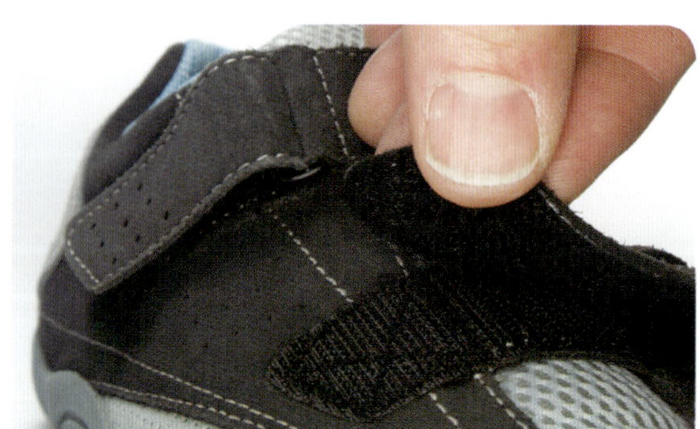

Now people who make clothes, bags, and shoes use Velcro a lot. Look at your clothes and your shoes. Are you wearing anything with Velcro today?

Velcro is the brand name of the most famous type of hook and loop fasteners.

Lesson 5 Nonfiction Reading

Lesson Objective: Read a nonfiction text to practice unit language.
Vocabulary Review: house, clothes, plant, animal, astronaut
Grammar Review: past tense verbs
Materials: Audio **Track 21**, small pieces of Velcro, and a magnifying glass for each group

Start the Class

10 min

Put students in four groups. Give two of the groups the soft side of the Velcro and the other two groups the side with the more abrasive "teeth." Ask students if they know what the material is called and if they have anything that has Velcro on it (either in class or at home). Ask students to look at the Velcro with the magnifying glass and also to rub it gently against their skin. Ask *How does it feel?* Ask them to fold the piece of Velcro in half. Ask *Does it stick? Why not?* Ask groups to exchange their pieces of Velcro, making sure that the groups get the opposite side of the Velcro this time. Repeat the activity.

1 What did George de Mestral see on his walk?

10 min

Have students look at the pictures in their books without reading the text. Ask them to predict what the text is going to be about. Then ask *What did George de Mestral see on his walk?* Tell a student to read the options, then have students circle what they think he saw.

Next, tell students they are going to read "The Story of Velcro." Ask students to scan the text (give students about one minute) to find the answer to the question (*a plant*).

2 21 Read and listen.

15 min

Tell students to read the text as they listen to the track. Play **Track 21**. Ask students if their predictions appeared in the text. Then have them read the text again as you play the track once more. Ask students to underline all the past tense verbs in the text. Say the past tense verbs and ask students to give the main verb, such as *was/be*, *went/go*, and so on.

Put students in groups of four. Give one paragraph of the text to each student in the group and have them read the text. Walk around the classroom to monitor and help with pronunciation.

Try This! 10 min

Have students close their books. Write the following pairs of words on the board: *dog, walk*; *plant, stuck*; *useful, idea*; *open, close*; *NASA, Velcro*. Ask students to work in pairs and write complete sentences about the text using both words. Monitor as students work, and help if necessary. Have students read one of their sentences. Ask the rest of the class if they wrote the same sentence or a different one. If they chose a different one, ask the class which sentence is better.

Finish the Class

5 min

Brainstorm all the items of clothing students can remember and write them on the board. Next, ask students to help you make two groups of clothing: those with a fastening that could use Velcro, for example *shorts* or *shoes* and those that couldn't use Velcro, for example, *a shirt*.

Use the **Presentation Kit** for interactive activities in this lesson.

Lesson 6 Reading Comprehension / Writing

Lesson Objectives: Identify specific information in a text. Write about your clothing invention.
Vocabulary Review: house, clothes, plant, animal, astronaut
Grammar Review: She sat in the office. I talked to a movie star.
Materials: Audio **Track 21**, large sheets of paper

Start the Class

5 min

Have students work in groups of four. Give one member of each group a large sheet of paper. Tell students to fold paper in half then in half again the other way. Draw an oval in the center of the paper and write *Velcro* in the oval. Have each student write his or her name at the outside edge of one of the squares as well as one fact, word, or idea that he or she remembers from "The Story of Velcro" in Lesson 5.

Have volunteer groups share their ideas with the class.

1 21 Listen again to The Story of Velcro.

5 min

Tell students they are going to listen to "The Story of Velcro" again. Tell them to listen to make sure that all the information they wrote on their groups' papers was correct. Play **Track 21**. Monitor and help as needed.

2 Circle *True* or *False*.

5 min

Ask volunteers to read the statements one at a time. Pause between each statement to allow students time to refer back to the text, decide if the statement is true or false, and circle the correct answer. Check answers with the class by having students say their answers. If a statement is false, ask them to correct it.

Try This! 5 min

Ask students to write their own true or false statements about the text. Then have them work in pairs. Students will take turns reading their statements aloud to their partners. The partner will say if the statement is true or false, and will point to the evidence in the text. Partners will then correct false statements.

3 Writing Time! Invent a new item for your clothing.

10 min

Explain that students are going to think of a new clothing invention, say what it does, and explain how to use it. Tell them they will fill in the chart. Encourage them to be imaginative. Give them some time to come up with an idea and complete the chart. Walk around the classroom to help as needed. You may find it useful to think of a few ideas yourself as examples. When they have finished, have students share their ideas with a partner. Have a few pairs share with the class.

4 Write about your clothing invention.

10 min

Tell students to use the information in their charts to write a paragraph about their inventions. Encourage them to read their paragraphs when they have finished to check for and correct any mistakes. Then have them exchange their paragraphs with a partner. Ask students to say one thing they really like about their partners' paragraphs.

Finish the Class

10 min

Have students take turns reading their paragraphs to the class. Remind them to stand up and speak clearly. Have the rest of the class listen and take notes about the inventions they like. Write a list of the inventions on the board as each student presents. Then have students vote for the best clothing invention.

To prepare for Lesson 7, ask students who their favorite movie stars are. Then pair students according to their favorite movie stars. Alternatively, ask pairs to choose their movie star. Ask each pair to find information about their movie star on the Internet or from books and/or magazines. If possible, ask students to print a picture of the movie star to the next class (if they have access to the Internet).

Use the **Presentation Kit** for interactive activities in this lesson.

For additional class time, use **Pages 18 and 19** of the Skills Book. Go to **Page 167** in the Happy Campers Teacher's Edition for teacher notes for this lesson. You may also choose to assign these pages as homework.

Lesson 6

1 21 Listen again to **The Story of Velcro.**

2 **Circle *True* or *False*.**

1. George de Mestral was a doctor in Switzerland. True (False)
2. He noticed parts of a plant were stuck on his pants. (True) False
3. Velcro is easy to open and close. (True) False
4. NASA astronauts didn't like Velcro on their clothes. True (False)

3 **Writing Time! Invent a new item for your clothing.**

De Mestral's Clothing Invention	Your Clothing Invention
Invention: Velcro **What it does:** makes it easy to open and close things **How it's used:** little "teeth" work like a sticker	**Invention:** (Students' own **What it does:** answers.) **How it's used:**

4 **Write about your clothing invention.**

My clothing invention is (Students' own answers) .

Lesson 7

Lesson 7

ON STAGE!

PROJECT:
Interview a Movie Star

1 **Plan** to Interview a Movie Star. Write questions.

Did you always want to be an actor?
Did you learn your lines every day?
Did you have to rehearse many scenes?

(Students' own answers.)

2 **Prepare** and practice your interview.

3 **On Stage!** Act out your interview for the class.

Lesson 7 Creative, Collaborative, and Critical Thinking Activity

Lesson Objective: Plan and act out an interview with a movie star.
Vocabulary review: movie star, rehearse a scene, be on time, learn your lines
Grammar review: Did you stay up last night? Yes, I did.
Materials: glue, dress-up clothes (optional)

Start the Class

5 min

Tell students to look at the information they discovered about their favorite movie stars after the last lesson. Have them get into the pairs you organized. Ask pairs to share who their movie star is, say something interesting about the person, and show a picture if they have one. Have the rest of the class suggest questions to ask the movie star in an interview. Remind students to ask the questions in the past tense to practice the language they have been learning in this unit.

1 Plan to Interview a Movie Star. Write questions.

10 min

Tell the pairs they are going to plan and act out an interview with the movie star they have chosen. Have volunteers read the questions in their books aloud.

Remind them of the word order for past tense questions.

Tell students to write at least five questions to ask their movie stars. They must make sure they know the answers to their questions. Once they have their final lists of questions, have them copy their lists neatly on a new sheet of paper (and if they have a picture, glue it to the page).

2 Prepare and practice your interview.

10 min

Have pairs decide who is going to be the interviewer and who is going to be the movie star. Give students time to rehearse the interview. Walk around the classroom to give help and encouragement as needed. Make sure the student who is acting as the movie star can answer the questions without hesitation. Coach students to act out their roles dramatically.

3 On Stage! Act out your interview for the class.

10 min

Tell students to look at the photo of the boy and girl acting out the interview. Ask two confident students to read the example dialogue and encourage them to be dramatic.

Ask each pair to act out their interview for the class. If you have brought any dress-up clothes, encourage students to use them. Have the class applaud after each interview.

As each pair acts out their interview, write down an interesting fact about each movie star for the Try This! activity.

Try This! 5 min

Using the interesting information you collected while students presented their interviews to the class, say facts about the movie stars and have students say who the movie star is each time. You could have volunteers take over your role.

Finish the Class

10 min

To practice present and past tense questions, play a game of Twenty Questions. Think of one of the movie stars who has been "interviewed" in this lesson. Tell students you are going to pretend to be a movie star and they can ask you 20 *yes/no* questions in the present or past tense to find out who you are, for example, *Are you a man or a woman? Are you American? Were you in the Harry Potter movies?*

Use the **Presentation Kit** for interactive activities in this lesson.

Lesson 8 Review

Lesson Objective: Review language from Unit 3.
Vocabulary Review: sweatshirt, sweatpants, cardigan, vest, leggings, tights, hoodie, dress, pay attention, go to bed, waste (your) time, rehearse a scene, be on time, learn your lines
Grammar Review: I didn't want to be late. I didn't have any money. Did you stay up late last night? Yes, I did. Did he learn his lines? No, he didn't.
Materials: board markers (one for each team)

Start the Class

5 min

Play the Shark Game (see **Page T 28**) with the movie and clothing vocabulary from Units 2 and 3. After two or three times, have a volunteer take over your role.

1 Spelling! Write.

10 min

Tell students to look at the pictures. Then have them work individually to label the pictures with the correct words. Check answers by having students write the words on the board. Ask the rest of the class if the words are spelled correctly.

Have students work in pairs to take turns asking a question in the past tense using one of the clothes words, for example, *Did you wear leggings yesterday?* The partner answers *Yes, I did / No, I didn't.* Monitor to make sure students are forming questions and answers correctly.

Try This!

10 min

Have students work in pairs to write down five scrambled verbs in the past tense. Have them exchange their words with another pair and then unscramble the words. Have the pairs check each other's answers. Then have pairs ask and answer questions using the verbs in the past tense.

2 Choose and complete.

5 min

Ask a volunteer to read the verbs in the box aloud. Have students work individually to choose the verbs and write it to complete the sentences correctly. Have students compare answers with a partner. Then check answers with the class.

3 Word Play! Find and circle the words from Unit 3 on Page 72.

10 min

Have students turn to **Page 72** and tell them to find and circle the clothing and commands vocabulary words from Unit 3. Then have students check the words they found with a partner.

Finish the Class

10 min

Play a game to practice the vocabulary and grammar in the unit. Put students in two teams and have them stand in two lines facing the board. Give a board marker to the first student in each team. Explain to students that you will say a sentence in the past tense. The student with the board marker has to go to the board and write the opposite of what you say as quickly as possible. For example, if you say *He learned his lines*, the students have to write *He didn't learn his lines*. The first student to write the opposite sentence correctly wins a point for his or her team. Then have the student hand his or her board marker to the next student in line and go to the back of the line. Keep a tally of the points, and when all students have participated, announce the winning team.

Use the **Presentation Kit** for interactive activities in this lesson.

For additional class time, use **Pages 20 and 21** of the Skills Book. Go to **Page 168** in the Happy Campers Teacher's Edition for teacher notes for this lesson. You may also choose to assign these pages as homework.

Lesson 8

Lesson 8

Round Up!

1 Spelling! Write.

1. tights

2. dress

3. hoodie

4. leggings

5. vest

6. cardigan

2 Choose and complete.

did	ate	learned	watch	play

1. Did they play soccer yesterday?
2. Did you watch TV last night?
3. We ate hamburgers for lunch.
4. She learned her lines last night.

3 Word Play! Find and circle the words from Unit 3 on Page 72.

Unit 4

Unit Objectives

By the end of the unit, students can:

- Identify movie genres.
- Ask and answer questions in the past tense.
- Identify the main idea and specific information in a story.

Student Book

Vocabulary

Types of Movies: action movie, comedy, horror, drama, science fiction, western, documentary, musical

Adjectives: serious, rude, polite, brave, grumpy, silly

Grammar

Who did you go with? When did you go?
What did you see? Where did you go?
Was he brave? Yes, he was.
Were they surprised? No, they weren't.

Skills

Listening: Listen for specific information.

Speaking: Ask and answer questions about movies. Talk about emotions and conditions.

Reading: Read a fiction text:
Uncle Bob's Jokes.
Identify the main idea and specific information in a text.

Writing: Write about the joke.

Creative, Collaborative, and Critical Thinking Competencies

Movie Billboard

Creativity: Develop self-expression and innovation. Determine how the information in the billboard will be presented in a visual and eye-catching way.

Collaboration: Use communication, negotiation, and problem-solving skills to complete the task. Agree on the type of movie, what to include on the billboard, how to present it effectively, and how each group member will contribute to the final product.

Critical Thinking: Analyze, select, and organize information to create an effective and dramatic final product.

Skills Book

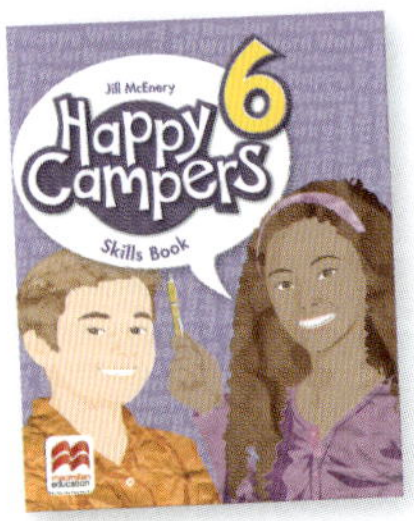

Extra Skills Practice

Speaking and Listening: Ask and answer questions about a picture.

Reading and Writing: Draw conclusions. Write an opinion. Identify multi-syllable words. Recognize spelling patterns. Read clues to identify words.

Teacher Workshop

Teaching with Technology

Ask the class which websites they visit regularly. They may be familiar with many websites that could be useful for class projects. Museum websites are extremely instructive and have information about a wide variety of topics. Students can use these websites to research, create projects, and make posters or presentations. Museum websites are updated regularly and usually have appropriate materials to add to lessons.

Teaching with Games

Words from Words

Write a vocabulary word on the board. Try to choose a longer word with a lot of letters. Put students in pairs or small teams and ask them to make as many words as they can using only the letters in the word. For example, from the word *ringmaster* students could make *ring, master, name, rat, me, string, as, sat, eat, ate*, and so on. The pair or team with the most words wins.

Happy Teacher

During a school year, students will cover a lot of new vocabulary terms. In addition to the My Dictionary section in their notebooks, you could encourage students to review vocabulary frequently by telling them to write new words on small cards and place them in a "Vocab Bag." This can be a plastic bag or any other kind of bag. When students are traveling to school or are at home, they can review the words with a family member or ask a friend to test them. This helps to commit new vocabulary words to memory and also encourages regular study habits.

Happy Class

The dynamics among your students is very important to ensure that learning is fun and motivating. In order to encourage good relationships in class, make a poster with all your students' names on it and display it in your classroom. Explain that when you see or hear a student helping another student without being told to do so, you will place a sticker next to his or her name on the poster. At the end of the school year, count who has the most stickers and reward that student. Rewards could be extra credit, or allow a student to lead a class game.

By Libby Williams

UNIT 4

Lesson 1

1 22 Listen. Then echo.

action movie
comedy
horror
drama
science fiction
western
documentary
musical

2 23 Listen and number.

Movie Fans

3 Page 13 The Language Lodge

Lesson 2

1 23 Sing: Movie Fans.

2 Who did you go with?
I went with my friend Sam!
We saw a lovely musical,
We watch them when
we can!

3 When did you go?
We went on Friday night,
We went to see a
horror film,
It gave us such a fright!

4 What did you see?
We saw a comedy,
We laughed a lot until
we cried,
It was funny to see!

1 Where did you go?
We went to Movie City,
A science fiction
movie played,
The actress was so pretty!

GRAMMAR PASS

Who did you go with?
When did you go?
What did you see?
Where did you go?

2 **Look at the Grammar Pass. Complete.**

1. ________ did you go? Movie City.
2. ________ did you eat? Pizza.
3. ________ did you go with? David.
4. ________ did you go? Yesterday.
5. We use *Where, What, When, Who* + ________ in questions about the past.

3 **Ask and answer about the movies.**

When did you go to the movies?

I went yesterday.

4 Page 14 The Language Lodge

UNIT 4 Lesson 1

1 **Write.**

1. documentary
2. science fiction
3. drama
4. action movie

2 **Read and write the movie types.**

MOVIE REVIEWS

1. It's an exciting story about a cowboy! western
2. It's very, very funny! comedy
3. We sang, too! musical
4. There was a monster in a lake! horror

My Dictionary
Add the new words to your dictionary.

Student Book Page 32

Lesson 1

This may also be completed for homework.

Lesson 1 Vocabulary

Unit 4

Lesson Objective: Identify movie genres.
New Vocabulary: action movie, comedy, horror, drama, science fiction, western, documentary, musical
Materials: Audio **Tracks 22 and 23**

Start the Class

10 min

Start the class with a quick stretch and ask students *Are you ready to learn?* They should say *Yes!* or *Yes, we are!* If they say it quietly, ask them to repeat louder and more enthusiastically.

Ask students what they like to do in their free time. Tell them that you like to go to the movies by saying *I like going to the movies.* Ask them when they went to the movies last and what movie they saw.

1 22 Listen. Then echo.

5 min

Tell students to listen, point to the pictures, and read the words. Play **Track 22**. Then listen and repeat the words. Play **Track 22** again.

Try This! 5 min

Play **Track 22** again, but this time stop after each word and ask the class to spell the words aloud.

2 23 Listen and number.

10 min

Ask students to close their books and try to remember all of the types of movies from Activity 1. Have them open their books to check.

Tell students that they are going to listen to a song about going to the movies. Explain that the verses of the song are not in the correct order in their books. Tell them to listen and number the verses in order. Play **Track 23**. Check answers with the class. Then ask students to listen again and raise their hands when they hear a type of movie. Play **Track 23** again. Finally, tell students to read the song as they listen to the song once more, and play **Track 23** again.

3 Page 13 The Language Lodge

15 min

Have students flip to The Language Lodge **Page 13**.

1 Write.

Tell students to look at the pictures and label each one with the type of movie it represents. Have them check their answers with a partner.

2 Read and write the movie types.

Tell students to read the descriptions of movie types aloud. Have a volunteer read the first sentence as an example, and have the class guess the movie type. Elicit *western.* Then have students write the movie types in their books. Check answers by asking volunteers to read their answers.

My Dictionary

Tell students to turn to the dictionary section in their notebooks. Ask them to write and illustrate the new vocabulary. If they have seen any of the types of movies, have them write the names of the movies, too.

Finish the Class

5 min

Tell the class that you are going to mime watching a movie, and they have to guess what type of movie it is. For example, mime laughing to elicit *comedy*, mime looking very scared to elicit *horror*, or mime riding a horse to elicit *western.* Ask students to say all of the movie types again and end the class.

Use the **Presentation Kit** for interactive activities in this lesson.

Have students use the **Happy Campers app** for additional practice with the new vocabulary.

The Language Lodge Page 13 may also be completed for homework.

Lesson 2 Grammar

Lesson Objective: Ask and answer questions in the past tense about going to the movies.
New Grammar: Who did you go with? When did you go? What did you see? Where did you go?
Vocabulary Review: action movie, comedy, horror, drama, science fiction, western, documentary, musical
Materials: Audio **Track 23**

Start the Class 5 min

Tell the class get in pairs. Write the beginning letters of the movie types on the board: *W, S/F, D, C, M, H, D, A/M*. Tell the pairs to write down the movie types as quickly as they can. Ask the first pair to finish to stand up and read their list.

1 23 Sing: Movie Fans. 10 min

Tell students they are going to read and listen to the song from Lesson 1 again. Play **Track 23**. Tell students to sing along, and play **Track 23** again.

Ask students to look at the lyrics and find and circle all the *wh-* question words. Write them on the board: *Who, When, What, Where*. Tell students to close their books, and try to say each of the four questions from the lyrics. Then tell students to only sing along with the questions. Play **Track 23** again.

Try This! 5 min

Play **Track 23** again, but this time ask boys to sing the four questions and girls to sing the rest of the verses. Then have them switch roles.

2 Look at the Grammar Pass. Complete. 10 min

Ask students to look at the board and say the question words. Then you will repeat the question words. Ask *Is the song is about the present or the past?* Elicit *the past*. Have students look at the Grammar Pass. Ask if they notice the word order of the questions. Have students read and complete the sentences. Check answers with the class.

3 Ask and answer about the movies. 5 min

Have two students read the example dialogue aloud. Have students work in pairs to ask and answer questions about going to the movies using the questions from the song. Walk around the classroom and help as needed. Have one pair demonstrate for the rest of the class.

4 Page 14 The Language Lodge 10 min

Have students flip to The Language Lodge **Page 14**. Have a volunteer read the Grammar Pass aloud.

1 Choose and complete.

Have students look at the Grammar Pass. Tell students to use the words in the box to complete the questions. Ask students to check their answers with a partner.

2 Write questions.

Model the activity by writing *Where/go* on the board and asking students to complete the question in the past tense. Then tell students to write the complete questions in their books, and check their answers with a partner.

Finish the Class 5 min

To finish the class, tell students to stand up. Explain that you are going to play a game. They have to do what you say, but they must not copy what you are doing. For example, say *Touch your nose!* while you are touching your ear. Students who copy what you are doing have to sit down. The last student standing is the winner.

Use the **Presentation Kit** for interactive activities in this lesson.

The Language Lodge Page 14 may also be completed for homework.

For additional class time, use **Pages 22 and 23** of the Skills Book. Go to **Page 169** in the Happy Campers Teacher's Edition for teacher notes for this lesson. You may also choose to assign these pages as homework.

UNIT 4

Lesson 1

1 22 Listen. Then echo.

2 23 Listen and number.

Movie Fans

3 Page 13 The Language Lodge

Lesson 2

1 23 Sing: Movie Fans.

☐ Who did you go with?
I went with my friend Sam!
We saw a lovely musical,
We watch them when
we can!

☐ When did you go?
We went on Friday night,
We went to see a
horror film,
It gave us such a fright!

☐ What did you see?
We saw a comedy,
We laughed a lot until
we cried,
It was funny to see!

☐ Where did you go?
We went to Movie City,
A science fiction
movie played,
The actress was so pretty!

GRAMMAR PASS

Who did you go with?
When did you go?
What did you see?
Where did you go?

2 Look at the Grammar Pass. Complete.

1. Where did you go? Movie City.
2. What did you eat? Pizza.
3. Who did you go with? David.
4. When did you go? Yesterday.
5. We use *Where, What, When, Who* + did in questions about the past.

3 Ask and answer about the movies.

When did you go to the movies?

I went yesterday.

4 Page 14 The Language Lodge

Lesson 2

GRAMMAR PASS

Who did you go with?
When did you go?
What did you see?
Where did you go?

1 Choose and complete.

Where What Who When

1. When did you go to the movies? Last weekend.
2. Where did you go yesterday? To the park.
3. Who did you go with? My cousins.
4. What did you do last night? We watched TV.

2 Write questions.

1. Where/go?
Where did you go ?
2. Who/go?
Who did you go with ?
3. When/go?
When did you go ?
4. What/see?
What did you see ?

Student Book Page 33

Lesson 2

This may also be completed for homework.

Lesson 3

THE HAPPY CAMPERS

1 Were they inside all day?

2 24 Read and listen.

3 25 **Dictation!** Listen and write. Then say.

1. The girls weren't silly, they were serious.
2. The girls were grumpy.
3. Who was brave?
4. He wasn't rude, he was polite.

4 Page 15 The Language Lodge

Lesson 4

1 24 Listen again to **The Happy Campers.**

2 **Grammar Pass!** Write questions.

1. Hamlet was there. Was Hamlet there?
2. He was brave. ______?
3. They were scared. ______?

3 26 Listen and cheer!

Was he brave? Yes, he was!
Were they silly? No, they weren't!

CHEER BOX!

4 Page 16 The Language Lodge

Lesson 3

1 **Match.**

1. rude
2. serious
3. polite
4. brave
5. grumpy
6. silly

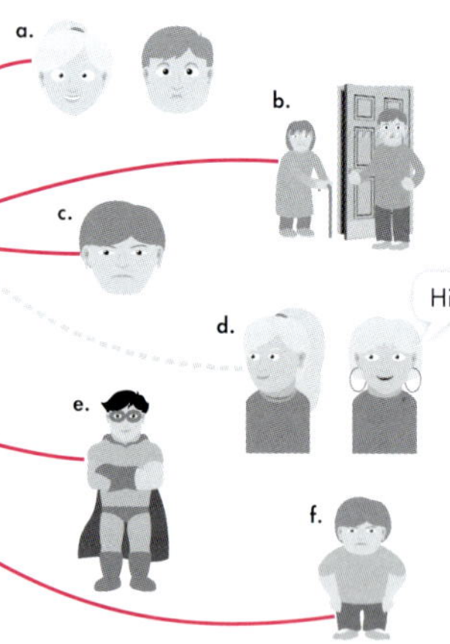

2 **Complete with words from Activity 1.**

1. Rita is always happy. She's never grumpy.
2. Danny is never rude. He's always polite.
3. Terry and Sheila don't do silly things. They're very serious.
4. Rob jumped into the lake and helped the boy. He's very brave.

My Dictionary
Add the new words to your dictionary.

Student Book Page 34

Lesson 3

This may also be completed for homework.

Lesson 3 Vocabulary in Context

Lesson Objective: Talk about emotions and conditions using past tense verbs.
New Vocabulary: serious, rude, polite, brave, grumpy, silly
Vocabulary Review: action movie, comedy, horror, drama, science fiction, western, documentary, musical
Materials: Audio **Tracks 24 and 25**, vocabulary flashcards with Lesson 3 emotions, a stuffed toy dog

Start the Class

5 min

Show the stuffed toy dog to the class and say that his name is Hamlet. Tell them that this is your toy, but that you always seem to lose it! Tell them to close their eyes and hide the toy somewhere in the classroom. Tell students to open their eyes. Ask *Where did Hamlet go?* Repeat once or twice.

1 Were they inside all day?

5 min

Tell students to look carefully at the comic strip illustrations, but not to read it yet. Ask *What is the dog's name?* and elicit *Hamlet*. Ask *Where did Hamlet go?* Elicit *In the water.*

2 24 Read and listen.

10 min

Have students read the comic strip as they listen to the audio. Play **Track 24**. Ask the class if their predictions in Activity 1 were correct. Play **Track 24** again, but this time pause after each frame and ask students questions about the comic strip, for example, Did *Hamlet run after a cat? Did he run into the ocean?*

Have students read the dialogue and underline adjectives. Say the words, write them on the board, and have students repeat. Check understanding of the new words by starting sentences and having students complete them with the appropriate word, for example, *I saw a horror movie and I was … scared!* Tell students that the new words are describing words, or adjectives.

3 25 Dictation! Listen and write. Then say.

10 min

Tell students they will hear sentences and write what they hear. Play the first sentence of **Track 25** and pause the audio to allow students time to write. Repeat with the other sentences. Tell the class that they are going to hear the audio again and this time they will say the sentences after they hear them. Play **Track 25** again and monitor student pronunciation. Then have volunteers write the sentences on the board for the class to check.

*Audio script **Track 25***
1. The girls weren't silly, they were serious.
2. The girls were grumpy. 3. Who was brave?
4. He wasn't rude, he was polite.

4 Page 15 The Language Lodge

15 min

Have students flip to The Language Lodge **Page 15**.

1 Match.

Have students look at the pictures, then match the words to the pictures. Have them check answers with a partner, then check answers with the class.

2 Complete with words from Activity 1.

Tell students to look at the sentences. Have students complete the sentences in their books. Check answers by asking the class to read the complete sentences together.

My Dictionary

Tell students to turn to the dictionary section in their notebooks. Have them write the new adjectives and draw a picture to illustrate the meaning of each one.

Finish the Class

5 min

Ask a student to come to the board and show them a vocabulary flashcard. Tell him or her to mime the adjective, for example, make a silly face for the word *silly*, for the rest of the class to guess. Repeat with the other flashcards.

Use the **Presentation Kit** for interactive activities in this lesson.

Have students use the **Happy Campers app** for additional practice with the new vocabulary.

The Language Lodge Page 15 may also be completed for homework.

Lesson 4 Grammar in Context

Lesson Objective: Ask and answer questions about past activities.
New Grammar: Was he brave? Yes, he was. Were they surprised? No, they weren't.
Vocabulary Review: serious, rude, polite, brave, grumpy, silly
Materials: Audio **Tracks 24 and 26**

Start the Class (5 min)

Energize students by telling them to keep standing after they come into class. Tell them that they can only sit down when they have said a word that begins with a letter that you say. Then say a letter. The first student to raise his or her hand and say a word beginning with that letter can sit down. Continue until all students are sitting.

1 24 Listen again to *The Happy Campers.* (10 min)

Ask students to tell you what they can remember about the comic strip about Hamlet. Remind them about the lake and try to elicit some of the new vocabulary, for example, *brave*. Tell students they are going to listen to the comic strip again. Play **Track 24** and have students read along as they listen.

2 Grammar Pass! Write questions. (5 min)

Ask volunteers to read the first sentence and example question. Write the question on the board and ask students to notice how the word order changes in the question. Have students write the other questions. Check answers with the class.

Try This! (5 min)

Make statements and have students ask you how you felt by using one of the new words, for example, *I missed the last bus home. Were you grumpy? I spoke to a police officer. Were you polite?* Then ask students to make statements.

3 26 Listen and cheer! (5 min)

Tell students to listen to the cheer and read along in their books. Play **Track 26**. Tell students to say the cheer without the audio. Then tell students to clap to the beat, and play **Track 26** again. Tell students to tap their feet, and play **Track 26** again. Then tell them to clap and tap their feet at the same time. Play **Track 26** one last time and see if they can do it!

4 Page 16 The Language Lodge (10 min)

Have students flip to The Language Lodge **Page 16**. Have a volunteer read the Grammar Pass aloud.

1 Choose and complete.
Have students work in pairs. Tell them to use the verbs in the box to complete the sentences. Check answers with the class.

2 Complete.
Ask a student to read the example question. In pairs, have students complete the questions. Check answers with the class.

Finish the Class (10 min)

Tell students they are going to play Swivel. Have students sit in chairs in groups of three. Tell students that the middle student in each group is going to turn left and then right but not get out of the chair—this is a swivel. Explain that when you clap your hands, the middle student should turn to the left and ask the student next to him or her a question about the past, such as *Were you rude yesterday?* The other student replies with a short answer, such as *No, I wasn't.* When you clap your hands again, tell the middle students to turn to the right and ask another question. Have students switch positions with their group members to change who sits in the middle.

Use the **Presentation Kit** for interactive activities in this lesson.

The Language Lodge Page 16 may also be completed for homework.

Lesson 3

THE HAPPY CAMPERS

1 Were they inside all day?

2 24 Read and listen.

3 25 Dictation! Listen and write. Then say.

1. ______________________ .

2. ______________________ .

3. ______________________ ?

4. ______________________ .

4 Page 15 The Language Lodge

Lesson 4

1 24 Listen again to The Happy Campers.

2 Grammar Pass! Write questions.

1. Hamlet was there. Was Hamlet there ?

2. He was brave. Was he brave ?

3. They were scared. Were they scared ?

3 26 Listen and cheer!

Was he brave? Yes, he was!

Were they silly? No, they weren't!

CHEER BOX!

4 Page 16 The Language Lodge

Lesson 4

This may also be completed for homework.

Lesson 4

GRAMMAR PASS

Was he brave?
Yes, he was.

Were they surprised?
No, they weren't.

1 Choose and complete.

was were wasn't weren't

1. Were you at the lake yesterday?
   No, we weren't . We were at the mall.
2. Was Tina with you?
   Yes, she was .
3. Was Jake with you?
   No, he wasn't . He was at home all afternoon.
4. Were you polite to the director?
   Yes, I was .

2 Complete.

1. Was he at school yesterday? No, he wasn't.
2. Was she polite to the teacher? Yes, she was.
3. Were they grumpy last night? No, they weren't.
4. Was he cold and wet? Yes, he was.
5. Was she silly? Yes, she was.

Student Book Page 35

Lesson 5

1 **Who did Uncle Bob send a gift to?**

Gary (circled) Mom frogs Andrea

2 27 **Read and listen.**

Uncle Bob's Jokes

Yesterday was Gary's birthday. He got a special gift from Uncle Bob. The gift box had a joke book, a water bottle, and a stone inside. It was an unusual gift, but jokes can be fun!

He opened the book and started reading a joke. It was called "How to Change Stones into Frogs!" It looked interesting. And Uncle Bob gave him all the things he needed to play the joke on his little sister, Andrea.

Gary and Andrea went into the yard. Gary put the stone in the gift box. Then he put the gift box next to the tree. He poured the water over the stone. "Close your eyes and count to 10, Andrea!" Gary said.

"OK!" Andrea said. She was very excited. She closed her eyes and counted to 10. Gary quietly took the stone out of the box, and put in a frog.

"Ready? OK, look!" Gary said. Andrea opened her eyes, and out jumped a big, fat frog. "Wow! A frog! That's amazing!" she said. "Now I'm going to try one of Uncle Bob's jokes!"

Lesson 5 Fiction Reading

Lesson Objectives: Read a fiction text to practice unit language.
Grammar Review: past tense verbs
Materials: Audio **Track 27**, an object wrapped several times in gift wrap or newspaper with a clue written on each layer

Start the Class

5 min

Ask students who their favorite comedians are or which movie or TV stars they think are funny. Tell the class that you think you are funny, and say *I think I'm funny!* Then tell them a simple joke, for example, *What is the best day to go to the beach? Sun-day, of course!* Tell students that they are going to read about a birthday and a joke.

1 Who did Uncle Bob send a gift to?

5 min

Tell students to look at the pictures. Elicit what is happening in each picture and pre-teach important vocabulary, such as *joke book, stone, frog.* Ask students to predict what the story is about. Write some of their predictions on the board.

Ask a student to read the question. Then have students scan the text to find the answer.

2 27 Read and listen.

20 min

Tell students to read and listen to the story. Play **Track 27**. Ask students if their predictions about the story were correct. Then ask students to tell you what Gary's joke was.

Put students in groups of five. Have students in each group take turns reading one paragraph of the story. Monitor and help with pronunciation and vocabulary.

Try This!

10 min

Have students read the text again, but this time ask a student to read the first sentence, the student next to him or her to read the second sentence, and so on. Continue until students have read the whole story sentence by sentence.

Finish the Class

10 min

Use the object wrapped in paper you prepared before class. For example, if the object is a stuffed toy elephant, the clues you provide could be one of the following: *I am an animal, I have big ears, I am gray, I am very big,* or *I have a very long nose.* Show the wrapped object to the class, and have students guess what it is. Give the object to a student and have him or her unwrap one layer of paper and read the clue. Tell students to guess what the object is again. Do not tell them if they are correct or not. Continue with other students until the object is completely unwrapped. Congratulate students who guessed correctly.

Use the **Presentation Kit** for interactive activities in this lesson.

Lesson 6 Reading Comprehension / Writing

Lesson Objectives: Identify specific information. Write about the joke.
Grammar Review: *wh-* questions in the past
Materials: Audio **Track 27**

Start the Class

5 min

Play a Chain Memory Game (see **Page T 53**) with birthday gifts.

Start the game by saying *I got a toy for my birthday.* Go around the class and have students continue the game.

1 27 Listen again to Uncle Bob's Jokes.

10 min

Ask students to tell you what they remember about the story in the last lesson.

Tell students to listen to the story again and read along. Play **Track 27**. Ask if they remembered the details correctly.

2 Answer the questions.

10 min

Ask a volunteer to read the questions. Tell students to read the text silently once again. Have students work in pairs to discuss and answer the questions. Once everyone has finished, have students share their answers with the class. Ask the rest of the class if they agree. For each answer, ask students to point to and say the evidence for their answers in the text.

3 Writing Time! Think of the joke that Gary played on Andrea.

10 min

Ask a volunteer to read the directions. Then have three students read the questions. Have students complete the questions individually. Then have them compare their answers with a partner. Tell students to share their answers with the class.

4 Write about the joke.

10 min

Tell students that they are going to write a paragraph about the joke that Gary played on Andrea. Tell them to use the information from Activity 3 to write their paragraphs. Walk around the classroom to monitor as students work and provide help as needed. When students have finished writing, encourage them to read their work, correct any mistakes, and rewrite a clean version of their paragraphs. Group students into pairs and have them read their paragraphs to each other. Encourage them to help their partners correct any remaining mistakes and to give positive feedback.

Finish the Class

5 min

Write a sentence from the story on a piece of paper. Tell students that they are going to play the Telephone Game. The game involves whispering a sentence from one student to the next without shouting or changing the sentence. First, divide the class in two groups and ask students to stand in two lines. Stand behind the lines (farthest away from the board) and show the last two students in each line the paper with the sentence from the story written on it. Tell them to whisper the sentence to the student in front of them, and so on. The students closest to the board will write the sentence they heard on the board. Read the sentence you wrote and ask students if it is exactly the same as the sentences on the board.

Use the **Presentation Kit** for interactive activities in this lesson.

For additional class time, use **Pages 24 and 25** of the Skills Book. Go to **Page 170** in the Happy Campers Teacher's Edition for teacher notes for this lesson. You may also choose to assign these pages as homework.

Lesson 6

Lesson 6

1 27 **Listen again to Uncle Bob's Jokes.**

2 **Answer the questions.**

1. When was Gary's birthday? It was yesterday.
2. Who sent Gary a gift? Uncle Bob.
3. What was the gift? A joke book, a water bottle, and a stone.
4. Did the stone change into a frog? No, it didn't.

3 **Writing Time!** **Think of the joke that Gary played on Andrea.**

1. What joke did he play? "How to Change Stones into Frogs!"
2. When did he do it? He did the joke yesterday.
3. Where did he do it? He did it in the yard.

4 **Write about the joke.**

Gary played a joke called How to Change Stones into Frogs.
(Students' own answers)

Lesson 7

Lesson 7

ON STAGE!

PROJECT: Movie Billboard

1 **Plan a Movie Billboard.**

What type of movie was it? (Students'

Who was in it? own

Where was it? answers.)

What happened in the movie?

2 **Prepare a Movie Billboard.**

3 **On Stage! Present your Movie Billboard to the class.**

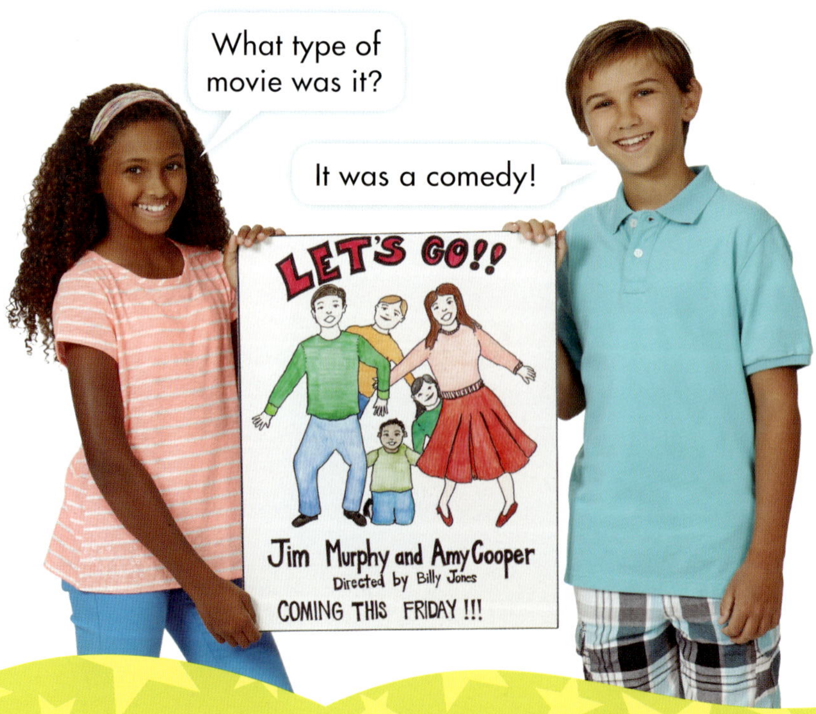

Lesson 7 Creative, Collaborative, and Critical Thinking Activity

Lesson Objective: Plan, create, and present a Movie Billboard.
Vocabulary Review: action movie, comedy, horror, drama, science fiction, western, documentary, musical
Grammar Review: Who did you go with? When did you go? What did you see? Where did you go?
Materials: an example of a movie billboard, scissors, construction paper, pens, tape, pencils

Start the Class

5 min

Show students an example of a movie billboard. If you don't have an actual poster, find one on the Internet and print it. Ask students to look at the poster and identify the type of information it contains, such as a photo or illustration, the title of the movie, the movie stars, the director, and so on. Ask students if they have seen the movie and if they liked it. If they haven't seen it, ask *Would you like to see the movie?*

1 Plan a Movie Billboard.

10 min

Tell students that they are going to create their own Movie Billboards. Put them in groups, or ask them to get into their project groups if they have been assigned.

Ask a volunteer to read the questions in Activity 1. Tell groups to discuss and choose the movie they are going to make a Movie Billboard for. When they have chosen a movie, tell students to plan their Movie Billboards by answering the questions about it.

2 Prepare a Movie Billboard.

20 min

Ask volunteers to hand out the materials. Tell the groups to use the information from Activity 1 to prepare their billboards. Have them look at the billboard in the photo to give them an idea of what they need to do. Encourage them to decide how they are going to present the information and what each student in the group is going do. When they have reached a decision, tell them to create their billboards. Monitor their work, particularly to make sure that every student in each of groups is participating equally; offer help and support when necessary.

3 On Stage! Present your Movie Billboard to the class.

10 min

Tell students to look at the photo of the girl and boy presenting their Movie Billboard. Tell two students to read the example dialogue.

Have each group take turns to come to the board to present their Movie Billboard. Tell the rest of the class to listen carefully so that they can ask any questions or give opinions at the end. Encourage applause at the end of each presentation.

Display the Movie Billboards around the classroom.

Finish the Class

5 min

Keep students in their groups. Tell them to imagine that they can go to one of the movies advertised on the billboards—but not their own! Give them two or three minutes to discuss and decide which movie they want to go to. Then ask each group to tell the class which movie they chose, and why.

Use the **Presentation Kit** for interactive activities in this lesson.

Lesson 8 Review

Lesson Objective: Review language from Unit 4.
Vocabulary Review: action movie, comedy, horror, drama, science fiction, western, documentary, musical, serious, rude, polite, brave, grumpy, silly
Grammar Review: Who did you go with? When did you go? What did you see? Where did you go? Was he brave? Yes, he was. Were they surprised? No, they weren't.
Materials: flashcards with the vocabulary words from Unit 4

Start the Class

10 min

Give students one minute to write down as many new vocabulary words from this unit as they can. Ask them to count their words and tell the class. The student with the most words is the winner. Have the winning student write his or her words on the board. Ask the other students to check spelling.

Divide the class into teams of three or four. Say one of the words on the board and ask students to write a correct sentence using the word as quickly as possible. Have them raise their hands as soon as they have written a sentence. Ask a volunteer from that team to read their sentence aloud. If it is correct, the team wins a point.

1 Spelling! Read the clues. Complete the puzzle.

10 min

Have students work in pairs. Tell them to look at the puzzle, read the clues, and write the words in the puzzle. To check answers, call out a clue number, such as *1 Down*, and a volunteer to say the answer.

2 Write questions.

10 min

Ask a volunteer to read the sentences on the right side of the page. Explain to students that they have to write the questions. Model the first one with the class to make sure everyone understands what to do. Then have students work individually to write the questions. Check answers with the class.

Dictate a few similar sentences, but use students' names in order to personalize the activity, for example, *(Gabriel) played tennis yesterday*. Ask students to ask the question: *Did (Gabriel) play tennis yesterday?*

3 Word Play! Find and circle the words from Unit 4 on Page 72.

10 min

Have students turn to **Page 72** and tell them to find and circle the movie and adjective vocabulary words from Unit 4. Then have students check the words they found with a partner.

Try This!

5 min

Write the letters from each of the new vocabulary words from Unit 4 randomly all over the board. Have students work in pairs use the letters to make as many words from the unit as possible. Ask each pair to say how many words they have and to spell them out. The pair with the most words wins.

Finish the Class

5 min

Ask a student to come to the board and show him or her a vocabulary flashcard. Have the student mime the word for the other students to guess. Have as many students mime as time allows.

Use the **Presentation Kit** for interactive activities in this lesson.

For additional class time, use **Pages 26 and 27** of the Skills Book. Go to **Page 171** in the Happy Campers Teacher's Edition for teacher notes for this lesson. You may also choose to assign these pages as homework.

Lesson 8

Lesson 8

Round Up!

1 Spelling! Read the clues. Complete the puzzle.

↓ Down

1. The movie hero was ____ .
2. Amy says please and thank you. She's ____ .
4. He's not happy. He's ____ .

→ Across

3. She looks ____ . She's not smiling.
5. They're not polite. They're ____ .
6. The comedy was funny and ____ .

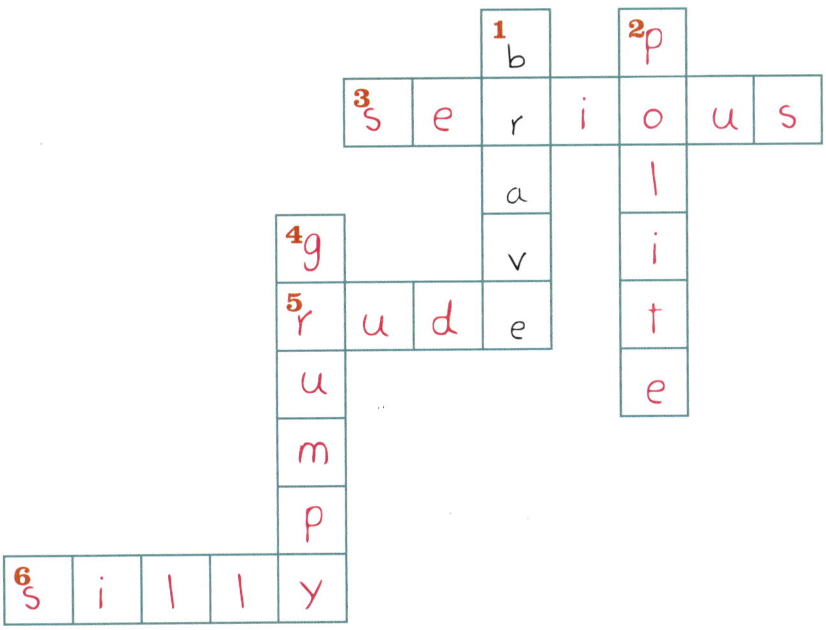

2 Write questions.

1. When did you go ? I went last Saturday.
2. What did they play ? They played soccer.
3. What did he drink ? He drank soda.
4. Where was it ? It was on the table.
5. What was it ? It was a sweatshirt.

3 Word Play! Find and circle the words from Unit 4 on Page 72.

Unit 5

Unit Objectives

By the end of the unit, students can:

- Identify elements of the solar system and astronomy.
- Compare and ask and answer questions about planets using superlatives.
- Talk about the solar system.

Student Book

Vocabulary

Solar System: universe, solar system, planet, Mercury, Neptune, Jupiter, Saturn, Earth

Astronomy: astronomer, telescope, moon, comet, meteor, crater

Grammar

The nearest planet to the sun is Mercury.
The largest planet is Jupiter.
Is it the nearest mall? Which is the smallest moon?

Skills

Listening: Listen for the main idea and specific information.

Speaking: Describe planets. Ask and answer questions about the solar system.

Reading: Read a nonfiction text (social studies): **Galileo and His Telescope**. Identify specific information. Read and correct false information.

Writing: Write about a famous person.

Creative, Collaborative, and Critical Thinking Competencies

The Solar System

Creativity: Develop self-expression, innovation, and problem-solving skills to plan the poster and present information effectively.

Collaboration: Use communication and negotiation skills to discuss and decide on what information to include, how to present it, and how each group member will contribute to the project.

Critical Thinking: Use problem-solving skills to analyze and organize information to create the final product.

Skills Book

Extra Skills Practice

Speaking and Listening: Ask and answer questions about a picture.

Reading and Writing: Identify the sequence of events. Recall details. Recognize spelling patterns. Categorize words. Read clues to identify words.

Teacher Workshop

Teaching with Technology

There are free educational websites that enable students to create virtual posters. These can be fun learning tools. Students can put together video clips, pictures, and texts from the Internet to make their virtual posters.

Teaching with Games

Word Tennis

Divide the class into two teams. Tell students that they have to keep "hitting" words or facts between the teams as though playing tennis with words. When one team cannot think of another word or fact to say, the other team scores a point. Give a category such as *food*. Each team says the name of a food until one team has run out of ideas.

Happy Teacher

If you feel that the motivation in your class is decreasing, set up a competition that can run for a few weeks and award prizes. For example, as this unit's theme is space, you could set up a competition to create a class wall display about the solar system and space. Encourage students to add to the display with pictures, drawings, interesting information, and so on. Award a prize to the student who contributed the most to the display.

Happy Class

During the school year, write brief letters to each student in class. The first letter could be welcome letter to let students know how happy you are to have them in class, and how excited you are to help them learn and have fun during their English lessons. This personalized welcome reduces student anxiety and creates a positive atmosphere. In the middle of the school year, send another letter encouraging students and recognizing their achievements. These letters demonstrate your investment and awareness of student progress and can bring you closer to your students.

By Angela Llanas

UNIT 5

Lesson 1

1 28 **Listen. Then echo.**

universe
solar system
planet
Mercury
Neptune
Jupiter
Saturn
Earth

2 29 **Listen and circle.**

Off We Go!

In our spaceship off we go,
Around the solar system / universe we know!

1. There's the sun! It's a star!
   It has eight planets, near and far!
   The nearest planet to the sun
   Is Jupiter / Mercury — the smallest one!
   Then there's the farthest planet, too!
   Its name is Saturn / Neptune, and it's blue!
2. The largest planet near our sun
   Is Neptune / Jupiter — the giant one!
   Look! Saturn's / Earth's rings are very nice.
   Wow! They're rings of rock and ice!
   And now it's time for us to go
   Back to planet Earth, we know!

3 Page 17 **The Language Lodge**

Lesson 2

1 29 **Sing: Off We Go!**

GRAMMAR PASS

The nearest planet to the sun is Mercury.

The largest planet is Jupiter.

2 **Look at the Grammar Pass. Circle.**

1. The sentences compare two planets / many planets.
2. We use *the* + adjective + *-est* / *-er* to compare more than two things.

3 **Make true sentences and tell a friend.**

Mercury is the smallest planet in our solar system.

Mercury is the nearest planet to the sun.

4 Page 18 **The Language Lodge**

UNIT 5 Lesson 1

1 **Find and circle eight solar system words in the puzzle.**

E	X	P	N	E	P	T	U	N	E	A
A	Z	L	M	E	R	C	U	R	Y	F
R	X	A	V	Z	Y	G	J	K	F	E
T	U	N	I	V	E	R	S	E	W	S
H	W	E	G	K	P	F	T	J	K	I
S	A	T	U	R	N	X	A	Z	Q	T
Q	J	U	P	I	T	E	R	Z	X	O
W	T	B	A	G	U	P	N	V	J	R
S	O	L	A	R	S	Y	S	T	E	M

2 **Choose and complete.**

Earth Mercury planets universe

1. The universe has many solar systems.
2. There are eight planets around the sun.
3. We live on planet Earth.
4. Mercury is the smallest planet.

My Dictionary
Add the new words to your dictionary.

Student Book Page 40

Lesson 1

This may also be completed for homework.

Lesson 1 Vocabulary

Unit 5

Lesson Objective: Identify solar system vocabulary.
New Vocabulary: universe, solar system, planet, Mercury, Neptune, Jupiter, Saturn, Earth
Materials: Audio **Tracks 28 and 29**

Start the Class

5 min

Draw a big circle on the board and ask students to guess what it is. Give clues, such as *It has water. It's big. We live here!* When students have guessed *Earth*, brainstorm words they know about space and write them on the board.

1 28 Listen. Then echo.

10 min

Ask students *Where are all the planets in the universe?* Elicit *The solar system*. Then ask *What is the center of the solar system?* Elicit *The sun*. Ask students if they know the names of all the planets in order from the sun. Say the order if they don't know, and draw a simple diagram on the board labeled with the names of the sun and planets: *Sun, Mercury, Venus, Earth, Mars, Jupiter, Saturn, Uranus, Neptune.*

Have students look at the pictures and identify as many words as they can. Tell them to listen to the audio and point to the pictures as they hear the words. Play **Track 28**. Then play **Track 28** again and have students echo the words.

Try This!

5 min

Tell students that American children learn the order of the planets by making a sentence using the first letter of each planet, for example, *My Very Excellent Mother Just Served Us Nachos!* Ask the class to make their own sentence in English to remember the order of the planets.

2 29 Listen and circle.

10 min

Ask students to look at the main photo. Tell them they are going to listen to a song about the solar system. Play **Track 29**. Then tell students to look at the song lyrics in their books. This time, tell them to listen, read the song lyrics, and circle the correct words
Play the song again. Check answers with the class.

3 Page 17 The Language Lodge

15 min

Have students flip to The Language Lodge **Page 17**.

1 Find and circle eight solar system words in the puzzle.

Have students look at the pictures. Elicit the vocabulary words. Then tell students to find and circle the words in the puzzle as quickly as they can. Check answers by pointing to the pictures and asking students to point to the words in the puzzle.

2 Choose and complete.

Tell students to look at the words in the box. Read Item 1 and elicit *universe*. Have students complete the other sentences. Check answers with the class.

My Dictionary

Tell students to turn to the dictionary section in their notebooks. Have them write the new words and draw a picture to illustrate each one.

Finish the Class

5 min

Review the order of the planets from the sun. Then play Word Tennis (see **Page T 89**) with space vocabulary.

Use the **Presentation Kit** for interactive activities in this lesson.

Have students use the **Happy Campers app** for additional practice with the new vocabulary.

The Language Lodge Page 17 may also be completed for homework.

Lesson 2 Grammar

Lesson Objective: Compare planets using superlatives.
New Grammar: The nearest planet to the sun is Mercury. The largest planet is Jupiter.
Vocabulary Review: universe, solar system, planet, Mercury, Neptune, Jupiter, Saturn, Earth
Materials: Audio **Track 29**; flashcards with the solar system vocabulary words; prepare *true/false* statements about the solar system for a quiz

Start the Class

5 min

Give flashcards of the solar system to volunteer students. Ask the volunteers to line up in the correct order from the sun. Ask the rest of the class *Which planet is nearest to the sun?* Elicit *Mercury*. Then ask *Which planet is farthest from the sun?* Elicit *Neptune*.

1 29 Sing: Off We Go!

10 min

Tell students they are going to listen to "Off We Go!" again. Play **Track 29** and have students listen and read the song lyrics. Play **Track 29** again and have the class sing along.

Ask students to look at the song lyrics and underline examples of words ending in *-est*. Tell students that these words are called superlatives.

Try This! 5 min

Tell students to sing the song again, but this time to stand up when they hear a word ending in *-est*. Play **Track 29**.

2 Look at the Grammar Pass. Circle.

5 min

Ask a volunteer to read the Grammar Pass. Have students work in pairs to look at the sentences in the activity and circle the correct answers. Have the pairs say their answers aloud for the class to check. Write *the* + ____*-est* on the board. Point out to the class that the word *the* is an important part of the structure.

3 Make true sentences and tell a friend.

10 min

Tell volunteers to read the example dialogue. Have students work in pairs and take turns making sentences about the solar system. Tell them to look at the song lyrics for ideas. Monitor that students are forming and using superlatives correctly.

Have pairs say their sentences for the class.

4 Page 18 The Language Lodge

10 min

Have students flip to The Language Lodge **Page 18**. Have a volunteer read the Grammar Pass aloud.

1 Choose and complete.

Write *small* and *brave* on the board. Ask students to say the superlative for each word. Elicit *the smallest* and *the bravest*. Point out that there is only one *-e* in *bravest*.
Tell students to look at the pictures and the words in the box. Have students choose words from the box and use them to complete the sentences with superlatives. Check answers with the class.

2 Write sentences.

Write *Earth / green / planet* on the board Ask students to make a superlative sentence. Then have students work in pairs to write the sentences. Have one pair say their answers for the class to check.

Finish the Class

5 min

Have the class take a quick *true/false* quiz about the solar system. Divide the class into two teams. Using the *true/false* statements you prepared, say sentences about the solar system. Tell students to raise their hands to say if each sentence is *true* or *false*. Select a student to answer each time and make sure that both teams have chances to answer. Each correct answer earns one point for the student's team.

Use the **Presentation Kit** for interactive activities in this lesson.

The Language Lodge Page18 may also be completed for homework.

For additional class time, use **Pages 28 and 29** of the Skills Book. Go to **Page 172** in the Happy Campers Teacher's Edition for teacher notes for this lesson. You may also choose to assign these pages as homework.

UNIT 5

Lesson 1

1 28 Listen. Then echo.

2 29 Listen and circle.

Off We Go!

In our spaceship off we go,
Around the solar system / universe we know!

1. There's the sun! It's a star!
   It has eight planets, near and far!
   The nearest planet to the sun
   Is Jupiter / Mercury — the smallest one!
   Then there's the farthest planet, too!
   Its name is Saturn / Neptune, and it's blue!

2. The largest planet near our sun
   Is Neptune / Jupiter — the giant one!
   Look! Saturn's / Earth's rings are very nice.
   Wow! They're rings of rock and ice!
   And now it's time for us to go
   Back to planet Earth, we know!

3 Page 17 The Language Lodge

Lesson 2

1 29 Sing: Off We Go!

GRAMMAR PASS

The nearest planet to the sun is Mercury.

The largest planet is Jupiter.

2 Look at the Grammar Pass. Circle.

1. The sentences compare two planets / (many planets).
2. We use *the* + adjective + (-est) / -er to compare more than two things.

3 Make true sentences and tell a friend.

Mercury is the smallest planet in our solar system.

Mercury is the nearest planet to the sun.

4 Page 18 The Language Lodge

Lesson 2

GRAMMAR PASS

The nearest planet to the sun is Mercury.

The largest planet is Jupiter.

1 Choose and complete.

large cold high near

1. The highest mountain in the world is Mount Everest.

2. The largest ocean in the world is the Pacific Ocean.

3. The coldest place on the Earth is in Antarctica.

4. The nearest star to the Earth is the sun.

2 Write sentences.

1. Earth / green / planet — Earth is the greenest planet.
2. Jupiter / large / planet — Jupiter is the largest planet.
3. Neptune / cold / planet — Neptune is the coldest planet.

Student Book Page 41

Lesson 2

This may also be completed for homework.

Lesson 3

THE HAPPY CAMPERS

1 What does Greg like to do?

2 30 Read and listen.

3 31 Dictation! Listen and write. Then say.

1. It's hit telescope.
2. There is a big crater on the moon.
3. Comets and meteors fly in space.
4. I want to be an astronomer.

4 Page 19 The Language Lodge

42

Lesson 4

1 30 Listen again to The Happy Campers.

2 Grammar Pass! Match.

1. Is our moon the biggest?	Jupiter.
2. Which is the closest moon to Earth?	Yes, it is.
3. Which is the largest planet?	Our moon.
4. Is Earth the greenest planet?	No, it isn't.

3 32 Listen and cheer!

Is Jupiter the biggest planet? Yes, it is!
Which is the smallest planet? Mercury!

CHEER BOX!

4 Page 20 The Language Lodge

43

Lesson 3

1 Look and complete.

1.  There is a big crater on the moon.
2.  We use a telescope to look at planets.
3.  There was a big, beautiful moon last night.
4.  An astronomer studies planets, moons, and solar systems.
5.  A meteor has a long tail.
6.  A comet flies across the sky in a flash.

My Dictionary
Add the new words to your dictionary.

Student Book Page 42

19

Lesson 3

This may also be completed for homework.

Lesson 3 Vocabulary in Context

Lesson Objective: Identify astronomy vocabulary.
New Vocabulary: astronomer, telescope, moon, comet, meteor, crater
Vocabulary Review: universe, solar system, planet, Mercury, Neptune, Jupiter, Saturn, Earth
Materials: Audio **Tracks 30 and 31**

Start the Class

5 min

Ask students how we can see stars and planets. Mime using a telescope and pretend to study something far away. As you are miming, give students clues about what you are looking at, for example, *It's big. It's hot. It's yellow.* Elicit *the sun.*

1 What does Greg like to do?

5 min

Ask a volunteer to read the question. Tell students to look at the pictures in the comic strip, and ask them to guess what Greg likes to do.

2 30 Read and listen.

10 min

Write *astronomer* on the board and discuss the meaning with the class. Tell students to read the comic strip as they listen to the audio. Play **Track 30**. Ask students if their guesses in Activity 1 were correct. Ask the question again and elicit *He likes to study the universe.* Ask *What does an astronomer use to look at the universe?* Elicit *a telescope.*

Tell students to read again and listen for what Patty wanted to see. Play **Track 30** again. Ask *What did Patty want to see?* Elicit *Jupiter.* Then ask *Did Patty see Jupiter?* Elicit *no.* Ask *Why couldn't Patty see Jupiter?* Elicit *It was daytime!*

3 31 Dictation! Listen and write. Then say.

10 min

Tell students they will hear sentences and write what they hear. Play the first sentence of **Track 31** and pause the audio to allow students time to write. Repeat with the other sentences. Tell the class that they are going to hear the audio again and this time they will say the sentences after they hear them. Play **Track 31** again and monitor student pronunciation. Then have volunteers write the sentences on the board for the class to check.

Audio script ***Track 31***
1. It's his telescope. 2. There is a big crater on the moon. 3. Comets and meteors fly in space. 4. I want to be an astronomer.

Try This! 5 min

Tell students they are going to say the sentences from Dictation! again, but this time they should whisper the first and third sentences, and speak loudly for the second and fourth sentences. Play **Track 31** again, pausing for students to say the sentences quietly or loudly.

4 Page 19 The Language Lodge

10 min

Have students flip to The Language Lodge **Page 19**.

1 Look and complete.
Have students work in pairs. Tell them to look at the pictures and complete the sentences. Have pairs read their sentences aloud for the class to check their answers.

My Dictionary
Tell students to turn to the dictionary section in their notebooks. Have them write the new words and draw a picture or write a sentence for each one.

Finish the Class

5 min

Have a volunteer use the imaginary telescope. Whisper one of the new vocabulary words to the student. Have him or her use the imaginary telescope and give clues to the class about what he or she is looking at, for example, *It has a long tail.* Repeat with other students.

Use the **Presentation Kit** for interactive activities in this lesson.

Have students use the **Happy Campers app** for additional practice with the new vocabulary.

The Language Lodge Page 19 may also be completed for homework.

Lesson 4 Grammar in Context

Lesson Objective: Ask and answer questions using superlatives.
New Grammar: Is it the nearest mall? Which is the smallest moon?
Vocabulary Review: universe, solar system, planet, Mercury, Neptune, Jupiter, Saturn, Earth, astronomer, telescope, moon, comet, meteor, crater
Materials: Audio **Tracks 30 and 32**

Start the Class

5 min

Write the words *Earth*, *Jupiter*, *Saturn*, and *Neptune* on the board. Put students in pairs to think of one or two facts about each word. After a few minutes, ask students to say their facts. Write a few facts on the board in the superlative form, for example, *Mercury is the nearest planet to the sun.* Ask students to repeat the sentences.

1 30 Listen again to The Happy Campers.

5 min

Before telling students to open their books, brainstorm what they remember about the comic strip from Lesson 3. Tell students to read and listen to the comic strip again. Play **Track 30**. Tell students to listen again and underline all the superlatives in the text. Play **Track 30** again.

Try This! 5 min

To prepare students for the Grammar Pass! activity, play **Track 30** again and pause it after each question. Have students repeat the questions.

2 Grammar Pass! Match.

10 min

Write the question *Is our moon the biggest?* on the board, and then say it. Model pronunciation for students, pointing out that the intonation of the question rises at the end. Then write *Which is the closest moon to Earth?* and model pronunciation, pointing out that intonation in *wh-* questions falls at the end.

Tell students to read the questions in the Grammar Pass! activity, using the correct rising or falling intonation. Then have students work in pairs to match the questions with the answers. Check by having different students read the questions and the answers.

3 32 Listen and cheer!

5 min

Tell students to listen to the cheer as they read along. Play **Track 32**. Then tell them to say the cheer along with the audio and play **Track 32** again.

4 Page 20 The Language Lodge

10 min

Have students flip to The Language Lodge **Page 20**. Have a volunteer read the Grammar Pass aloud.

1 Write questions.

Read Item 1 aloud with the class. Read the answer and ask students to say what the question is. Elicit *Which is the hottest planet?*

Then have students work in pairs to write the other questions. Check by reading the answers and having students ask the questions. Correct intonation if necessary.

Finish the Class

10 min

Put the class into four teams. Give each team four sheets of paper. Ask the teams to write a question on each sheet of paper using superlatives. Collect the papers. Ask each team at least one question, but make sure you do not ask them the questions they wrote. The team with the most correct answers wins.

Use the **Presentation Kit** for interactive activities in this lesson.

The Language Lodge Page 20 may also be completed for homework.

Lesson 3

THE HAPPY CAMPERS

1 What does Greg like to do?

2 30 Read and listen.

3 31 **Dictation!** Listen and write. Then say.

1. ______________________________.
2. ______________________________.
3. ______________________________.
4. ______________________________.

4 Page 19 The Language Lodge

Lesson 4

1 30 Listen again to The Happy Campers.

2 **Grammar Pass!** Match.

1. Is our moon the biggest?
2. Which is the closest moon to Earth?
3. Which is the largest planet?
4. Is Earth the greenest planet?

Jupiter.
Yes, it is.
Our moon.
No, it isn't.

3 32 Listen and cheer!

Is Jupiter the biggest planet? Yes, it is!
Which is the smallest planet? Mercury!

CHEER BOX!

4 Page 20 The Language Lodge

Lesson 4

This may also be completed for homework.

Lesson 4

GRAMMAR PASS

Is it the nearest mall?

Which is the smallest moon?

1 **Write questions.**

1. Which is the hottest planet?
   Venus is the hottest planet.
2. Is the Amazon the longest river?
   Yes, the Amazon is the longest river.
3. Which is the highest mountain?
   Mount Everest is the highest mountain.
4. Is Mercury the smallest planet?
   Yes, Mercury is the smallest planet.
5. Which is the coldest place?
   Antarctica is the coldest place.
6. Which is the biggest country?
   Russia is the biggest country.
7. Is an elephant the largest land animal?
   Yes, an elephant is the largest land animal.

Student Book Page 43

Lesson 5

1 What did Galileo study?

telescopes   moons and planets   astronomers   spaceships

2 33 Read and listen.

Galileo and His Telescope

Galileo was an Italian astronomer who lived a long time ago. He was one of the smartest astronomers in history. He was the very first astronomer to learn about the solar system with a telescope!

One of the first things he looked at was the moon. He saw the deepest craters and the highest mountains on the moon with his telescope.

Then Galileo studied the planets. He looked at Mercury, the smallest planet, and Jupiter, the biggest planet. He discovered that the planets don't circle the Earth. They circle the sun. Galileo was the first person to see Jupiter's moons. There are 64 moons, but he didn't see all of them! He only saw four moons with his telescope. Then he saw something that looked like ears on the planet Saturn. He didn't know he saw the famous rings of Saturn.

Some people think Galileo is the father of modern astronomy. In 1989, a spaceship started a trip to study Jupiter and its moons. The name of this spaceship was *Galileo*!

Lesson 5 Nonfiction Reading

Lesson Objective: Read a nonfiction text to practice unit language.
Vocabulary Review: astronomer, solar system, telescope, moon, crater, planet, Mercury, Jupiter, Saturn, Earth, sun
Materials: Audio **Track 33**, yellow and black construction paper

Start the Class

10 min

Play the Shark Game (see **Page T 28**) with the new vocabulary from the unit. Play a couple of times, then have students come to the board and take over your role.

1 What did Galileo study?

5 min

Tell students to look at the title of the text and the pictures and then ask students to predict what the text is going to be about. Write a few of their suggestions on the board. Then ask *What did Galileo study?* and read the answer options. Have students give their answers, but don't tell them if they are correct or not.

2 33 Read and listen.

20 min

Point to the picture of Galileo and ask the class what they already know about him. Tell students to read the text as they listen to the audio. Play **Track 33**. Refer to students' predictions about the text on the board, and ask if they were correct or not. Then tell students to read and listen again, and underline the discoveries that Galileo made. Play **Track 33** again. Tell students to read the phrases or sentences they underlined.

Put students in groups of four and have each group take turns reading a paragraph of the text. Walk around the classroom to help with pronunciation and vocabulary as necessary. Have one group read the text to the class.

Try This! (5 min)

Ask students to read through the text and circle all of the superlatives. Review the superlatives in the text with the class.

Finish the Class

10 min

Tell the class that Galileo was a very famous person from Italy. Brainstorm the names of famous people from the past and write a list on the board. The famous people should only come from the students' own country. Hand out the yellow stars you prepared and tell students to choose one of the famous people on the board that they know five things about. Tell them to write the name of the person in the center of the star, and write an interesting fact about the person on each of the five arms of the star. Have as many students as possible read their five facts, and ask the rest of the class to guess who the person is. Display the stars on black paper on a classroom wall to look like stars in the night sky.

Use the **Presentation Kit** for interactive activities in this lesson.

Lesson 6 Reading Comprehension / Writing

Lesson Objectives: Identify specific information. Write about a famous person.
Vocabulary Review: astronomer, solar system, telescope, moon, crater, planet, Mercury, Jupiter, Saturn, Earth
Materials: Audio **Track 33**, a prepared paragraph about a famous person from the past

Start the Class

5 min

Divide the class into two teams. Play Word Tennis (see **Page T 89**) with facts they can remember from the text in Lesson 5. If one team cannot say a fact, they lose.

1 33 Listen again to Galileo and His Telescope.

10 min

Make sure students have their books closed. Tell them to listen again to the text about Galileo. Play **Track 33**. Tell students to work in pairs and take turns to tell each other as much as they can remember about the text. Have students tell the class something they remember. Then tell students to read the text again and see how much they could remember.

2 Correct the false sentences.

5 min

Write a false statement about the text on the board, such as *Galileo was Mexican.* Ask if this sentence is *true* or *false*. Because this is false, ask a student to correct the sentence. Elicit *Galileo was Italian.*

Tell students to look at the sentences, and ask them to read the sentences aloud. Have students work in pairs to correct the false sentences. Check answers by telling students to say *true* or *false* for each sentence, and then say their corrected sentences.

Try This! 5 min

Have students work in pairs to write another false sentence about the text. Have each pair take turns reading their sentence. Ask the rest of the class to correct it.

3 Writing Time! Complete the chart about a famous person from the past.

10 min

Tell students to look at the chart and how the notes about Galileo are organized. Have students choose a famous person from the past to write about, and write similar notes about them. Remind them about the famous people they wrote about on the stars at the end of the last lesson. Tell students that they can complete the chart about that person, or they can choose a different person from the past.

4 Write about a famous person.

10 min

Prepare a short paragraph about a famous person from the past, omit the person's name but say where he or she came from and three important facts about the person. See if the class can guess who your famous person is. If students can't guess correctly, tell them.

Tell students to use the information from their charts in Activity 3 to write about a famous person. Make sure they start with the person's name and where they were from, then include at least four important facts about the person. Help with vocabulary and spelling as necessary.

When they have finished, have them exchange their paragraphs with a partner. Have them read each other's work, and suggest corrections and improvements. If there is time, encourage students to rewrite a clean version of their paragraphs.

Finish the Class

5 min

Play a game of Twenty Questions. Ask a student to come to the board. Whisper the name of a famous person to him or her. Tell the rest of class to only ask *yes/no* questions to find out who the person is, for example, *Was she a woman? Was she American? Was she a scientist?* Check that students are forming the questions correctly. When the class has guessed the person, or has run out of questions, repeat with a different student.

Use the **Presentation Kit** for interactive activities in this lesson.

For additional class time, use **Pages 30 and 31** of the Skills Book. Go to **Page 173** in the Happy Campers Teacher's Edition for teacher notes for this lesson. You may also choose to assign these pages as homework.

Lesson 6

Lesson 6

1 33 **Listen again to Galileo and His Telescope.**

2 **Correct the false sentences.**

1. Galileo was an artist.
   Galileo was an astronomer.
2. He didn't see the deepest craters.
   He saw the deepest craters.
3. He studied Earth.
   He studied the planets.
4. Galileo didn't see Jupiter's moons.
   Galileo saw four of Jupiter's moons.

3 **Writing Time!** **Complete the chart about a famous person from the past.**

Who: Galileo	Who: (Students' own answers.)
Where: Italy	Where:
1. was an astronomer	1.
2. saw Jupiter's moons	2.
3. saw craters on the moon	3.

4 **Write about a famous person.**

______ was a ______.

He/She (Students' own answers)

______.

Lesson 7

Lesson 7

ON STAGE!

PROJECT: The Solar System

1 **Plan** your Solar System. Write a sentence to describe each planet.

Mercury	(Students'
Earth	own
Jupiter	answers.)
Saturn	
Neptune	

2 **Prepare** your Solar System.

3 **On Stage!** Tell the class about your Solar System.

Lesson 7 Creative, Collaborative, and Critical Thinking Activity

Lesson Objective: Plan, create, and present a Solar System poster.
Vocabulary Review: universe, planet, Mercury, Neptune, Jupiter, Saturn, Earth, meteor, crater
Grammar Review: superlatives
Materials: construction paper, markers, crayons, stickers or a small prize

Start the Class

5 min

Write these scrambled words on the board: *rinevsue, elapnt, otemer, racret.*

Put students into teams and tell them to unscramble the words as quickly as possible. Tell the teams to raise their hands as soon as they have finished. Ask the first team to finish to write the words on the board: *universe, planet, meteor, crater.*

1 Plan your Solar System. Write a sentence to describe each planet.

10 min

Put students into groups. Tell them to look at the chart and the example sentence. Then have them discuss and choose a sentence to describe each of the five planets. Have the groups choose one student to write the sentences. Monitor as the groups are working.

2 Prepare your Solar System.

10 min

Tell students to look at the photo of the boys' poster of the solar system. Tell the groups that they are going to make their own Solar System poster. Ask volunteers to hand out the materials.

Tell the groups to use the information in the chart from Activity 1 to help plan their posters. Tell them that they can also include other planets and facts that they know. Encourage them to discuss and agree on how they are going to present their information, what drawings or illustrations are going to be included, and how each student in the group is going to contribute to the project. Walk around the classroom to monitor and provide ideas and help as needed.

Try This!

5 min

Before the presentations, tell each group to think of one question to ask the other groups about their poster. After each presentation, have the other groups ask their question.

3 On Stage! Tell the class about your Solar System.

15 min

Have one student read the example dialogue aloud. Allow time for students to practice giving their presentations. Then ask each group to present their poster to the class. Encourage applause and constructive feedback.

Finish the Class

5 min

Display all of the Solar System posters around the classroom. Take a class vote on the best poster. Award the winners a sticker or small prize.

Use the **Presentation Kit** for interactive activities in this lesson.

Lesson 8 Review

Lesson Objective: Review language from Unit 5.
Vocabulary Review: universe, solar system, planet, Mercury, Neptune, Jupiter, Saturn, Earth, astronomer, telescope, moon, comet, meteor, crater
Grammar Review: The nearest planet to the sun is Mercury. The largest planet is Jupiter. Is it the nearest mall? Which is the smallest moon?

Start the Class

5 min

Start the class by reviewing vocabulary from the unit. Tell students you are going to slowly spell a word from the unit letter by letter. Students should say the word as soon as they know it. For example, you say *t … e … l …* and students say *telescope!* Repeat with different words.

1 Spelling! Write.

10 min

Tell students to look at the pictures quickly and then close their books. Ask them to say as many of the pictures as they can remember. Then have them open their books and write the words next to the pictures. Ask students for their answers and have them spell the words each time.

Try This!

10 min

Repeat the Start the Class activity, but this time nominate students to spell the words for the rest of the class to guess.

2 Choose and complete with the superlative form of the adjectives.

10 min

Write a noun and an adjective on the board, such as *cheetah* and *fast*. In pairs, have students think of and write a complete superlative sentence, such as *A cheetah is the fastest animal*. Ask a volunteer to say how the superlative is formed, *the* + adjective + *-est*. Remind them that the final *-e* in adjectives is dropped before adding *-est*.

Tell students to look at the adjectives in the box and the sentences with blank spaces. Tell them to complete the sentences with the correct superlative form. Check answers by having students read their sentences. Ask the rest of the class if they agree.

3 Word Play! Find and circle the words from Unit 5 on Page 72.

10 min

Have students turn to **Page 72** and tell them to find and circle the solar system and astronomy words from Unit 5. Then have students check the words they found with a partner.

Finish the Class

5 min

Stand in the middle of the class and point to objects, such as the board, or point to students in the classroom. Say an adjective, for example, *big*, and ask students to make a superlative sentence, *The board is the biggest thing in our classroom!* Repeat several times. Then write *class* and *smart* on the board to elicit *Our class is the smartest class!* Ask students to repeat this as they leave the classroom.

Use the **Presentation Kit** for interactive activities in this lesson.

For additional class time, use **Pages 32 and 33** of the Skills Book. Go to **Page 174** in the Happy Campers Teacher's Edition for teacher notes for this lesson. You may also choose to assign these pages as homework.

Lesson 8

Lesson 8

Round Up!

1 Spelling! Write.

1. telescope

2. comet

3. planet

4. meteor

5. Earth

6. astronomer

2 Choose and complete with the superlative form of the adjectives.

large	fast	cold	near	slow

1. Mercury is the nearest planet to the sun.
2. Elephants are the largest animals on land.
3. Cheetahs are the fastest animals.
4. Sloths are the slowest animals on land.
5. Neptune is the coldest planet in our solar system.

3 Word Play! Find and circle the words from Unit 5 on Page 72.

Unit 6

Unit Objectives

By the end of the unit, students can:

- Identify new personal technology devices.
- Make comparisons using superlative forms of long and short adjectives.
- Ask and answer questions using superlative adjectives.

Student Book

Vocabulary

Technology: smartphone, smartwatch, MP3 player, gaming system, laptop, tablet, wireless, digital camera

Superlatives: best, worst, generous, careful, thoughtful, peaceful

Grammar

It's the most amazing smartphone.
It's the most exciting laptop.
Is this the best tablet?

Skills

Listening: Listen for specific information.

Speaking: Describe objects and people using superlative adjectives.
Ask and answer questions using superlative adjectives.
Talk about a new gadget.

Reading: Read a fiction text: **The Dog Walker**.
Identify the main idea and specific information.

Writing: Write about your robot.

Creative, Collaborative, and Critical Thinking Competencies

A New Gadget

Creativity: Develop self-expression, innovation, and problem-solving skills to invent a new gadget, and plan how to present the gadget effectively.

Collaboration: Use communication and negotiation skills to discuss and decide on a new gadget and how each group member will contribute to the final project at all stages.

Critical Thinking: Use problem-solving skills to analyze ideas and organize information about the new gadget. Identify the best method of presenting the gadget to the class.

Skills Book

Extra Skills Practice

Speaking and Listening: Ask and answer questions about a picture.

Reading and Writing: Recall details.
Read clues to identify words.
Identify one- and multi-syllable words.

Teacher Workshop

Teaching with Technology

If students in your class have email accounts, emailing is a great way to communicate with them outside the classroom. You can send welcoming or encouraging notes, review progress, and send homework assignments. However, if some students do not have an email account, it may be better not to use email at all, which will avoid creating a sense of inequality.

Teaching with Games

Stand Up When

Stand Up When is a great game to use with listening or reading activities. Ask students to stand up when they hear or read target vocabulary words or grammar structures. If standing is too noisy, you could ask students to raise their hands instead. The purpose of the game is to encourage students to listen and look for specific language.

Happy Teacher

Using the board effectively is an important skill. The board is a useful tool for teachers, but it is important not to become over-reliant on the board and spend too much time at it rather than engaging directly with the class.

If you find yourself spending too much time at the board, think creatively about other ways of conveying the information necessary for students to do each activity. Before class, plan what you are going to use the board for. By using the board effectively, you can structure the class while providing a learning tool for your students to highlight the key points of the lesson.

Happy Class

To foster a supportive learning environment in your class, set up "homework buddies." These are paired students who check that they know what to do for homework, help each other with homework, and check each other's work. Having a homework buddy motivates students to do homework and can prevent intimidation or confusion about what they have to do.

By Libby Williams

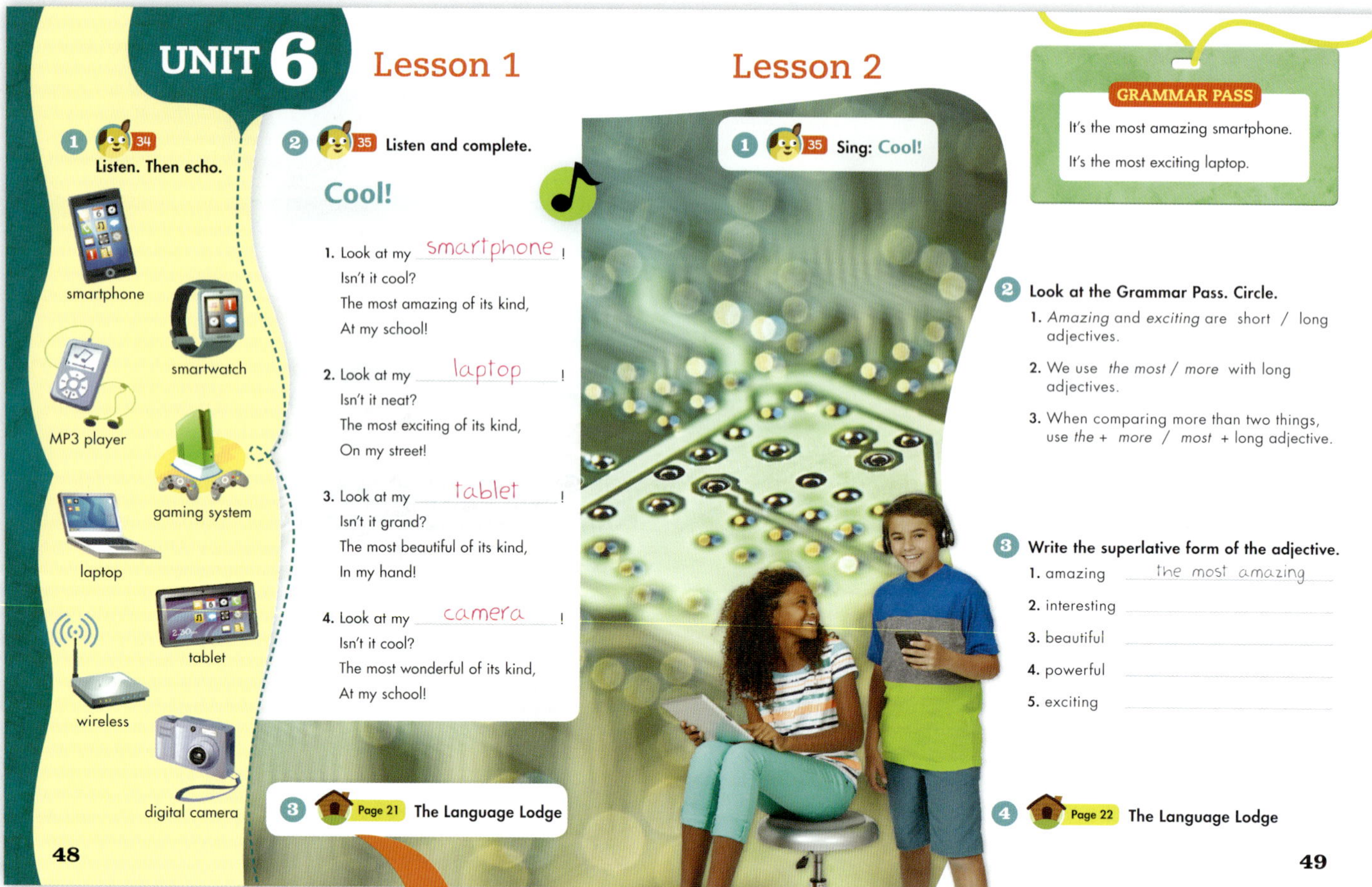

UNIT 6

Lesson 1

1 34 Listen. Then echo.

smartphone
smartwatch
MP3 player
gaming system
laptop
tablet
wireless
digital camera

2 35 Listen and complete.

Cool!

1. Look at my smartphone !
Isn't it cool?
The most amazing of its kind,
At my school!

2. Look at my laptop !
Isn't it neat?
The most exciting of its kind,
On my street!

3. Look at my tablet !
Isn't it grand?
The most beautiful of its kind,
In my hand!

4. Look at my camera !
Isn't it cool?
The most wonderful of its kind,
At my school!

3 Page 21 The Language Lodge

Lesson 2

1 35 Sing: Cool!

GRAMMAR PASS

It's the most amazing smartphone.

It's the most exciting laptop.

2 Look at the Grammar Pass. Circle.

1. *Amazing* and *exciting* are short / long adjectives.
2. We use *the most* / *more* with long adjectives.
3. When comparing more than two things, use *the* + *more* / *most* + long adjective.

3 Write the superlative form of the adjective.

1. amazing the most amazing
2. interesting
3. beautiful
4. powerful
5. exciting

4 Page 22 The Language Lodge

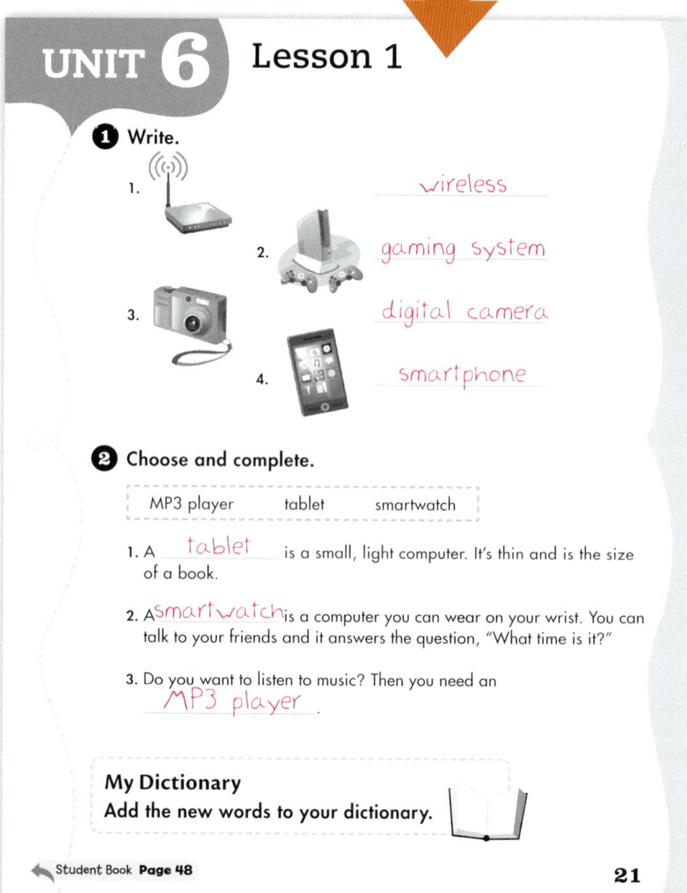

UNIT 6 Lesson 1

1 Write.

1. wireless
2. gaming system
3. digital camera
4. smartphone

2 Choose and complete.

MP3 player tablet smartwatch

1. A tablet is a small, light computer. It's thin and is the size of a book.
2. A smartwatch is a computer you can wear on your wrist. You can talk to your friends and it answers the question, "What time is it?"
3. Do you want to listen to music? Then you need an MP3 player .

My Dictionary
Add the new words to your dictionary.

Student Book Page 48

Lesson 1

This may also be completed for homework.

Lesson 1 Vocabulary

Unit 6

Lesson Objective: Identify new personal technology devices.
New Vocabulary: smartphone, smartwatch, MP3 player, gaming system, laptop, tablet, wireless, digital camera
Materials: Audio **Tracks 34 and 35**

Start the Class

5 min

Show students a smartphone, laptop, tablet, or digital camera. Ask students to think of as many personal technology devices as they can. Discuss the devices with the class. Ask what the different devices are used for, which is their favorite, and which device they would most like to own.

1 34 Listen. Then echo.

5 min

Have students look at the pictures and identify as many words as they can. Tell them to listen to the audio and point to the pictures as they hear the words. Play **Track 34**. Then play **Track 34** again and have students echo the words.

Try This! 5 min

Tell students to close their books and say as many of the new vocabulary words as they can remember. See if they can remember how to spell them. Then have them check in their books.

2 35 Listen and complete.

10 min

Ask students to look at the photos on **Pages 48 and 49** and identify what they see. Tell the class they are going to hear a song about technology. Tell them to listen and complete the blanks in the song lyrics. Play **Track 35**. Then play **Track 35** again for students to check their answers. Check answers with the class.

3 Page 21 The Language Lodge

15 min

Have students flip to The Language Lodge **Page 21**.

1 Write.

Have students look at the pictures and write the correct words. Check answers with the class.

2 Choose and complete.

Have students look at the words in the box. Then have them work individually to complete the sentences with the correct words. Put students in pairs to compare their answers. Then check answers with the class.

My Dictionary

Tell students to turn to the dictionary section in their notebooks. Have them write the new words and draw pictures or write sentences to help them remember the meanings.

Finish the Class

10 min

Write the new vocabulary words on the board and draw a circle around each word. Point to and say each word, and then have students repeat. Tell students to close their eyes, and then erase one of the words on the board, but leave the circle. Tell students to open their eyes and say all the words, including the one that has been erased. Continue until all the words have been erased and students can say them from memory.

Use the **Presentation Kit** for interactive activities in this lesson.

Have students use the **Happy Campers app** for additional practice with the new vocabulary.

The Language Lodge Page 21 may also be completed for homework.

Lesson 2 Grammar

Lesson Objective: Describe personal technology devices using superlatives.
New Grammar: It's the most amazing smartphone. It's the most exciting laptop.
Vocabulary Review: smartphone, smartwatch, MP3 player, gaming system, laptop, tablet, wireless, digital camera
Materials: Audio **Track 35**, slips of paper

Start the Class

5 min

Put students in pairs. Have them rank personal technology devices by how much they need them from one (device they need the most) to eight (device they need the least), and write why they need each device. Say an example sentence, such as *I need a laptop. I make my lesson plans on it.* Have pairs share their ideas with the class.

1 35 Sing: Cool!

10 min

Tell students they are going to listen to "Cool" again. Play **Track 35** and have students listen and read the lyrics. Play **Track 35** again and have the class sing along. Ask students to find and underline examples of superlative forms using *the most* in the song.

Try This! 5 min

Play a game of Stand Up When (see **Page T 107**) to provide movement and help students recognize the target grammar. Ask students to stand up when they hear superlative forms of adjectives in the song. Play **Track 35**.

2 Look at the Grammar Pass. Circle.

10 min

Say *a - maz - ing*. Have students repeat and count the syllables. Explain that comparative and superlative forms of adjectives with three or more syllables are different than the forms for shorter adjectives such as *small*, *nice*, and *big*.
Tell students to look at the Grammar Pass. Have volunteers read the sentences to the class. Do the activity aloud with the class first. Read the sentences and elicit the correct answers. Then have students circle the answers in their books.

3 Write the superlative form of the adjective.

5 min

Ask students to look at the example answer. Then have them write the superlative forms of the other adjectives. Check answers with the class.

4 Page 22 The Language Lodge

10 min

Have students flip to The Language Lodge **Page 22**. Have a volunteer read the Grammar Pass aloud.

1 Complete.
Have students work in pairs to fill in the blanks in the sentences with the superlative form of the adjectives in parentheses. Check answers with the class.

2 Unscramble.
Have students look at the scrambled sentences. Then have students unscramble and write the sentences. Check answers by having volunteers read the unscrambled sentences.

Finish the Class

5 min

Show students a personal technology device from the Lesson 1 vocabulary. "Sell" it to the class by saying, for example, *This is the best smartphone. It has the most interesting features.* Have a pair of students come to the board. Give one of them a slip of paper with the name of a personal technology device written on it. Have the student "sell" the device to his or her partner using superlatives. Ask the other student if he or she wants to buy it or not. Continue with other pairs and items of vocabulary.

Use the **Presentation Kit** for interactive activities in this lesson.

The Language Lodge Page 22 may also be completed for homework.

For additional class time, use **Pages 34 and 35** of the Skills Book. Go to **Page 175** in the Happy Campers Teacher's Edition for teacher notes for this lesson. You may also choose to assign these pages as homework.

UNIT 6

Lesson 1

1 [34] Listen. Then echo.

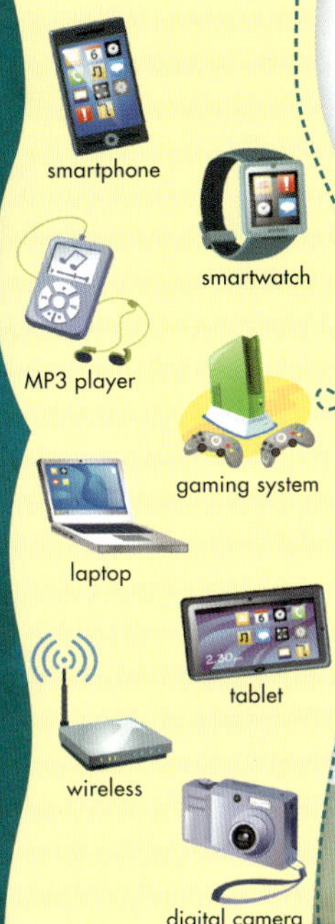

2 [35] Listen and complete.

Cool!

1. Look at my ______________!
Isn't it cool?
The most amazing of its kind,
At my school!

2. Look at my ______________!
Isn't it neat?
The most exciting of its kind,
On my street!

3. Look at my ______________!
Isn't it grand?
The most beautiful of its kind,
In my hand!

4. Look at my ______________!
Isn't it cool?
The most wonderful of its kind,
At my school!

3 Page 21 The Language Lodge

Lesson 2

1 [35] Sing: Cool!

GRAMMAR PASS

It's the most amazing smartphone.

It's the most exciting laptop.

2 Look at the Grammar Pass. Circle.

1. *Amazing* and *exciting* are short / (long) adjectives.
2. We use (*the most*) / *more* with long adjectives.
3. When comparing more than two things, use *the* + *more* / (*most*) + long adjective.

3 Write the superlative form of the adjective.

1. amazing — the most amazing
2. interesting — the most interesting
3. beautiful — the most beautiful
4. powerful — the most powerful
5. exciting — the most exciting

4 Page 22 The Language Lodge

Lesson 2

GRAMMAR PASS

It's the most amazing smartphone.

It's the most exciting laptop.

1 **Complete.**

1. My dad wants the most powerful computer in the store. (powerful)
2. My mom got the most colorful MP3 player in the store. (colorful)
3. My parents gave me the most amazing digital camera! (amazing)
4. My drawing game is the most exciting game on my tablet. (exciting)

2 **Unscramble.**

1. generous / Lisa / the / is / girl / most
Lisa is the most generous girl.
2. laptop / is / most / the / expensive / This
This is the most expensive laptop.
3. My / delicious / most / is / sandwich / the
My sandwich is the most delicious.
4. snake / This / is / the / dangerous / most
This is the most dangerous snake.

Student Book **Page 49**

Lesson 2

This may also be completed for homework.

Lesson 3

THE HAPPY CAMPERS

1 Where are The Happy Campers?

2 36 Read and listen.

3 37 **Dictation!** Listen and write. Then say.

1. The best laptop is the worst color.
2. She is very generous and thoughtful.
3. Be careful with my smartphone.
4. It isn't the most peaceful place.

4 Page 23 The Language Lodge

Lesson 4

1 36 Listen again to The Happy Campers.

2 **Grammar Pass!** Complete.

1. It's the most powerful laptop.
2. Adam thinks pink is ______ color for a laptop.
3. The pizza place is ______.

3 38 Listen and cheer!

Pizza, pizza! Is it the worst?
No, it isn't! It's the most delicious! It's the best!

CHEER BOX!

4 Page 24 The Language Lodge

Lesson 3

1 Find and circle six adjectives in the puzzle. Then write.

W	O	R	S	T	V	B	K	L	R
S	Q	P	E	A	C	E	F	U	L
U	G	A	J	E	X	S	C	E	H
T	H	O	U	G	H	T	F	U	L
B	I	D	C	A	R	E	F	U	L
G	E	N	E	R	O	U	S	A	H
Z	X	I	B	Q	T	S	A	R	W

1. worst
2. best
3. peaceful
4. thoughtful
5. careful
6. generous

2 Answer the questions.

1. Is it the worst gaming system? ✗ No, it isn't.
2. Is she the most generous girl? ✓ Yes, she is.
3. Is Earth the greenest planet? ✓ Yes, it is.
4. Is he the most careful unicyclist? ✗ No, he isn't.

My Dictionary
Add the new words to your dictionary.

Student Book Page 50

Lesson 3

This may also be completed for homework.

Lesson 3 Vocabulary in Context

Lesson Objective: Identify superlative adjectives.
New Vocabulary: best, worst, generous, careful, thoughtful, peaceful
Vocabulary Review: laptop
Materials: Audio **Tracks 36 and 37**, pictures of the Lesson 1 vocabulary words

Start the Class

5 min

Print pictures from the Internet or cut them out of magazines or catalogs of new vocabulary from Lesson 1.

Display the pictures for all students to see. Tell them to look at the pictures for 30 seconds, memorize them, and then close their eyes. Remove one of the pictures, and ask them to open their eyes. Ask *What's missing?* Repeat with other pictures.

1 Where are The Happy Campers?

5 min

Have a volunteer read the question. Then tell students to look at the pictures in the comic strip, and ask them to say where The Happy Campers are. Elicit *The mall.*

2 36 Read and listen.

5 min

Have students read the comic strip as they listen to the track. Play **Track 36**. Tell students to underline the superlative adjectives whenever they hear them in the comic strip. Play **Track 36** again.

3 37 Dictation! Listen and write. Then say.

10 min

Tell students they will hear sentences and write what they hear. Play the first sentence of **Track 37** and pause the audio to allow students time to write. Repeat with the other sentences. Tell the class that they are going to hear the audio again and this time they will say the sentences after they hear them. Play **Track 37** again and monitor student pronunciation. Have volunteers write the sentences on the board. Tell the class to correct the sentences in their notebooks if necessary.

*Audio script **Track 37***

1. The best laptop is the worst color. 2. She is very generous and thoughtful. 3. Be careful with my smartphone. 4. It isn't the most peaceful place.

Try This! 5 min

Erase the sentences from the dictation in Activity 3 from the board. Tell students to close their notebooks. Have them work in pairs to remember and rewrite one of the sentences from the dictation on a piece of paper. Then have pairs check the sentence they have written against the one in their notebooks.

4 Page 23 The Language Lodge

15 min

Have students flip to The Language Lodge **Page 23**.

1 Find and circle six adjectives in the puzzle. Then write.

Tell students to find and circle the six adjectives in the puzzle. Have students point in the book, say the words, and then write the words. Then check answers with the class.

2 Answer the questions.

Ask volunteers to read the example question and answer. Have students work individually to answer the other questions. Then check answers by asking the questions and having students answer.

My Dictionary

Ask students to turn to the dictionary section in their notebooks. Have them add the new superlative adjectives and write a sentence using each one.

Finish the Class

5 min

Ask a volunteer to come to the board and mime using a personal technology device from the vocabulary in Lesson 1. The rest of students have to guess what the device is. Repeat with different students.

Use the **Presentation Kit** for interactive activities in this lesson.

Have students use the **Happy Campers app** for additional practice with the new vocabulary.

The Language Lodge Page 23 may also be completed for homework.

Lesson 4 Grammar in Context

Lesson Objective: Ask questions using superlative adjectives.
New Grammar: Is this the best tablet?
Vocabulary Review: best, worst, generous, careful, thoughtful, peaceful
Materials: Audio **Tracks 36 and 38**, pictures of personal technology devices from Lesson 3

Start the Class

5 min

Play a Chain Memory Game with things you can buy from a computer store. Start by saying *I'm going to a computer store and I want to buy a tablet.* Then have students continue the chain until they have recalled all the personal technology devices.

1 36 Listen again to The Happy Campers.

10 min

Ask students to tell you everything they can remember about the comic strip from Lesson 3. Then tell them to listen again and read along in their books. Play **Track 36**. Tell them to listen again, and underline all the superlative adjectives in the comic strip. Play **Track 36** again.

2 Grammar Pass! Complete.

5 min

Ask a volunteer to read the example sentence. Then have students complete the sentences in their books. Check answers with the class.

Try This!

5 min

Ask students to think of something that they own or like and write a sentence about it using a superlative adjective. Give an example such as *Mario's is the best restaurant!* Ask students to share their sentences with the class.

3 38 Listen and cheer!

5 min

Tell students to listen to the cheer as they read along. Play **Track 38**. Then tell them to say the cheer along with the audio, and play **Track 38** again.

4 Page 24 The Language Lodge

10 min

Have students flip to The Language Lodge **Page 24**. Have a volunteer read the Grammar Pass aloud.

1 Write questions.

Ask a student to read the first sentence. Elicit the question *Is it the best pizza?* Write it on the board and tell students to notice the order of the verb and subject. Then have students work in pairs to write the questions. Check answers by saying the statements and having students say the questions.

2 Complete.

Tell students to read the sentences. Have them use superlative forms of the adjectives to complete the sentences. Check answers with the class.

Finish the Class

10 min

Use the pictures of personal technology devices from Lesson 3. Put the pictures on the walls, but hide parts of them with pieces of paper so that students can only see a small amount of detail of each picture. Have students work in pairs to figure out what each picture is. The first pair to figure out what all of the pictures are wins.

Use the **Presentation Kit** for interactive activities in this lesson.

The Language Lodge Page 24 may also be completed for homework.

Lesson 3

1 Where are The Happy Campers?

2 36 Read and listen.

3 37 **Dictation!** Listen and write. Then say.

1. ______________________________.
2. ______________________________.
3. ______________________________.
4. ______________________________.

4 Page 23 The Language Lodge

Lesson 4

1 36 Listen again to **The Happy Campers**.

2 **Grammar Pass!** Complete.

1. It's the most powerful laptop.
2. Adam thinks pink is the worst color for a laptop.
3. The pizza place is the best.

3 38 Listen and cheer!

Pizza, pizza! Is it the worst?
No, it isn't! It's the most delicious! It's the best!

CHEER BOX!

4 Page 24 The Language Lodge

Lesson 4

This may also be completed for homework.

Lesson 4

GRAMMAR PASS

Is this the best tablet?

1 Write questions.

1. It is the best pizza.
   Is it the best pizza?
2. Sue is the most thoughtful person.
   Is Sue the most thoughtful person?
3. Mom is the most careful person.
   Is mom the most careful person?
4. Charlie is the most generous friend.
   Is Charlie the most generous friend?

2 Complete.

1. Is it the best tablet in the store? (good)
2. Are these the most colorful smartwatches you have? (colorful)
3. Which is the most expensive laptop bag you have? (expensive)
4. Is this the most popular gaming system you have? (popular)
5. Is this the worst camera in the store? (bad)

Student Book Page 51

Lesson 5

Lesson 5

1 Circle the dog walker.

Joshua Joshua's mom Joshua's robot

2 39 Read and listen.

The Dog Walker

"Joshua, where are you?" said his mom. Joshua wasn't in his bedroom, and he didn't answer. He was in the yard making a robot. "Sorry, I didn't hear you," Joshua said. "Can you walk the dogs, please?" his mom asked.

Joshua didn't like walking the dogs. They were bigger and stronger than him. But now he had the most talented and amazing robot. "Walk the dogs!" Joshua said to the robot. The robot walked out of the yard and the two big dogs followed him! Joshua was very happy, and went inside to watch TV.

"Walk the dogs," the robot repeated. Then the robot took Joshua's dogs, the small dog on the corner, the dog from the grocery store, and all of the dogs on the street out for a walk!

There were a lot of dogs in the yard, and a lot of angry people. "What did you do, Joshua?" Mom asked. "Oh, no, maybe this isn't the best robot!" Joshua said.

Lesson 5 Fiction Reading

Lesson Objective: Read a fiction text to practice unit language.
Vocabulary Review: best, worst, generous, careful, thoughtful, peaceful
Grammar Review: comparative and superlative adjectives
Materials: Audio **Track 39**

Start the Class

10 min

Play a game of Pictionary. Ask a volunteer to come to the board. Whisper the name of an animal to him or her, such as *cat*. The student draws the animal on the board without speaking. The rest of the class has to guess the animal. Repeat with other students.

1 Circle the dog walker.

5 min

Ask students to look at the story title and pictures and predict what the story is about. Write a few of their predictions on the board. Then ask a student to read the directions and answer options. Without reading the text, tell students to circle who they think the dog walker is in the story. Do not tell them the answer yet.

2 39 Read and listen.

20 min

Tell students to read the story as they listen to the audio. Play **Track 39**. Ask students if they circled the correct answer in Activity 1. Tell students to read and listen again, and underline the comparative and superlative adjectives in the story.

Put students in groups of four. Give a paragraph of the text to each student. Tell them to read their paragraphs carefully and memorize as much as they can. Then have each student take turns retelling the paragraph of the story to the other members of his or her group. Monitor and help as needed.

Try This! 5 min

Tell students to listen to the story again and stand up, or do another sort of movement of your choice, when they hear comparative and superlative adjectives in the story. Play **Track 39**.

Finish the Class

10 min

Put students in groups of four. Tell students to think of one chore that they do not like doing and that they would like a robot to do. Each member of the group must agree on the one chore they would like the robot to do. Then tell them to draw the robot doing the chore. Display the drawings and take a class vote on the robot they would most like to have. Keep the drawings for the next lesson.

Use the **Presentation Kit** for interactive activities in this lesson.

Lesson 6 Reading Comprehension / Writing

Lesson Objectives: Identify specific information. Write about your robot.
Vocabulary Review: best, worst, generous, careful, thoughtful, peaceful
Grammar Review: comparative and superlative adjectives
Materials: Audio **Track 39**, a small prize, a bag, small objects

Start the Class

5 min

Remind the class about the robot in the story in the last lesson. Put students into groups and tell them that you are going to describe your ideal robot to them, and they have to draw what you say. Describe your robot, for example, *It has a very big head. It has big eyes to see my students with. It has long arms. It has short legs and very big feet.* Have the groups hold up their pictures, and award one of the groups a small prize for the best drawing.

1 39 Listen again to The Dog Walker.

5 min

Ask students to tell the class as much as they can remember about the story in Lesson 5.

Tell students to listen to the story again. Play **Track 39**. Ask *Who was in the yard at the end of the story?* Answers include: *The robot.; Joshua and his mom.; A lot of dogs.; A lot of angry people.*

2 Make the sentences true.

10 min

Ask a volunteer to read Item 1. Ask *Is the sentence true or false?* Elicit *false*. Ask another volunteer to read the true sentence in the example.

Then have students work in pairs to read the other sentences and correct them so that they are true. Check answers with the class.

Try This!

5 min

Have students work in pairs to write two more false sentences about the story. Ask each pair to take turns reading their sentence aloud for the rest of the class to correct.

3 Writing Time! Write about a robot that can do your chores.

10 min

Remind students about the robot they drew in the Finish the Class activity in the last lesson. Tell students to complete the chart. Walk around the classroom to make sure that students are including the robot's name, the chores it does, and at least two or three adjectives to describe it.

4 Write about your robot.

10 min

Tell students to work individually to write a paragraph about their robots using the information from their charts in Activity 3. Make sure that students start with adjectives that describe the robot as well as include the robot's name, and the chores it does. Walk around the classroom and help as needed.

Ask volunteers to share their paragraphs with the class.

Finish the Class

5 min

Put small items, such as a pencil sharpener, a cell phone, an eraser, a calculator, and so on, into a bag. Have a student put one hand in the bag and describe one of the items he or she can feel. The other students guess what it is. Repeat with other students until all the objects have been guessed.

Use the **Presentation Kit** for interactive activities in this lesson.

For additional class time, use **Pages 36 and 37** of the Skills Book. Go to **Page 176** in the Happy Campers Teacher's Edition for teacher notes for this lesson. You may also choose to assign these pages as homework.

Lesson 6

Lesson 6

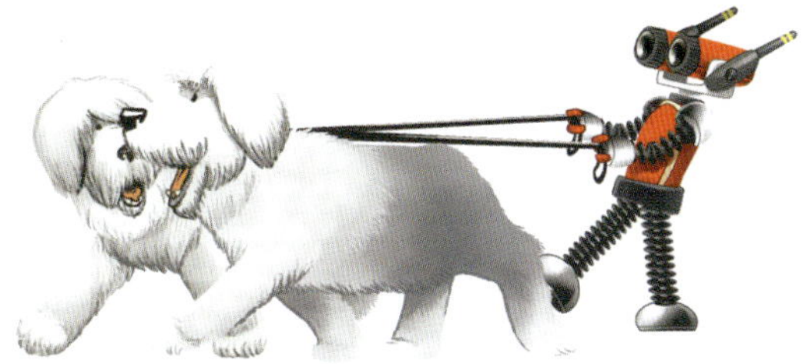

1 39 **Listen again to The Dog Walker.**

2 Make the sentences true.

1. Joshua didn't make a robot. Joshua made a robot.
2. Joshua liked walking the dogs. Joshua didn't like walking the dogs.
3. Joshua didn't watch TV. Joshua watched TV.
4. The robot walked two dogs. The robot took all of the dogs on the street for a walk.
5. The people were happy. The people were angry.

3 Writing Time! Write about a robot that can do your chores.

My Robot
Robot's name: (Students'
Chores it does: own
Adjectives that describe it: answers.)

4 Write about your robot.

My robot is the most (Students' own answers).

Lesson 7

ON STAGE!

PROJECT: A New Gadget

1 **Plan a New Gadget.**

What type of gadget is it?
How does it look?
How is it special?
What is its name?

(Students' own answers.)

2 **Prepare a poster to advertise your New Gadget.**

3 **On Stage! Sell your New Gadget to the class!**

Lesson 7 Creative, Collaborative, and Critical Thinking Activity

Lesson Objective: Plan, prepare, and create a New Gadget.
Vocabulary Review: smartphone, smartwatch, MP3 player, gaming system, laptop, tablet, wireless, digital camera
Grammar Review: It's the most amazing smartphone. It's the most exciting laptop.
Materials: construction paper, colored markers and crayons

Start the Class

5 min

Tell the class about one or two technology devices, also called gadgets, that you have at home, such as a smartphone, a digital camera, a tablet, and so on. Describe each gadget with a sentence or two using a superlative adjective, for example, *I have the most amazing smartphone. I keep all my music and photos on it.* Explain to students that a gadget is a small device that does a clever or unusual job for the user. Brainstorm gadgets with the class. Write a list on the board.

1 Plan a New Gadget.

10 min

Have students get into groups. Tell them that they are going to invent a New Gadget and make a poster about it to present to the class.

Tell students to look at the chart. Ask for volunteers to read the questions. Have groups discuss the questions and agree among themselves what their gadget is, how it looks, how it is special, and what its name is. Walk around the classroom to help as needed. Make sure that all opinions in the group are being considered. When they have reached an agreement, have groups complete the charts about their gadgets.

2 Prepare a poster to advertise your New Gadget.

15 min

Tell students to look at the example poster in the photo. Tell the class information an advertising poster should include, *the name of the product, a picture of the product,* and *the special features of the product that make it different from other products.*

Hand out materials. Tell the groups to work together to create their posters using the information in their charts in Activity 1. Remind them to "sell" their gadgets on the posters, and use superlative adjectives, for example, *It's the most powerful …* Tell them to decide what each member of the group is going to do before they start work. Monitor and help as students work.

3 On Stage! Sell your New Gadget to the class!

15 min

Ask the class what makes a good presentation. Write some ideas on the board, for example, *Speak clearly. Be enthusiastic. Smile! Look at the audience. Point to details on the poster.*

Allow time for the groups to practice presenting their posters. Make sure that each student in every group has a role in the presentation. Then have each group present their poster to the class. Tell the class to think of a question to ask other groups about their gadgets at the end of each presentation.

When all groups have presented, congratulate the class on their imaginative gadgets and presentations.

Finish the Class

5 min

Display the posters around the class. Take a class vote on the best poster.

Use the **Presentation Kit** for interactive activities in this lesson.

Lesson 8 Review

Lesson Objective: Review language from Unit 6.
Vocabulary Review: smartphone, smartwatch, MP3 player, gaming system, laptop, tablet, wireless, digital camera, best, worst, generous, careful, thoughtful, peaceful
Grammar Review: It's the most amazing smartphone. It's the most exciting laptop. Is this the best tablet?
Materials: pictures of personal technology devices from Lesson 3

Start the Class

5 min

Look around the classroom and say *What an interesting classroom!* Choose an object in the classroom, such as a backpack, and describe it using a superlative adjective, *It's the most colorful backpack in the classroom!* Select other objects and have students describe them using superlative adjectives.

1 Spelling! Write.

10 min

Tell students to look at the pictures in their books for one minute. Then point to the pictures randomly and elicit the vocabulary words.

Tell students to write the correct words next to the pictures. Check answers by having volunteers write their answers on the board. Ask the rest of the class to check the spelling.

Try This!

5 min

Ask a volunteer to stand up and spell one of the new words from this unit slowly to the class. The rest of the class has to guess as quickly as possible which word the student is spelling. The first student to guess correctly spells another word, and so on.

2 Choose and complete.

10 min

Tell students to close their books. Slowly spell out the four words in the box in Activity 2. Tell students to say the word as soon as they know what it is. When students have correctly said all the words, have them open their books. Tell them to choose the correct words from the box to complete the sentences. Check answers with the class.

3 Word Play! Find and circle the words from Unit 6 on Page 72.

10 min

Have students turn to **Page 72** and tell them to find and circle the technology and superlative words from Unit 6. Then have students check the words they found with a partner.

Finish the Class

10 min

Use the pictures of personal technology devices from Lesson 3. Ask a volunteer to come to the board. Show the rest of the class one of the pictures, and tell them not to say the name of the item. Tell them to gives clues about the item to the student at the board, and he or she has to guess what it is. Repeat with other students and pictures.

Use the **Presentation Kit** for interactive activities in this lesson.

For additional class time, use **Pages 38 and 39** of the Skills Book. Go to **Page 177** in the Happy Campers Teacher's Edition for teacher notes for this lesson. You may also choose to assign these pages as homework.

Lesson 8

Round Up!

1 Spelling! Write.

1. laptop

2. smartphone

3. digital camera

4. smartwatch

5. tablet

6. gaming system

7. wireless

8. MP3 player

2 Choose and complete.

thoughtful	careful	peaceful	generous

1. It was very loud at the concert. It wasn't very peaceful.
2. He didn't think about anyone else. He wasn't thoughtful.
3. She didn't help her friends. She wasn't very generous.
4. Be careful when you cross the street.

3 Word Play! Find and circle the words from Unit 6 on Page 72.

Unit 7

Unit Objectives

By the end of the unit, students can:

- Identify types of weather.
- Ask and answer questions about causes and consequences.
- Talk about the weather and appropriate clothing.

Student Book

Vocabulary

Weather: windy, bright, wet, foggy, mild, chilly, freezing, icy

Nature: trunk, branch, mud, puddle, wind

Grammar

Why are you wearing a hat? Because it's chilly.
Why did you stop? Because the wind took my hat!

Skills

Listening: Listen for and identify types of weather and nature words. Listen for the main idea and specific information.

Speaking: Talk about nature and clothing. Ask and answer questions using *why* and *because*.

Reading: Read a nonfiction text (social studies): **George Washington's False Teeth**.
Recall details in a story.

Writing: Write specific information about George Washington's dentist.

Creative, Collaborative, and Critical Thinking Competencies

Weather Report

Creativity: Develop self-expression, innovation, and problem-solving skills to plan a Weather Report.

Collaboration: Use communication and negotiation skills to discuss and decide on what to include in the Weather Report, how to present the information, and how each group member will contribute to the final product at all stages.

Critical Thinking: Use problem-solving skills to analyze what information should be included and how that information can be expressed graphically. Use organizational skills to present the information clearly and effectively.

Skills Book

Extra Skills Practice

Speaking and Listening: Ask and answer questions about a picture.

Reading and Writing: Draw conclusions. Write an opinion. Recognize rhyming words. Categorize words.

Teacher Workshop

Teaching with Technology

Encourage students to use trusted informational websites, such as news websites, to supplement their learning. Weather websites will be a particularly useful resource during this unit. Suggest that students consult weather websites at relevant times during the unit, particularly before Lesson 7.

Teaching with Games

Magic Bingo

Play the game with a basic 3x3 Bingo grid and vocabulary sets, such as *weather*, *clothing*, *food*, and so on.

Tell students to write a keyword in the center square of their grids, for example, *weather*.

Write a list of weather-related vocabulary items on the board, for example, *windy*, *chilly*, *mild*, etc. Tell students to choose and write eight of the words in any remaining squares of their grid.

Say the words in the list and tell students to cross out words they have in their grid. Say the center word last. All students should call out *Bingo!* at the same time.

Happy Teacher

For group work, you may want to give each group member a role. This ensures that every student has a clear responsibility and sense of purpose in the group and avoids confusion and duplication of effort. Some possible roles include: a monitor who makes sure everyone in the group has a chance to speak; a recorder who takes notes; a timekeeper who makes sure the group finishes on time; a question master who asks other groups or the teacher questions; a materials manager who collects, distributes, and puts materials away; and a reporter who will report what his or her group has achieved.

Happy Class

Feedback is an important element in the learning process. Corrective feedback focuses on language, and this can be provided by you or other students. Feedback can also focus on how well students have performed a task. Above all, feedback should be constructive and include praise for things students have done particularly well in addition to corrections or suggestions for improvement.

By Lesley Painter-Farrell

UNIT 7

1 (40) Listen. Then echo.

windy
bright
wet
foggy
mild
chilly
freezing
icy

Lesson 1

2 (41) Listen and number.

The Bicycle Ride!

2 Come on! Let's go outside!
It's a great day for a bicycle ride!
Why are you wearing a raincoat today?
Because it's windy and wet
they say!

3 Come on! Let's go outside!
It's a great day for a bicycle ride!
Why are you wearing sunglasses today?
Because it's chilly, but bright
they say!

1 Come on! Let's go outside!
It's a great day for a bicycle ride.
Why are you wearing a scarf today?
Because it's freezing and icy
they say!

3 Page 25 The Language Lodge

56

Lesson 2

1 (41) Sing: The Bicycle Ride!

GRAMMAR PASS
Why are you wearing a hat?
Because it's chilly.

2 Look at the Grammar Pass. Circle.
1. Why are you wearing a scarf?
a. Because it's freezing outside.
b. It's a red scarf.
2. Why are you going outside?
a. It's windy.
b. Because I want to ride my bike.
3. We use *why* / *because* to give a reason for doing things.

3 Unscramble.
1. are / sunglasses / wearing / Why / you
______________________________?
2. raincoat / are / a / Why / wearing / you
______________________________?
3. wearing / a / Why / are / you / hoodie
______________________________?

Why are you wearing sunglasses?
Because it's very bright today.

4 Page 26 The Language Lodge

57

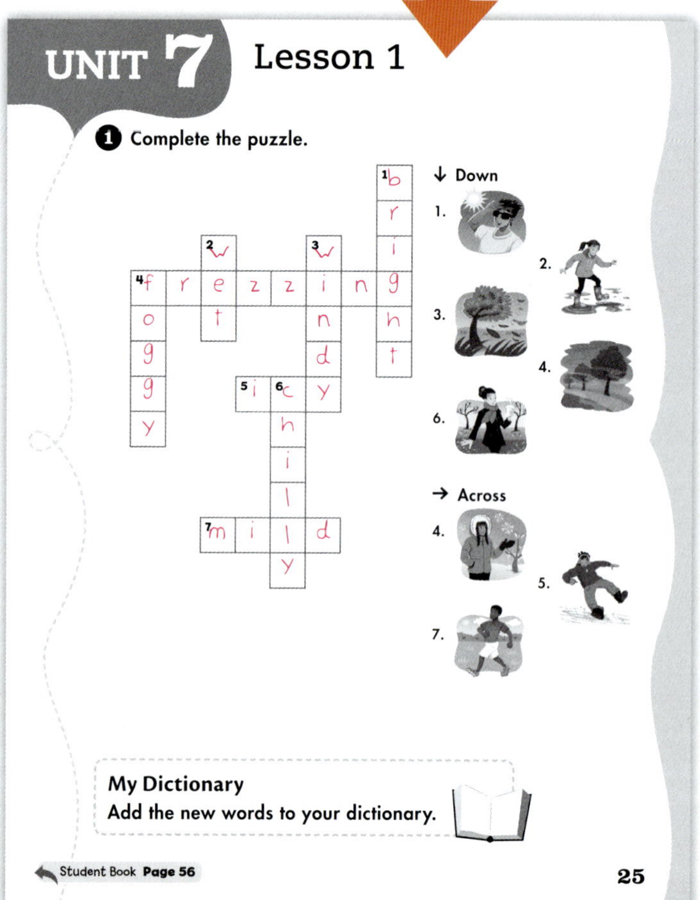
UNIT 7 Lesson 1

1 Complete the puzzle.

1 b r i g h t
2 w e t
3 w i n d y
4 f r e e z i n g
4 f o g g y
5 i c y
6 c h i l l y
7 m i l d

↓ Down
1. 2. 3. 4. 6.

→ Across
4. 5. 7.

My Dictionary
Add the new words to your dictionary.

Student Book Page 56

25

Lesson 1

This may also be completed for homework.

Lesson 1 Vocabulary

Unit 7

Lesson Objective: Identify types of weather.
New Vocabulary: windy, bright, wet, foggy, mild, chilly, freezing, icy
Materials: Audio **Tracks 40 and 41**

Start the Class

5 min

Draw a thermometer on the board and mark three temperatures, for example 30°C, 15°C, and 5°C, that are typically hot, average, or cold where you live. Point to the highest temperature and elicit *hot*. Ask students what clothes they wear when the weather is very hot. Do the same for the other temperatures.

1 40 Listen. Then echo.

10 min

Tell students they are going to listen to some weather words and they should raise their hands if they know any of the words. Play **Track 40**.

Tell students to open their books. Have them look at the pictures and identify as many words as they can. Tell them to listen to the audio and point to the pictures as they hear the words. Play **Track 40**. Then play **Track 40** again and have students echo the words.

Try This!

5 min

Give students clues about types of weather, and have them guess the weather word. For example, say *The leaves are blowing off the trees!* Elicit *windy*. Then say *It was very cold, I slipped and fell over!* Elicit *icy*. Then, in pairs, have students take turns to give clues of the new weather vocabulary words for their partner to guess.

2 41 Listen and number.

10 min

Tell the class they are going to hear a song about weather. Tell them to listen and number the verses in the correct order. Play **Track 41**. Check answers with the class. Then tell students to listen again and read along. Play **Track 41** again.

3 Page 25 The Language Lodge

15 min

Have students flip to The Language Lodge **Page 25**.

1 Complete the puzzle.

Have students look at the pictures. Point to them randomly and elicit the weather words.

Have students work in pairs to complete the puzzle. Check answers by calling out the number of the clues and have students say the answers.

My Dictionary

Tell students to turn to the dictionary section of their notebooks. Have them write the new vocabulary words. Play Magic Bingo (see **Page T 125**). Tell students to draw a Bingo grid in the dictionary section of their notebooks. Tell them to write *sunny* in the center square and complete the other squares with the new weather vocabulary words. Then say the words in any order, but remember to leave the word *sunny* to the end, so that the whole class calls out *Bingo!* at the same time.

Finish the Class

5 min

Write these words on the board: *freezing, mild, icy, windy, chilly*. Ask students to work in pairs and put the words in alphabetical order: *chilly, freezing, icy, mild, windy*. Then discuss what clothes students would wear for each type of weather.

Use the **Presentation Kit** for interactive activities in this lesson.

Have students use the **Happy Campers app** for additional practice with the new vocabulary.

The Language Lodge Page 25 may also be completed for homework.

Lesson 2 Grammar

Lesson Objective: Ask and answer questions about clothing and weather.
New Grammar: Why are you wearing a hat? Because it's chilly.
Vocabulary Review: windy, bright, wet, foggy, mild, chilly, freezing, icy
Materials: Audio **Track 41**

Start the Class

5 min

Brainstorm all the clothing vocabulary students know and write a list on the board. Write three headings on the board: *Hot, Mild, Cold*. Have volunteers write an item of clothing under the correct heading on the board. Explain that some items of clothing can go under more than one heading.

1 41 Sing: The Bicycle Ride!

5 min

Tell students they are going to listen to the song again. Play **Track 41** and have students listen and read the lyrics. Remind students of the correct order of the verses. Play **Track 41** again and have the class sing along.

Have students look at the song lyrics to find and underline examples of weather words in one color and clothing words in another color.

Try This!

5 min

Put students into groups. Have them read the song lyrics and agree on gestures to use with the different weather words. Each group will take turns standing up and singing along to the audio. Tell them to gesture or mime as they sing. Play **Track 41** one time for each group.

Take a class vote on the best choreography. Ask the winning group to teach their moves to the rest of the class. Play **Track 41** again and have the whole class sing and perform the choreography.

2 Look at the Grammar Pass. Circle.

10 min

Ask volunteers to read the question and the answer in the Grammar Pass. Write the question and answer on the board and underline *why* and *because*. Ask students to find and circle similar questions and answers in the song. Explain to students that we use *why* to ask for a reason and *because* to give a reason.

Tell students to look at Activity 2. Have them read each item and then circle the correct answers. Check answers with the class.

3 Unscramble.

10 min

Tell students to look at the first scrambled words. Elicit the unscrambled question. Have two students read the speech bubbles aloud.

Have students work in pairs to unscramble all the questions, then take turns asking and answering the questions. Check answers by having pairs ask and answer for the class.

4 Page 26 The Language Lodge

10 min

Have students flip to The Language Lodge **Page 26**. Have a volunteer read the Grammar Pass aloud.

1 Match.

Tell students to read and match the sentences. Have them check answers with a partner. Then check answers with the class.

2 Write questions and answers with information from Activity 1.

Have a volunteer read the example question and answer. Refer students to the information in Activity 1. Point out that they will write a *why* question and a *because* answer for each pair of matching sentences in Activity 1. Check answers with the class.

Finish the Class

5 min

Tell the class to sing the song and perform the winning choreography from the Try This! activity again. Play **Track 41**.

Use the **Presentation Kit** for interactive activities in this lesson.

The Language Lodge Page 26 may also be completed for homework.

For additional class time, use **Pages 40 and 41** of the Skills Book. Go to **Page 178** in the Happy Campers Teacher's Edition for teacher notes for this lesson. You may also choose to assign these pages as homework.

UNIT 7

1 (40) Listen. Then echo.

Lesson 1

2 (41) Listen and number.

The Bicycle Ride!

☐ Come on! Let's go outside!
It's a great day for a bicycle ride!
Why are you wearing a raincoat today?
Because it's windy and wet
they say!

☐ Come on! Let's go outside!
It's a great day for a bicycle ride!
Why are you wearing sunglasses today?
Because it's chilly, but bright
they say!

☐ Come on! Let's go outside!
It's a great day for a bicycle ride.
Why are you wearing a scarf today?
Because it's freezing and icy
they say!

3 Page 25 The Language Lodge

Lesson 2

1 (41) Sing: The Bicycle Ride!

GRAMMAR PASS

Why are you wearing a hat?

Because it's chilly.

2 Look at the Grammar Pass. Circle.

1. Why are you wearing a scarf?
   a. Because it's freezing outside. (circled)
   b. It's a red scarf.
2. Why are you going outside?
   a. It's windy.
   b. Because I want to ride my bike. (circled)
3. We use *why* / *because* (circled) to give a reason for doing things.

3 Unscramble.

1. are / sunglasses / wearing / Why / you
   Why are you wearing sunglasses?
2. raincoat / are / a / Why / wearing / you
   Why are you wearing a raincoat?
3. wearing / a / Why / are / you / hoodie
   Why are you wearing a hoodie?

Why are you wearing sunglasses?

Because it's very bright today.

4 Page 26 The Language Lodge

Lesson 2

This may also be completed for homework.

Lesson 2

GRAMMAR PASS

Why are you wearing a hat?

Because it's chilly.

1 Match.

1. The roads are icy. — It's snowing.
2. It's a perfect day to fly a kite. — It's windy and bright.
3. She's wearing a raincoat. — It's wet outside.
4. He's wearing a scarf and gloves. — It's very cold!
5. She is going to the beach. — It's always warm there!

2 Write questions and answers with information from Activity 1.

1. Why are the roads icy?
   Because it's snowing.
2. Why is it a perfect day to fly a kite?
   Because it's windy and bright.
3. Why is she wearing a raincoat?
   Because it's wet outside.
4. Why is he wearing a scarf and gloves?
   Because it's very cold.
5. Why is she going to the beach?
   Because it's always warm there.

Student Book Page 57

Lesson 3

THE HAPPY CAMPERS

1 Why is Greg's nose red?

2 42 Read and listen.

3 43 **Dictation!** Listen and write. Then say.

1. The branch fell in the mud
2. The dog jumped in a puddle
3. The tree trunk is big
4. The wind is strong today

4 Page 27 The Language Lodge

Lesson 4

1 42 Listen again to **The Happy Campers**.

2 **Grammar Pass!** Match.

1. Why did they do the scene outside?
2. Why does Zac say "cut"?
3. Why did Sue need a towel?

Because Hamlet jumped in a puddle.

Because it was foggy.

Because the monster's tooth fell in the mud.

3 44 Listen and cheer!

Why did they laugh?

Because he walked into a tree.

CHEER BOX!

4 Page 28 The Language Lodge

Lesson 3

1 Find and circle five differences in the pictures. Then complete the sentences.

freezing trunk wind branch puddles

1. In Picture B the trunk of the tree is thinner.
2. In Picture A there are two birds on the branch, and in Picture B there are three.
3. In Picture A there are three puddles, not two.
4. The wind in Picture A is very strong, but the weather in Picture B is mild.
5. In Picture B the man is hot, but in Picture A he's freezing.

My Dictionary

Add the new words to your dictionary.

Student Book **Page 58**

Lesson 3

This may also be completed for homework.

Lesson 3 Vocabulary in Context

Lesson Objective: Identify nature words.
New Vocabulary: trunk, branch, mud, puddle, wind
Vocabulary Review: windy, bright, wet, foggy, mild, chilly, freezing, icy
Materials: Audio **Tracks 42 and 43**

Start the Class

5 min

Consolidate students' understanding of cause and effect by making statements about consequences and asking students to suggest causes. For example, say *I'm all wet. Why?* Elicit causes, such as, *Because it's raining.* Or *Because I jumped into a swimming pool!*

1 Why is Greg's nose red?

5 min

Tell students to look at the pictures in the comic strip without reading the text. Ask them to describe details and what they think is happening in each frame. Introduce the new vocabulary for this lesson by pointing to details in the pictures and eliciting or saying the words. Then ask *Why is Greg's nose red?* Ask students to guess.

2 42 Read and listen.

10 min

Tell students to read the comic strip and listen for the answer to the question in Activity 1. Play **Track 42**. Elicit the answer *Because it's foggy and he walked into a tree trunk.*

Tell students to read and listen again. Play **Track 42**. Ask *What kind of movie are they making?* Elicit *A horror movie.* Then divide the class into two groups. Tell them you are going to play the audio again, and this time one group will repeat all the *why* questions and the other group will repeat all the *because* answers. Assign roles and play **Track 42** again, pausing after the questions and answers for students to repeat. Then have groups change roles and repeat.

3 43 Dictation! Listen and write. Then say.

10 min

Tell students they will hear sentences and write what they hear. Play the first sentence of **Track 43** and pause the audio to allow students time to write. Repeat with the other sentences. Tell the class that they are going to hear the audio again, and this time they will say the sentences after they hear them. Play **Track 43** again and monitor student pronunciation. Check answers by asking volunteers to write the sentences on the board.

Audio script ***Track 43***
1. The branch fell in the mud. 2. The dog jumped in a puddle. 3. The tree trunk is big. 4. The wind is strong today.

4 Page 27 The Language Lodge

15 min

Have students flip to The Language Lodge **Page 27**.

1 Find and circle five differences in the pictures. Then complete the sentences.

Tell students to look at the pictures and the words in the box. Have students work in pairs to circle all the differences in their books and choose the correct words from the box to complete the sentences. Check answers with the class.

My Dictionary

Ask students to turn to the dictionary section in their notebooks. Have them add the words and draw a picture to illustrate each one.

Finish the Class

5 min

Have students choose a new word they learned in this lesson and think of a *why* question using that word. Then have them work with a partner taking turns asking and answering their questions. Ask pairs to share their questions and answers with the class.

Use the **Presentation Kit** for interactive activities in this lesson.

Have students use the **Happy Campers app** for additional practice with the new vocabulary.

The Language Lodge Page 27 may also be completed for homework.

Lesson 4 Grammar in Context

Lesson Objective: Ask and answer questions about causes and consequences.
New Grammar: Why did you stop? Because the wind took my hat!
Vocabulary Review: windy, bright, wet, foggy, mild, chilly, freezing, icy, trunk, branch, mud, puddle, wind
Materials: Audio **Tracks 42 and 44**, prepare *true/false* sentences about the story from Lesson 3

Start the Class

5 min

Put students in groups and hand out sheets of paper with *true/false* sentences about the comic strip from the last lesson. Tell groups to decide if their sentence is true or false without opening their books. Ask each group to take turns reading their sentence and say whether they think it is true or false. Ask the rest of the class if they agree.

1 42 Listen again to The Happy Campers.

10 min

Tell students to listen again to the comic strip and check their answers in the Start the Class activity. Play **Track 42**. Ask groups if their answers were correct.

Tell the class to listen to the comic strip again, and this time they should underline all the *why* questions and circle all the *because* answers in the comic strip. Play **Track 42** again.

2 Grammar Pass! Match.

5 min

Ask one volunteer to read the questions in the activity and another to read the answers. Tell students to match the questions and answers. Check answers with the class.

3 44 Listen and cheer!

5 min

Tell students to listen to the cheer and read along in their books. Play **Track 44**. Tell students to say the cheer and play **Track 44** again. Then have students say the cheer without the audio, and tell them to clap on the words *why* and *because*.

4 Page 28 The Language Lodge

10 min

Have students flip to The Language Lodge **Page 28**. Have a volunteer read the Grammar Pass aloud.

1 Read. Then answer.

Ask students to look at the picture and describe it. Tell students to read the story. Then have them work in pairs to read the questions and write the answers. Check answers by telling students to read the questions and then let them nominate another student to read his or her answer each time.

Try This!

10 min

Write question prompts on the board such as *Who went to the park?* or *What happened at the park?*

Put students in groups and have them work together to write notes about the story in The Language Lodge. Have students use the prompts to help them organize the information. Elicit possible answers to any of the prompts if necessary such as *Robert went to the park, Wind blew the kite into tree, or Robert fell into a puddle.*

Have groups practice retelling the story by referring to their notes. Each group could nominate a reporter to retell the story, or they could take turns saying sentences. Ask a volunteer group to retell the story for the class.

Finish the Class

5 min

Tell the class to close their books. Ask *why* questions about the story in The Language Lodge and have students answer using *because*. Encourage the rest of the class to supply any other details they can remember.

Use the **Presentation Kit** for interactive activities in this lesson.

The Language Lodge Page 28 may also be completed for homework.

Lesson 3

THE HAPPY CAMPERS

1 Why is Greg's nose red?

2 42 Read and listen.

3 43 **Dictation!** Listen and write. Then say.

1. ______.
2. ______.
3. ______.
4. ______.

4 Page 27 The Language Lodge

Lesson 4

1 42 Listen again to The Happy Campers.

2 **Grammar Pass!** Match.

1. Why did they do the scene outside? — Because it was foggy.
2. Why does Zac say "cut"? — Because the monster's tooth fell in the mud.
3. Why did Sue need a towel? — Because Hamlet jumped in a puddle.

3 44 Listen and cheer!

Why did they laugh?

Because he walked into a tree.

CHEER BOX!

4 Page 28 The Language Lodge

Lesson 4

This may also be completed for homework.

Lesson 4

GRAMMAR PASS

Why did you stop?

Because the wind took my hat!

1 Read. Then answer.

It rained for days and days. But yesterday it wasn't rainy. It was a bright and sunny day, so Robert went to the park with his friends. It was chilly and windy so he wore his warm jacket. One of Robert's friends had a kite. It was a good day to fly a kite! But suddenly the wind blew the kite into a tree. Robert climbed the tree to get the kite. But the branch wasn't strong and he fell into a mud puddle! "Are you OK?" everyone shouted. "Yes, but I'm cold and wet. I want to go home!"

They all went back to Robert's house. Robert looked cold and wet. Robert's mother made a hot drink for everyone. Now everyone was happy again!

1. Why did Robert go to the park?
   Because it was a bright and sunny day.
2. Why did he wear his warm jacket?
   Because it was chilly and windy.
3. Why did Robert climb the tree?
   Because he wanted to get the kite.
4. Why did he fall into a mud puddle?
   Because the branch wasn't strong.

Student Book Page 59

Lesson 5

1 **What part of George Washington's body is the text about?**

arms   legs   (mouth)   feet   hands   tummy

2 45 **Read and listen.**

George Washington's False Teeth

On a bright day in April 1789, George Washington became the first president of the United States. He was a brave man and he wanted the United States to be a peaceful country. Washington was also a good man.

But he had a secret. He had bad teeth! This was because he was sick a lot as a young man. He took care of his teeth, but it didn't help. By the time he was president he only had one tooth of his own! George Washington didn't smile or talk much because his teeth hurt him a lot!

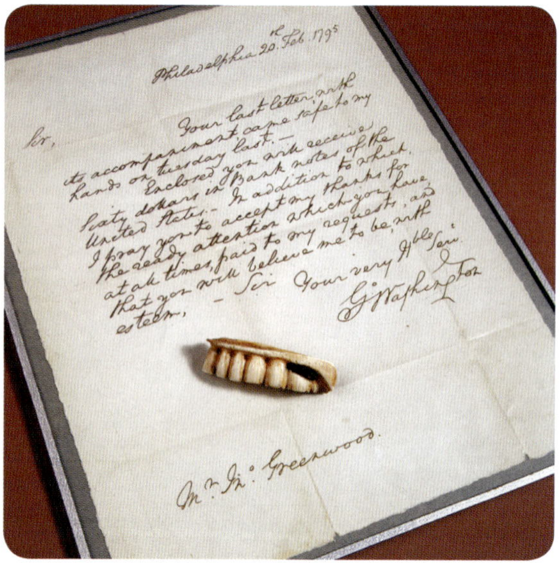

Washington didn't want anyone to know about his bad teeth. He looked for a dentist to make a set of false teeth. John Greenwood was an important dentist in New York. Washington asked him to make false teeth for him. Greenwood made them from the teeth of a hippopotamus. They were strong and white. They were expensive, too.

George Washington wore his new false teeth for his official portrait. Look at his picture on the American dollar bill. Do you think he was wearing his false teeth for that picture, too?

Lesson 5 Nonfiction Reading

Lesson Objective: Read a nonfiction text to practice unit language.
Vocabulary Review: arm, leg, mouth, foot/feet, hand, tummy
Materials: Audio **Track 45**

Start the Class

5 min

Tell students to open their books and scan the text. Tell them you are going to write the scrambled name of a famous person from history on the board, and they have to unscramble the name as quickly as possible.

Write *E R G O G E   S N T A G H W I O N* on the board. Have students raise their hands to answer. When a student has answered correctly, brainstorm anything students already know about George Washington.

1 What part of George Washington's body is the text about?

5 min

Ask students to look at the title of the text and the pictures and predict what the text is going to be about.

Then ask a student to read the question and the answer options. Without reading the text, tell students to circle the part of the body they think the text is about. Do not confirm the answer yet.

2 45 Read and listen.

20 min

Tell students to read the text as they listen to the audio. Play **Track 45**. Ask students if they circled the correct answer in Activity 1, *mouth*. Tell students to read and listen again, and play **Track 45** again. Ask *yes/no* questions to check understanding, for example, *Was George Washington the president in January 1789? Did he take care of his teeth? Is he smiling in his official portrait? Did he ask a doctor to help him?* Tell students to answer with full sentences, for example, *No, he wasn't. He became president in April 1789.*

Put students in groups of four. Assign a paragraph of the text to each student. Have each student read a paragraph from the text aloud to his or her group. Walk around the classroom to help with vocabulary and pronunciation as needed.

Try This! 10 min

Ask groups to think of an alternative title for the text. Encourage them to be imaginative, for example, suggest *The President* or *The Dentist and the Hippopotamus.* Ask each group to take turns telling the class their new title. Write the titles on the board. Take a class vote on the best new title.

Finish the Class

10 min

Keep students in their groups. Ask each group to write two *why* questions about the text. Collect the questions and read them to the class. Ask groups to answer the questions and point to the evidence in the text for their answers. Tell the groups they cannot answer their own question.

Use the **Presentation Kit** for interactive activities in this lesson.

Lesson 6 Reading Comprehension / Writing

Lesson Objectives: Identify specific information. Write about George Washington's dentist.
Materials: Audio **Track 45**

Start the Class

10 min

Tell the class to keep their books closed. Write *George Washington's False Teeth* on the board. Explain that you are going to select some students to participate. If a student hears his or her name, he or she will say a word or sentence from the text in Lesson 5 or ask a question about it. If the student asks a question, the rest of the class can try to answer it.

1 45 Listen again to George Washington's False Teeth.

5 min

Tell students to open their books. Tell them to listen to the text again, and follow in their books. Play **Track 45**. Discuss whether there are any important details in the text that the class missed in the Start the Class activity.

2 Answer.

5 min

Ask a volunteer to read the first question. Elicit the answer from the class. Have students work individually to answer the questions. Then check answers with the class.

Try This!

10 min

Draw a two-column chart on the board. Write *George Washington in* column 1 and *John Greenwood in* column 2. Have students work in pairs. Tell them to read the text again and make notes about each character. Ask pairs to read their notes. Add the information in note form to the chart on the board.

3 Writing Time! Answer the questions about Washington's dentist.

5 min

Ask volunteers to read the questions. Tell students to work individually to answer the questions. Then have them check their answers with a partner. Check answers with the class.

4 Write about John Greenwood.

10 min

Tell students to write a paragraph about John Greenwood using their answers from Activity 3. Monitor and help as needed.

Have students exchange their paragraphs with a partner. Tell them to read their partners' paragraphs. Encourage students to suggest any corrections. If time allows, have students rewrite their paragraphs, taking into account their partners' suggestions.

Have one or two volunteers read their paragraphs to the class.

Finish the Class

5 min

Play the Shark Game (see **Page T 28**) with words from the text, such as *president, peaceful, dentist, hippopotamus*.

Use the **Presentation Kit** for interactive activities in this lesson.

For additional class time, use **Pages 42 and 43** of the Skills Book. Go to **Page 179** in the Happy Campers Teacher's Edition for teacher notes for this lesson. You may also choose to assign these pages as homework.

Lesson 6

Lesson 6

1 45 **Listen again to George Washington's False Teeth.**

2 **Answer.**

1. What was George Washington's secret?
   He had bad teeth.
2. Why did he have bad teeth?
   Because he was sick a lot as a young man.
3. Why did the dentist use hippopotamus teeth?
   Because they were strong and white.

3 **Writing Time! Answer the questions about Washington's dentist.**

1. Who was he? John Greenwood.
2. Where did he live? New York.
3. What did he make? He made false teeth.
4. What did he use? The teeth of a hippopotamus.

4 **Write about John Greenwood.**

John Greenwood was an important dentist in New York.
(Students' own answers)

Lesson 7

Lesson 7

ON STAGE!

PROJECT: Weather Report

1 **Plan** your Weather Report.

Monday	Tuesday	Wednesday
Weather: Chilly **Clothes:** jacket	(Students' own answers.)	(Students' own answers.)

2 **Prepare** a Weather Report for the week.

3 **On Stage!** Give your Weather Report to the class.

Why do I need a jacket today?

Because it's chilly.

Lesson 7 Creative, Collaborative, and Critical Thinking Activity

Lesson Objective: Plan, create, and present a Weather Report.
Vocabulary Review: windy, bright, wet, foggy, chilly, freezing, icy, jacket,
Grammar Review: Why do I need a jacket today? Because it's chilly.
Materials: five- or seven-day graphic weather reports cut out from a newspaper or printed from the Internet, construction paper, scissors, glue, colored pencils/markers

Start the Class

10 min

Put students in their project groups. Give each group a weather report. Ask them to use the images and other information in the weather reports to describe the weather on particular days and ask what clothing students suggest to wear for each day. Monitor and help as needed.

1 Plan your Weather Report.

10 min

Tell the groups to look at the example Weather Report for Monday in their books. Ask *What information does the Weather Report show?* Elicit the following answers: *day, weather, temperature, clothes.*

Tell the groups to plan their own Weather Reports. Have them work together to decide on the type of weather, temperature, and clothes for each day, and what symbols they are going to use to represent the weather. Monitor and help as needed.

2 Prepare a Weather Report for the week.

15 min

Tell the groups to look at the example Weather Report in the photo. Explain that they are now going to prepare their own Weather Reports. Hand out materials.

Ask groups to work together to create their weather report using the information they planned in Activity 1. If there isn't enough time, tell them that they can prepare a Weather Report for three or four days rather than a whole week. Encourage the groups to agree on what each group member is going to do to complete the report. Monitor and help as needed.

3 On Stage! Give your Weather Report to the class.

10 min

Tell students to look at the photo of the girl and boy presenting their Weather Report. Have volunteers read the speech bubbles.

Give groups time to practice presenting their Weather Reports. Make sure that every student in each group has a role in the presentation. Then ask each group to present their Weather Report to the class. At the end of each presentation, encourage students to provide feedback or ask questions.

Finish the Class

5 min

Display the Weather Reports around the classroom where all students can see them clearly. Have students work individually to make three sentences about one of the Weather Reports. For example, *I need a hoodie on Tuesday. The temperature is 30 degrees on Wednesday. It's sunny on Thursday.* Tell them not to say which report it is. The rest of the class has to guess which weather report it is.

Use the **Presentation Kit** for interactive activities in this lesson.

Lesson 8 Review

Lesson Objective: Review language from Unit 7.
Vocabulary Review: windy, bright, wet, foggy, mild, chilly, freezing, icy, trunk, branch, mud, puddle, wind
Grammar Review: Why are you wearing a hat? Because it's chilly. Why did you stop? Because the wind took my hat!

Start the Class

10 min

Before students come into the classroom, label each corner in the room with a different weather word, such as *chilly*, wet, *bright*, *hot*.

Tell students you are going to say an item of clothing, such as *jacket*, *raincoat*, *sunglasses*, or *sandals*. Then have a volunteer stand in the appropriate corner. Ask him or her a question about the item of clothing, for example, *Why do I need sunglasses today?* The student should say *Because it's bright*. Continue this with several other students.

1 Spelling! Complete.

5 min

Tell students to look at the pictures and read the incomplete sentences in their books. Have them complete the sentences with a weather word. Check answers by asking students to read the complete sentences. Ask the rest of the class if they agree.

2 Match.

10 min

Ask volunteers to read the questions and the answer choices. Have students work individually to match the questions and answers. Check answers by asking students to read the questions and asking other students to read the matching answers.

Try This!

5 min

Ask students to create new *why* questions by substituting other words in the questions in Activity 2, for example, *Why don't you like action movies? Why did you put on your swimsuit?* Put students in pairs and have them take turns asking and answering the questions. Tell students that answers have to be a logical reply to the question, but answers do not have to be true for them.

3 Word Play! Find and circle the words from Unit 7 on Page 72.

10 min

Have students turn to **Page 72** and tell them to find and circle the weather and nature vocabulary words from Unit 7. Then have students check the words they found with a partner.

Finish the Class

10 min

Tell students to write about what clothes they wore after school yesterday. Have a student read the clothes they wore, for example, *jeans and a sweatshirt*. Have another student ask a *why* question about the clothes, such as *Why did you wear jeans and a sweatshirt after school yesterday?* The first student has to answer using *because*, for example, *Because it was chilly*. Continue by asking as many students to read their clothes as possible.

Use the **Presentation Kit** for interactive activities in this lesson.

For additional class time, use **Pages 44 and 45** of the Skills Book. Go to **Page 180** in the Happy Campers Teacher's Edition for teacher notes for this lesson. You may also choose to assign these pages as homework.

Lesson 8

Round Up!

1 Spelling! Complete.

1. I put on my scarf because I felt chilly .

2. Dad put on the car lights because it was foggy .

3. Yesterday was very cold, but today it's mild .

4. He put on his sunglasses because the sun was very bright .

2 Match.

1. Why don't you like horror movies? — Because I missed the bus.
2. Why did you put on your boots? — Because it's wet outside.
3. Why do you need a scarf? — Because they're scary.
4. Why were you late? — Because I have a cold.

3 Word Play! Find and circle the words from Unit 7 on Page 72.

Unit 8

Unit Objectives

By the end of the unit, students can:

- Identify air travel vocabulary.
- Talk about the future using future tense verbs.
- Talk about vacations and travel.

Student Book

Vocabulary

Air Travel 1: suitcase, hand luggage, bag tag, ticket, check-in, airline, window seat, boarding pass

Air Travel 2: gate, flight, aisle, flight attendant, emergency exit, seat belt

Grammar

I'll buy the tickets.
Will you sing for us today? Yes, we will.
Will you dance for us today? No, we won't.

Skills

Listening: Listen for and identify air travel vocabulary. Listen for the main idea and specific information.

Speaking: Talk about air travel and vacations. Ask and answer questions using future tense verbs.

Reading: Read a fiction text: **Adventure on Mount Juniper**.
Identify the main idea.

Writing: Write about your adventure.

Creative, Collaborative, and Critical Thinking Competencies

Vacation Checklist

Creativity: Develop self-expression, innovation, and problem-solving skills to plan a vacation checklist.

Collaboration: Use communication and negotiation skills to discuss and decide on what to include in the Vacation Checklist, how to present the information, and how each group member will contribute to the final product.

Critical Thinking: Use problem-solving skills to analyze, categorize, and order information.

Skills Book

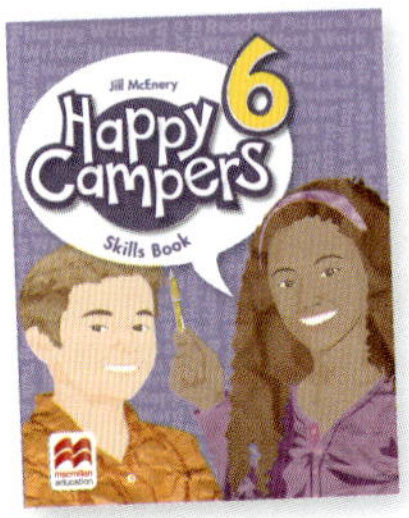

Extra Skills Practice

Speaking and Listening: Ask and answer questions about a picture.

Reading and Writing: Recall details. Read clues to identify words. Identify one- and multi-syllable words. Use visual clues to identify words.

Teacher Workshop

Teaching with Technology

Flashcards can provide students with a variety of images to better demonstrate understanding of vocabulary words. These flashcards can also be used as speaking and writing prompts for further practice.

Teaching with Games

Progressive Drawing

Students of this age enjoy predicting and problem solving. Progressive drawing is a great way to engage their attention while reviewing or consolidating vocabulary. Start by deciding which vocabulary set you want to practice. Choose a word and start by drawing just one line or a minor detail. Ask students to predict what you are drawing. Keep your drawings simple and linear and do not add so much detail that students can guess immediately. The first student to correctly guess what you are drawing takes your place at the board to draw another vocabulary item.

Happy Teacher

As you come to the end of the school year, there are several end-of-year activities that you can try with the class. For example, students can say what they have enjoyed learning about. Another activity is to review how much students have achieved in their English classes. The last activity could take place during the final class of the school year. Organize a class celebration. Have students play their favorite games or sing their favorite songs from *Happy Campers*.

Happy Class

When your students have been working hard, have them choose an activity to celebrate, such as singing a favorite song from the book, watching a video in English, or playing a game. Be sure to emphasize that this is a reward for their hard work.

By Gabriel Diaz Maggioli

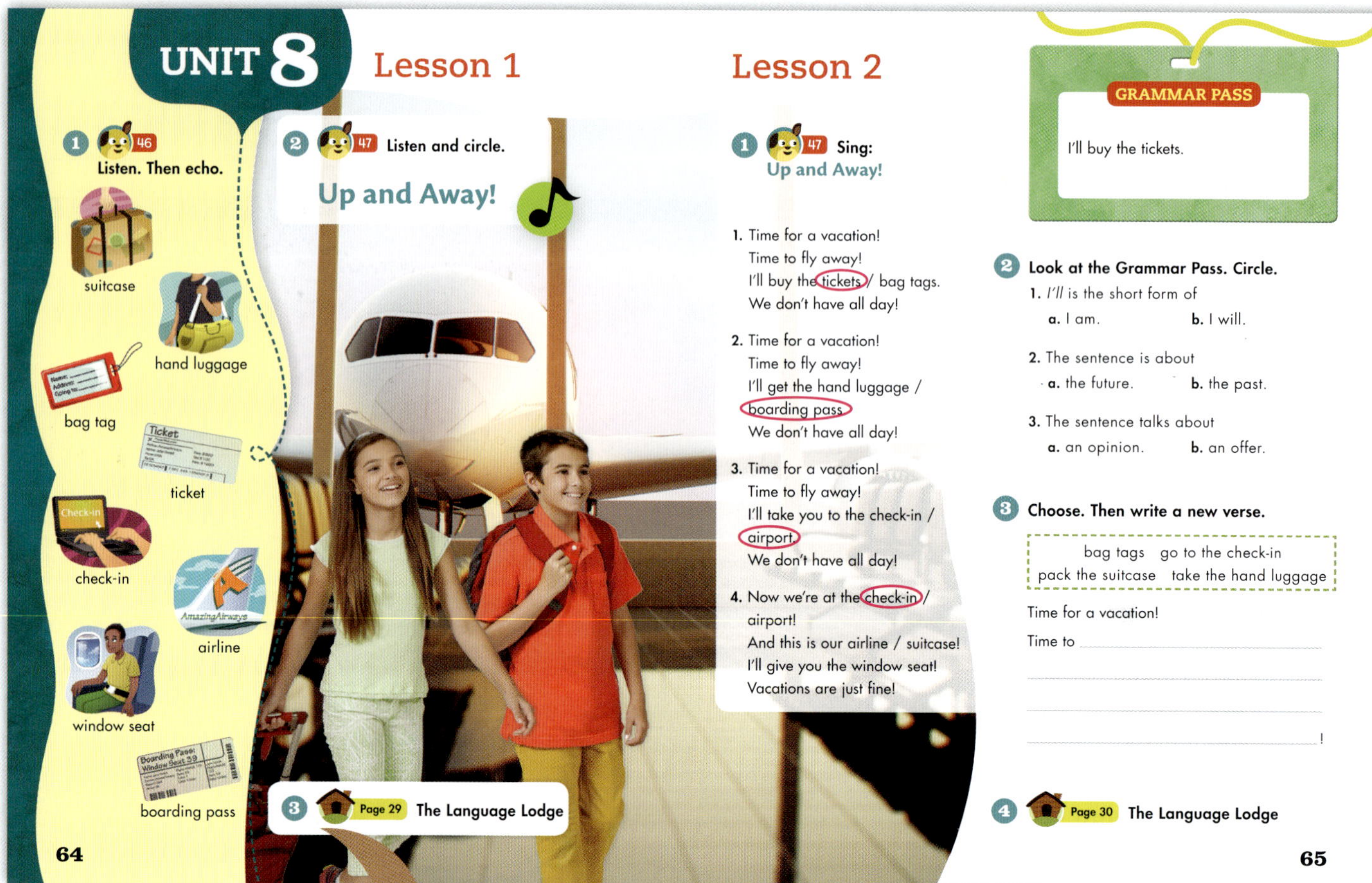

UNIT 8 Lesson 1

1 (46) Listen. Then echo.

suitcase
hand luggage
bag tag
ticket
check-in
airline
window seat
boarding pass

2 (47) Listen and circle.

Up and Away!

3 Page 29 The Language Lodge

Lesson 2

1 (47) Sing: Up and Away!

1. Time for a vacation!
   Time to fly away!
   I'll buy the tickets / bag tags.
   We don't have all day!
2. Time for a vacation!
   Time to fly away!
   I'll get the hand luggage / boarding pass.
   We don't have all day!
3. Time for a vacation!
   Time to fly away!
   I'll take you to the check-in / airport.
   We don't have all day!
4. Now we're at the check-in / airport!
   And this is our airline / suitcase!
   I'll give you the window seat!
   Vacations are just fine!

GRAMMAR PASS

I'll buy the tickets.

2 Look at the Grammar Pass. Circle.

1. *I'll* is the short form of
   a. I am. b. I will.
2. The sentence is about
   a. the future. b. the past.
3. The sentence talks about
   a. an opinion. b. an offer.

3 Choose. Then write a new verse.

bag tags go to the check-in
pack the suitcase take the hand luggage

Time for a vacation!
Time to ______
______
______
______!

4 Page 30 The Language Lodge

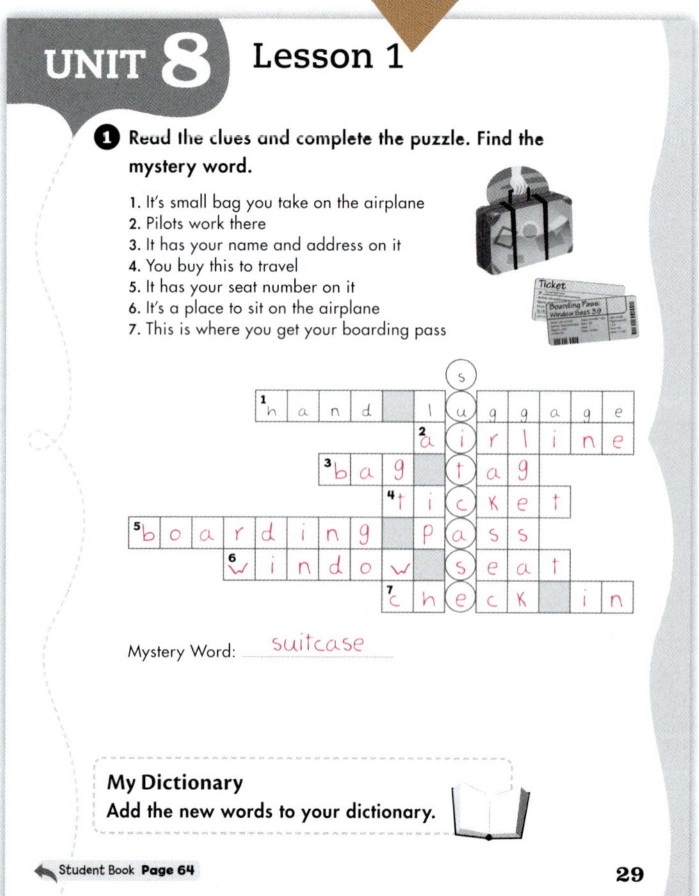

UNIT 8 Lesson 1

1 Read the clues and complete the puzzle. Find the mystery word.

1. It's small bag you take on the airplane
2. Pilots work there
3. It has your name and address on it
4. You buy this to travel
5. It has your seat number on it
6. It's a place to sit on the airplane
7. This is where you get your boarding pass

1	h a n d ■ l u g g a g e
2	a i r l i n e
3	b a g ■ t a g
4	t i c k e t
5	b o a r d i n g ■ p a s s
6	w i n d o w ■ s e a t
7	c h e c k ■ i n

Mystery Word: suitcase

My Dictionary
Add the new words to your dictionary.

Student Book Page 64

Lesson 1

This may also be completed for homework.

Lesson 1 Vocabulary

Lesson Objective: Identify air travel vocabulary.
New Vocabulary: suitcase, hand luggage, bag tag, ticket, check-in, airline, window seat, boarding pass
Materials: Audio **Tracks 46 and 47**

Start the Class

10 min

Say to the class *I went to France for my vacation last year!* Ask students to guess how you traveled to France. Elicit *airplane*. Ask students if they have ever flown in an airplane. Ask them to tell the class about their experience. Prompt them with questions, such as *Where did you fly to? Were you going on vacation? What did you like about flying? What didn't you like*?

1 46 Listen. Then echo.

5 min

Tell students to look at the pictures. Elicit any words students already know in English.

Tell students to listen to the audio and point to the pictures as they hear the words. Play **Track 46**. Then play **Track 46** again and have students echo the words.

Try This! 5 min

Put students in pairs and ask them to number the pictures in Activity 1 from 1 to 8. They will take turns saying a number for their partners to say the word.

2 47 Listen and circle.

10 min

Tell students to look at the photo. Ask them to describe it in as much detail as they can.

Tell the class they are going to hear a song about air travel. Tell them to listen, follow the song lyrics in their books, and circle the correct words. Play **Track 47**. Check that students have circled the correct words by reading out the options and asking students to say which word they circled each time. Then tell students to listen and sing along. Play **Track 47** again.

3 Page 29 The Language Lodge

15 min

Have students flip to The Language Lodge **Page 29**.

1 Read the clues and complete the puzzle. Find the mystery word.

Ask a volunteer to read the directions. Ask another volunteer to read the first clue. Elicit the answer *hand luggage*. Explain to students that they will read each clue then write individual letters in the squares and circles in order to complete the puzzle. Tell them to leave each gray box blank. Explain that when they have finished the puzzle correctly, they will be able to write the mystery word by looking at the letters in the circles.

Have students work in pairs to read the clues and complete the puzzle. Check answers by saying the clue numbers and asking students to say the words. Then ask the class to say the mystery word.

My Dictionary

Ask students to turn to the dictionary section in their notebooks. Tell them to write in the new words and draw a picture or write a sentence to illustrate the meaning of each one.

Finish the Class

5 min

Start drawing a suitcase with just one line on the board. Ask students to guess what you are drawing. Continue adding details to the drawing until a student guesses what it is. Ask him or her to come to the board to start drawing another word related to air travel for the class to guess.

Use the **Presentation Kit** for interactive activities in this lesson.

Have students use the **Happy Campers app** for additional practice with the new vocabulary.

The Language Lodge Page 29 may also be completed for homework.

Lesson 2 Grammar

Lesson Objective: Talk about the future using *I'll ...*
New Grammar: I'll buy the tickets.
Vocabulary Review: suitcase, hand luggage, bag tag, ticket, check-in, airline, window seat, boarding pass
Materials: Audio **Track 47**, flashcards of the new vocabulary from Lesson 1

Start the Class

5 min

Review the vocabulary from Lesson 1 using the flashcards. Cover each flashcard and reveal one letter at a time. Ask the student who guesses the word first to make a sentence with it.

1 47 Sing: Up and Away!

10 min

Tell students they are going to sing the song from Lesson 1. Play **Track 47** and have them follow in their books and sing along. Then put the class in three groups. Assign one of the first three verses to each group. Tell each group to sing their verse, and the whole class to sing verse 4. Play **Track 47** again.

Ask the class if the song is about the future or the past. Elicit *future*. Elicit an example of the future tense in the song. Then have students underline all the examples of the future tense in the song lyrics. Have volunteers read the sentences they have underlined.

2 Look at the Grammar Pass. Circle.

5 min

Ask a volunteer to read the sentence in the Grammar Pass. Write it on the board. Then write *I will buy the tickets*. Explain that the sentences mean the same and that *I'll* is a short form of *I will*. Tell the class that we use *I'll* when we are offering to help or when predicting based on speculation.

Have students work in pairs to read the sentences and circle the correct answers. Check answers with the class.

3 Choose. Then write a new verse.

10 min

Tell students to look at the words in the box. Put students in groups. Tell them to choose one of the words and use it to write a new verse for the song. Give time for each group to write their verse and practice singing it. Then have each group take turns singing their new verse to the class.

Try This! 5 min

Take a class vote on the best new verse from Activity 3. Have the whole class sing the winning verse.

4 Page 30 The Language Lodge

10 min

Have students flip to The Language Lodge **Page 30**. Have a volunteer read the Grammar Pass aloud.

1 Match.

Tell students to look at the pictures. Ask a volunteer to read the first sentence. Have students read all the sentences and match them with the pictures. Check answers by asking students to read the sentences and point to the correct pictures.

2 Choose and complete.

Tell students to look at the verbs in the box. Ask a volunteer to read them. Then read the first sentence and have another student read the example answer. Have students work in pairs to choose the correct verbs to complete the other sentences in the future tense. Check answers with the class.

Finish the Class

5 min

Say to the class *I'm thirsty. I'll drink some water!* Write *thirsty, hungry, tired, bored, scared, hot,* and *cold* on the board. Point to one of the words and ask a student to make similar sentences, for example, *I'm tired. I'll go to sleep.* Continue with other students and words.

Use the **Presentation Kit** for interactive activities in this lesson.

The Language Lodge Page 30 may also be completed for homework.

For additional class time, use **Pages 46 and 47** of the Skills Book. Go to **Page 181** in the Happy Campers Teacher's Edition for teacher notes for this lesson. You may also choose to assign these pages as homework.

UNIT 8

Lesson 1

1 46 Listen. Then echo.

2 47 Listen and circle.

Up and Away!

3 Page 29 The Language Lodge

Lesson 2

1 47 Sing: Up and Away!

1. Time for a vacation!
   Time to fly away!
   I'll buy the tickets / bag tags.
   We don't have all day!
2. Time for a vacation!
   Time to fly away!
   I'll get the hand luggage / boarding pass.
   We don't have all day!
3. Time for a vacation!
   Time to fly away!
   I'll take you to the check-in / airport.
   We don't have all day!
4. Now we're at the check-in / airport!
   And this is our airline / suitcase!
   I'll give you the window seat!
   Vacations are just fine!

GRAMMAR PASS

I'll buy the tickets.

2 **Look at the Grammar Pass. Circle.**

1. *I'll* is the short form of
   a. I am. b. (I will.)
2. The sentence is about
   a. (the future.) b. the past.
3. The sentence talks about
   a. an opinion. b. (an offer.)

3 **Choose. Then write a new verse.**

bag tags go to the check-in
pack the suitcase take the hand luggage

Time for a vacation!
Time to ______
(Students' own answers)
______
______!

4 Page 30 The Language Lodge

Lesson 2

This may also be completed for homework.

Lesson 2

GRAMMAR PASS

I'll buy the tickets.

1 **Match.**

1. I'll have the aisle seat. — Jim
2. I'll show you my boarding pass. — David
3. I'll check-in online now. — Betty

2 **Choose and complete.**

give help get buy

1. Lisa likes animals. *I'll get* her a dog.
2. Jerry is hungry. *I'll buy* him a pizza.
3. Julie has too much homework. *I'll help* her with it.
4. Tom wants to sit by the window. *I'll give* him my seat.

Student Book Page 65

Lesson 3

THE HAPPY CAMPERS

1 How are The Happy Campers going to New York City?

2 48 Read and listen.

3 49 Dictation! Listen and write. Then say.

1. The flight attendant is in the aisle.
2. I'll put on my seat belt.
3. This is the emergency exit.
4. Our flight is at Gate 2.

4 Page 31 The Language Lodge

Lesson 4

1 48 Listen again to The Happy Campers.

2 Grammar Pass! Circle.

1. Will you give me your seat? Yes, I will. / No, I won't.
2. Will the movie be fantastic? Yes, it will. / No, it won't.
3. Who will sing today? We will. / We won't.

3 50 Listen and cheer!

Will you sing for us today? Yes, we will! Yes, we will!
Will you dance for us today? No, we won't! No, we won't!

CHEER BOX!

4 Page 32 The Language Lodge

Lesson 3

1 Read the clues. Complete the puzzle.

↓ Down

1. Your seat on the airplane has this for safety
5. This is where you get on the airplane in the airport

→ Across

2. This is the exit we use to get out of the airplane fast
3. This person takes care of you on your flight
4. This is a trip by airplane
6. This is where you walk when you are on an airplane

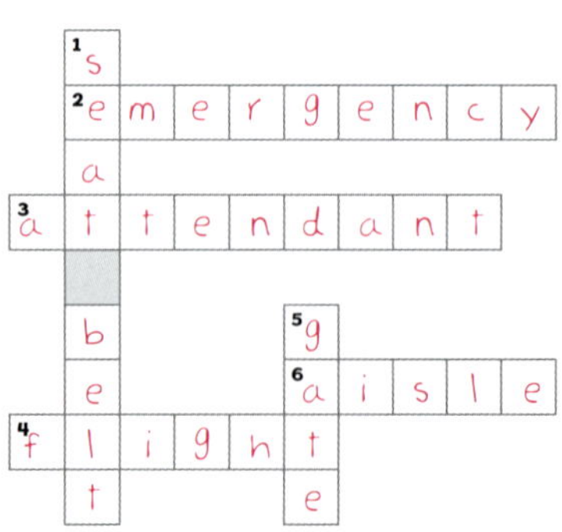

My Dictionary
Add the new words to your dictionary.

Student Book Page 66

Lesson 3

This may also be completed for homework.

Lesson 3 Vocabulary in Context

Lesson Objective: Identify more air travel vocabulary.
New Vocabulary: gate, flight, aisle, flight attendant, emergency exit, seat belt
Vocabulary Review: suitcase, hand luggage, bag tag, ticket, check-in, airline, window seat, boarding pass
Materials: Audio **Tracks 48 and 49**, flashcards from Lesson 1

Start the Class

5 min

Use the flashcards from Lesson 1 as prompts. Show a flashcard and ask a student to make a sentence using the word. Continue with other students and flashcards.

1 How are The Happy Campers going to New York City?

5 min

Tell students to look at the comic strip pictures without reading the text. Ask them to describe what is happening in each picture in as much detail as they can. Then ask *How are The Happy Campers going to New York City?* Have the class say the answer together.

2 48 Read and listen.

10 min

Have students read the comic strip as they listen. Play **Track 48**. Then ask them to read and listen again, and to listen for who will sing the song. Play **Track 48** again and ask *Who will sing the song?* Elicit *The Happy Campers.*

Check comprehension of the new vocabulary by asking questions, for example, *Where are The Happy Campers in the first picture?* Elicit *Gate 2. What is the walk area between the seats in an airplane called?* Elicit *aisle.*

Try This!

5 min

Write the new words on the board and underline the stressed syllables, for example, *emergency exit.* Say the words, emphasizing the stressed syllables, and have the class repeat. Then erase the underlining on the board, point to words, and have the class say the words, stressing the correct syllables.

3 49 Dictation! Listen and write. Then say.

10 min

Tell students they will hear sentences and write what they hear. Play the first sentence of **Track 49** and pause the audio to allow students time to write. Repeat with the other sentences. Tell the class that they are going to hear the audio again and this time they will say the sentences after they hear them. Play **Track 49** again and monitor student pronunciation. Check answers by asking volunteers to write the sentences on the board.

*Audio script **Track 49***
1. The flight attendant is in the aisle. 2. I'll put on my seat belt. 3. This is the emergency exit. 4. Our flight is at Gate 2.

4 Page 31 The Language Lodge

10 min

Have students flip to The Language Lodge **Page 31**.

1 Read the clues. Complete the puzzle.

Have a student read the first clue. Elicit the answer from the class. Tell students to work in pairs to read the clues and complete the puzzle. Remind them to follow the direction of the arrows when completing the puzzle. Check answers by saying clue numbers and asking students to say the answers.

My Dictionary

Have students turn to the dictionary section in their notebooks. Have them write the new words and draw a picture or write a sentence to show the meaning of each one.

Finish the Class

5 min

Play the Shark Game (see **Page T 28**) with the new vocabulary from Lessons 1 and 3.

Use the **Presentation Kit** for interactive activities in this lesson.

Have students use the **Happy Campers app** for additional practice with the new vocabulary.

The Language Lodge Page 31 may also be completed for homework.

Lesson 4 Grammar in Context

Lesson Objective: Ask and answer questions about the future.
New Grammar: Will you sing for us today? Yes, we will. Will you dance for us today? No, we won't.
Vocabulary Review: suitcase, hand luggage, bag tag, ticket, check-in, airline, window seat, boarding pass, gate, flight, aisle, flight attendant, emergency exit, seat belt
Materials: Audio **Tracks 48 and 50**

Start the Class

5 min

Tell students not to open their books. Ask several students to tell the class everything they can remember about the comic strip from Lesson 3. Encourage the other students to provide additional details.

1 48 Listen again to The Happy Campers.

10 min

Tell students they are going to listen to the comic strip again. Tell them to listen and see how much they remembered in the Start the Class activity. Play **Track 48**. Then tell them to underline all the questions and answers in the comic strip as they listen again. Play **Track 48** again.

Try This! 10 min

Tell the class they are going to role play the press conference in frame four of the comic strip. Put students in groups. Assign the roles of the female reporter, Zac, Madison, the male reporter, and The Happy Campers to each group member. Give them time to learn their lines and practice the scene. Have groups role play the scene for the class.

2 Grammar Pass! Circle.

5 min

Tell students to look back at the questions and answers they underlined in the comic strip. Write *Will you give me your seat? and No, I won't* on the board. Explain that *won't* is a short form of *will not*.

Tell students to work in pairs to read the questions and circle the correct answers. Read the questions and ask volunteers to say the correct answers. Ask students to notice how the word order is different in the *who* question.

3 50 Listen and cheer!

5 min

Tell students to listen to the cheer and read along in their books. Play **Track 50**. Tell students to say the cheer, and play **Track 50** again. Then have students say the cheer again, and clap when they hear the words *sing*, *will*, *dance*, and *won't*. Play **Track 50** again.

4 Page 32 The Language Lodge

10 min

Have students flip to The Language Lodge **Page 32**. Have a volunteer read the Grammar Pass aloud.

1 Look. Then write questions and answers.

Tell students to look at the example question and answer. Remind students that a check mark indicates a positive answer and an X indicates a negative answer. Have students work in pairs to write the questions and answers. Check answers by asking students to read the questions and having other students read their answers to the questions.

Finish the Class

5 min

Tell students to flip back through their books to look at all "The Happy Campers" comic strips again. Have a class discussion about them. Ask students who their favorite characters are, what their favorite episodes are, and what the funniest moments are. Encourage them to support their opinions about their favorites.

Use the **Presentation Kit** for interactive activities in this lesson.

The Language Lodge Page 32 may also be completed for homework.

Lesson 3

1 How are The Happy Campers going to New York City?

2 48 Read and listen.

3 49 **Dictation!** Listen and write. Then say.

1. ______________________________.
2. ______________________________.
3. ______________________________.
4. ______________________________.

4 Page 31 The Language Lodge

Lesson 4

1 48 Listen again to The Happy Campers.

2 **Grammar Pass!** Circle.

1. Will you give me your seat? Yes, I will. / (No, I won't.)
2. Will the movie be fantastic? Yes, it will. / (No, it won't.)
3. Who will sing today? We will. / (We won't.)

3 50 **Listen and cheer!**

Will you sing for us today? Yes, we will! Yes, we will!
Will you dance for us today? No, we won't! No, we won't!

CHEER BOX!

4 Page 32 The Language Lodge

Lesson 4

GRAMMAR PASS

Will you sing for us today?
Yes, we will.

Will you dance for us today?
No, we won't.

1 **Look. Then write questions and answers.**

1. ✓ learn / solar system / Will / she / the / about
   Will she learn about the solar system?
   Yes, she will.
2. ✗ Sara / book / a / Will / write
   Will Sara write a book?
   No, she won't.
3. ✓ Will / pictures / many / paint / he
   Will he paint many pictures?
   Yes, he will.
4. ✗ play / Will / they / basketball
   Will they play basketball?
   No, they won't.
5. ✓ vacation / Will / take / you / a
   Will you take a vacation?
   Yes, we will.

Student Book Page 67

Lesson 4

This may also be completed for homework.

Lesson 5

1 **What kind of transportation do the kids use?**

airplane (helicopter) car boat train

2 51 **Read and listen.**

Adventure on Mount Juniper

Olivia, Zoe, Noah, and Gavin are in the school walking club. Last Saturday the club planned to visit Mount Juniper. But it was a chilly day and many children stayed at home. But not Olivia, Zoe, Noah, and Gavin. They wanted to see the mountain. "Let's go anyway," Noah said.

It was easy and a lot of fun going up the mountain. Then, it started to snow. It was scary! "This is dangerous," Noah said. "Let's go back!"

"Now we won't be able to see!" Gavin said.

"What are we going to do?" Olivia asked.

"I'll call for help. I have a smartphone," Noah said.

"Who will you call?" Zoe asked.

"The fire station," Noah said.

Soon they heard a noise! It was a helicopter! The firefighters helped them into the helicopter. "Thank you!"

"Now fasten your seats belts and let's go! We'll be home soon!" the pilot said.

Lesson 5 Fiction Reading

Lesson Objective: Read a fiction text to practice unit language.
Grammar Review: present, past, and future tenses
Materials: Audio **Track 51**

Start the Class

10 min

Tell students to keep their books closed. Tell them they are going to read a story called "Adventure on Mount Juniper" about four children who are classmates. Put students in groups of four and ask them to create a short story with the same title but using only three sentences. Ask each group to take turns telling their story to the class.

1 What kind of transportation do the kids use?

10 min

Ask students to look at the story pictures and predict what the story is going to be about. Write some of their ideas on the board.

Then ask a student to read the question and the answer options. Without reading the text, tell students to circle the kind of transportation they think the children in the story use. Do not confirm the answer yet.

2 51 Read and listen.

15 min

Tell students to read the story as they listen to the track. Play **Track 51**. Ask students if they circled the correct word, *helicopter*, in Activity 1. Tell students to read and listen again, and play **Track 51** again. To check understanding, make *true/false* statements about the story. Ask students to answer *True!* or *False!* and have them correct the false statements, for example, *It was a hot day last Saturday. False! It was a chilly day.*

Put students in groups of four. Assign a paragraph of the story to each student. Have them take turns reading their paragraphs aloud in their groups. Walk around the classroom and help with vocabulary and pronunciation as much as necessary.

Try This! 5 min

Tell students to listen to the story again and stand up when they hear the future tense. Play **Track 51**.

Finish the Class

10 min

Ask students to close their books. Ask students to tell you a sentence from the story. Write the sentences on the board in any order. Then have students work in pairs to order the sentences according to the story. Check answers by having students come to the board to number the sentences in order.

Use the **Presentation Kit** for interactive activities in this lesson.

Lesson 6 Reading Comprehension / Writing

Lesson Objectives: Listen for specific information. Write about your adventure.
Vocabulary Review: weather words, scary, dangerous, smartphone, fire station, helicopter, seat belts, pilot
Grammar Review: present, past, and future tenses
Materials: Audio **Track 51**

Start the Class

5 min

Tell students to keep their books closed. Ask them to think back to the story from Lesson 5. Tell students you are going to say sentences of direct speech from the story, and they have to tell you which character said them, for example, *This is dangerous.* Elicit *Noah.* Say *Now we won't be able to see!* Elicit *Gavin.* If any students give the wrong answer, don't tell them the correct answer yet.

1 51 Listen again to Adventure on Mount Juniper.

5 min

Tell students to open their books. Have them listen to the story again and follow in their books. Play **Track 51**. Ask students to give the correct answers to any characters they got wrong in the Start the Class activity.

2 Answer.

5 min

Ask students to cover **Page 68** in their books so that they cannot see the story text. Have students work in pairs to read the questions and answer them from memory. Have them check answers with another pair.

Try This! 5 min

Have students uncover the text on **Page 68** and reread the story to make sure that their answers in Activity 2 are correct. Then check answers with the class by having students read the questions and different students to read their answers and point to the evidence in the text.

3 Writing Time! Plan a short adventure story.

10 min

Ask students to look at the chart. Tell them they are going to plan an adventure story. Demonstrate what they have to do by writing the chart on the board and eliciting brief information about the plot of the story on **Page 68** to complete the chart.

Then tell students to plan their own stories. They should: think of a title and make notes about who is in the story, where it happened, when it happened, and what happened. Encourage them to be imaginative. Monitor and help with vocabulary and ideas as needed. When students have finished, tell them to exchange charts with a partner. Encourage students to comment on how interesting their partners' stories will be.

4 Write about your adventure.

10 min

Tell students to write a paragraph about their adventures using the information in their charts in Activity 3. Monitor and help as needed.

Have students exchange their paragraphs with a partner. Tell them to read their partner's paragraph. Write the following criteria on the board, *Is the story written in the past? Does it say where the action happened? Does it say when the actions happened? Does it say what happened?*

Encourage students to suggest corrections or suggestions for their partners' stories. If possible, allow time for students to rewrite their own paragraphs, taking into account their partners' suggestions. Ask volunteers to read their paragraphs to the class.

Finish the Class

10 min

Display the stories around the classroom. Have students read each of them, and then take a class vote on the best adventure story. Congratulate the class on their exciting adventure stories.

Use the **Presentation Kit** for interactive activities in this lesson.

For additional class time, use **Pages 48 and 49** of the Skills Book. Go to **Page 182** in the Happy Campers Teacher's Edition for teacher notes for this lesson. You may also choose to assign these pages as homework.

Lesson 6

1 51 **Listen again to Adventure on Mount Juniper.**

2 **Answer.**

1. Where did Olivia, Zoe, Noah, and Gavin want to go?
   They wanted to go to Mount Juniper.
2. What was the weather like?
   It was a chilly day.
3. Why did they want to go back?
   It started to snow.
4. Who helped them get home?
   Firefighters helped them get home.

3 **Writing Time! Plan a short adventure story.**

My Story: (Students' own answers.)
When:
Where:
Who:
What happened:

4 **Write about your adventure.**

(Students' own answers)

Lesson 7

Lesson 7

ON STAGE!

PROJECT: Vacation Checklist

1 **Plan what you need for your Vacation Checklist.**

Things I'll buy: (Students'

Activities I'll do: own

Things I'll pack: answers.)

Things I won't forget:

2 **Prepare a Vacation Checklist.**

3 **On Stage! Share your Vacation Checklist.**

Lesson 7 Creative, Collaborative, and Critical Thinking Activity

Lesson Objective: Plan, create, and present a Vacation Checklist.
Vocabulary Review: suitcase, hand luggage, ticket, book, sunglasses, T-shirt,
Grammar Review: future tense
Materials: Audio **Track 47**, construction paper, colored markers and crayons

Start the Class

10 min

Tell the class that you went to the beach on your last vacation. Brainstorm other popular places to go on vacation, such as *mountains, the country, cities, national parks*, and so on. Then brainstorm activities to do on vacation, such as *swimming, hiking, visiting old buildings*, and so on. Ask the class if they need different clothes for different vacations. Brainstorm clothes to take on different vacations, such as *swimsuit, sandals, shorts, hiking boots*, or *ski jacket*.

Say *There's a lot of things to remember before you go on vacation! How do you remember what to take?* Elicit a *checklist*.

1 Plan what you need for your Vacation Checklist.

10 min

Tell students to get into their project groups. Tell them they are going to plan their own Vacation Checklist. First, tell the groups to decide what kind of place they are going to go to on vacation.

When groups have decided, tell them to look at the chart. Ask volunteers to read the categories of things they'll need to do. Have groups discuss and agree on things they'll buy, activities they'll do, and things they'll pack. Walk around the classroom to help with vocabulary if needed.

2 Prepare a Vacation Checklist.

10 min

Tell groups to look at the example Vacation Checklist in the photo. Explain that they are now going to prepare their own Vacation Checklists. Hand out materials.

Tell the groups to work together to create their Vacation Checklists using the information they planned in Activity 1. Encourage them to think about how they are going to organize and present the information. Then tell them to agree on what each group member is going to do to complete the task. Monitor and help as needed.

3 On Stage! Share your Vacation Checklist.

15 min

Refer students to the photo of the two girls and have a student read the speech bubble.

Give groups time to practice presenting their Vacation Checklists. Monitor to make sure students are using full sentences when talking about the items on their checklists, for example, *We'll buy hiking boots, We'll go swimming*, or *We'll pack our sunglasses.*

Have each group take turns presenting their Vacation Checklist to the class. At the end of each presentation, encourage the class to ask questions.

Finish the Class

5 min

Tell students they are going to sing "Up and Away!" again. Tell them to imagine they are going on a dream vacation as they sing along. Play **Track 47**.

Use the **Presentation Kit** for interactive activities in this lesson.

Lesson 8 Review

Lesson Objective: Review language from Unit 8.
Vocabulary Review: suitcase, hand luggage, bag tag, ticket, check-in, airline, window seat, boarding pass, gate, flight, aisle, flight attendant, emergency exit, seat belt
Grammar Review: I'll buy the tickets. Will you sing for us today? Yes, we will. Will you dance for us today? No, we won't.

Start the Class

10 min

Ask students to brainstorm words, phrases, and sentences they remember from this unit. Write them on the board. Put students in pairs and have them write four sentences about a vacation using any of the words on the board. Ask several pairs to share their sentences with the class.

1 Spelling! Write.

10 min

Tell students to look at the pictures and elicit the word for each one. Then have students work individually to write the words. Have them compare answers with a partner.

Check answers with the class by asking students to write the words on the board. Ask the class if they are spelled correctly.

2 Write a sentence to say how you will help.

10 min

Ask a student to read the first sentence. Elicit the answer orally from the class. Then have students work in pairs to write the other answers. Check answers by saying the statements and having students read their answers saying how they will help.

3 Word Play! Find and circle the words from Unit 8 on Page 72.

10 min

Have students turn to **Page 72** and tell them to find and circle the air travel words from Unit 8. Then have students check the words they found with a partner.

Finish the Class

10 min

Ask students to flip through their books and choose their favorite lessons. Ask as many students as possible to share about their favorite lessons and give reasons why they chose them.

Congratulate the class on how well they are speaking English and how much they have learned during the course.

Use the **Presentation Kit** for interactive activities in this lesson.

For additional class time, use **Pages 50 and 51** of the Skills Book. Go to **Page 183** in the Happy Campers Teacher's Edition for teacher notes for this lesson. You may also choose to assign these pages as homework.

Lesson 8

Round Up!

1 Spelling! Write.

1. bag tag

2. hand luggage

3. airline

4. ticket

5. check-in

6. window seat

7. boarding pass

8. suitcase

2 Write a sentence to say how you will help.

1. Sandra is going on vacation. I'll help her pack.
2. Lisa is hungry. (Students' own answers).
3. Tom has a test tomorrow. (Students' own answers).
4. Angela can't find her book. (Students' own answers).
5. Bob feels cold. (Students' own answers).

3 Word Play! Find and circle the words from Unit 8 on Page 72.

Unit 1 Skills Book Picture Talk

Lesson Objective: Make statements about a picture and respond.

Start the Class

10 min

Review circus vocabulary with a game of Ready, Steady, Draw! Have students take turns coming to the board and draw circus vocabulary words for the class to guess.

1 Look at the picture. Find and complete.

15 min

Have students look carefully at the picture on **Page 5**. Explain that the text on **Page 4** is about the circus vocabulary in the picture. Have students work in pairs to complete the blanks. Check answers by asking different students to read a complete sentence.

2 Talk about the picture.

10 min

Tell students to look again at the picture and ask them to describe it. Point to details in the picture to elicit unit vocabulary and grammar. Encourage students to use full sentences.

Have volunteers read the example dialogue in the speech bubbles on **Page 5**. Model the example dialogue with a confident student. Have students work in pairs to talk about the picture by pointing to details and asking and answering questions. Have volunteers talk about the picture for the class.

Finish the Class

15 min

Have students write a short paragraph about the circus in the picture. Have volunteers read their descriptions to the class.

UNIT 1 Picture Talk

1 Look at the picture. Find and complete.

Home Page | Homework | About Me

Julie's Journal
My Trip to the Circus

The 1. circus was in town yesterday. Everyone watched the show from under the red and white 2. big top. The 3. clown was funny. He had a large red nose and blue hair. The elephants were amazing. They walked together in a 4. parade for the audience. The 5. ringmaster talked to the audience with his microphone and announced the performers. The 6. tightrope walker was very talented. She walked on a very thin rope high in the air. The powerful 7. trapeze artist was on a swing with two other people. The 8. unicyclist juggled bananas. The circus had many amazing performers—it was great!

4

2 Talk about the picture.

5

Skills Book Happy Reader

Lesson Objectives: Recall details in a fiction text. Summarize part of the text.
Materials: Audio **Track 52**

Start the Class

5 min

Say a letter of the alphabet and ask students to say a word or words from the unit starting with that letter. Continue with different letters.

1 52 Read and listen.

20 min

Have students look at the title and the pictures and predict what the text is going to be about. Do not tell them if they are correct or incorrect yet.

Tell students to read along as they listen to the text. Play **Track 52**. Ask students whether or not their predictions were correct.

Have the class read the text again in pairs. Then check understanding with comprehension questions about what Maggie won, how she felt when she began singing, and who helped her sing her song.

2 Circle the act that was not in The Smith Brothers Circus.

5 min

Have students work in pairs to read the circus acts in Activity 2 and circle the act that is not mentioned in the text. Check the answer with the class.

Page 52 Happy Writer

15 min

Tell the class that they will write about Maggie's performance in the story. Encourage students to give details about how Maggie felt at the beginning and then how the performance ended. Have volunteers share their ideas with the class.

Finish the Class

5 min

Have students say their favorite circus acts. Take a class vote on the most popular circus act.

Page 52 (Students' own answers)

Happy Reader

1 52 **Read and listen.**

Maggie's Song

1
There was a song contest at a radio station to win tickets to the circus and to perform. Maggie loved to sing, and it was her dream to sing in front of an audience. She wrote a song about a circus and practiced every day. A week later, she went to the radio station to sing her song—and she won!

2
Maggie and her family went to The Smith Brothers Circus the next day. It was amazing with all of the unicyclists, jugglers, clowns, and tightrope walkers. And on that day, Maggie was one of the performers, too!

6

3
After a few acts, it was Maggie's turn. The ringmaster called her name. The audience went quiet. Maggie walked into the middle of the ring and took the microphone. She was very nervous. The band started to play her song, but Maggie didn't sing! Everyone looked at her, and waited. Maggie closed her eyes and listened to the music. But she still didn't sing!

Then, something unusual happened. All of the performers walked into the ring to stand with Maggie. Suddenly, she started to sing. The audience cheered, and the performers cheered, too! Maggie's circus song was a hit! Now The Smith Brothers Circus opens all its shows with Maggie's song!

2 **Circle the act that was not in The Smith Brothers Circus.**

	unicyclists	ringmaster	Maggie
clowns	jugglers	tightrope walkers	(trapeze artists)

Happy Writer Page 52

7

Skills Book Word Work

Lesson Objectives: Recognize spelling patterns. Read clues to identify words. Compare and contrast verb forms.

Start the Class

5 min

Review circus vocabulary with a miming game. Call out circus acts and have students mime them.

1 Unscramble the names.

10 min

Explain that the circus performers' names are scrambled versions of the circus acts. Refer students to the example answer. In pairs, have students unscramble the other names and write the circus acts on the lines. Check answers with the class.

2 Read and answer.

5 min

Have volunteers read the clues in the riddle aloud. Ask *What Am I?* and have students write the answer. Check the answer with the class.

3 Complete the verb chart puzzle.

10 min

Explain to students that they have to complete each pair of verbs—the base form, present tense, and past tense of the same verb. Do Item 1 as an example with the class and elicit the first letters of each verb to complete *go* and *went*. Have students work in pairs to complete the puzzle. Check answers with the class.

4 Make a verb chart puzzle.

15 min

Have students work in pairs to create their own verb chart puzzles by using Activity 3 as a model. Have each student switch his or her puzzle with a partner to solve.

Finish the Class

5 min

Ask volunteers to say true sentences about themselves using verbs in the past tense.

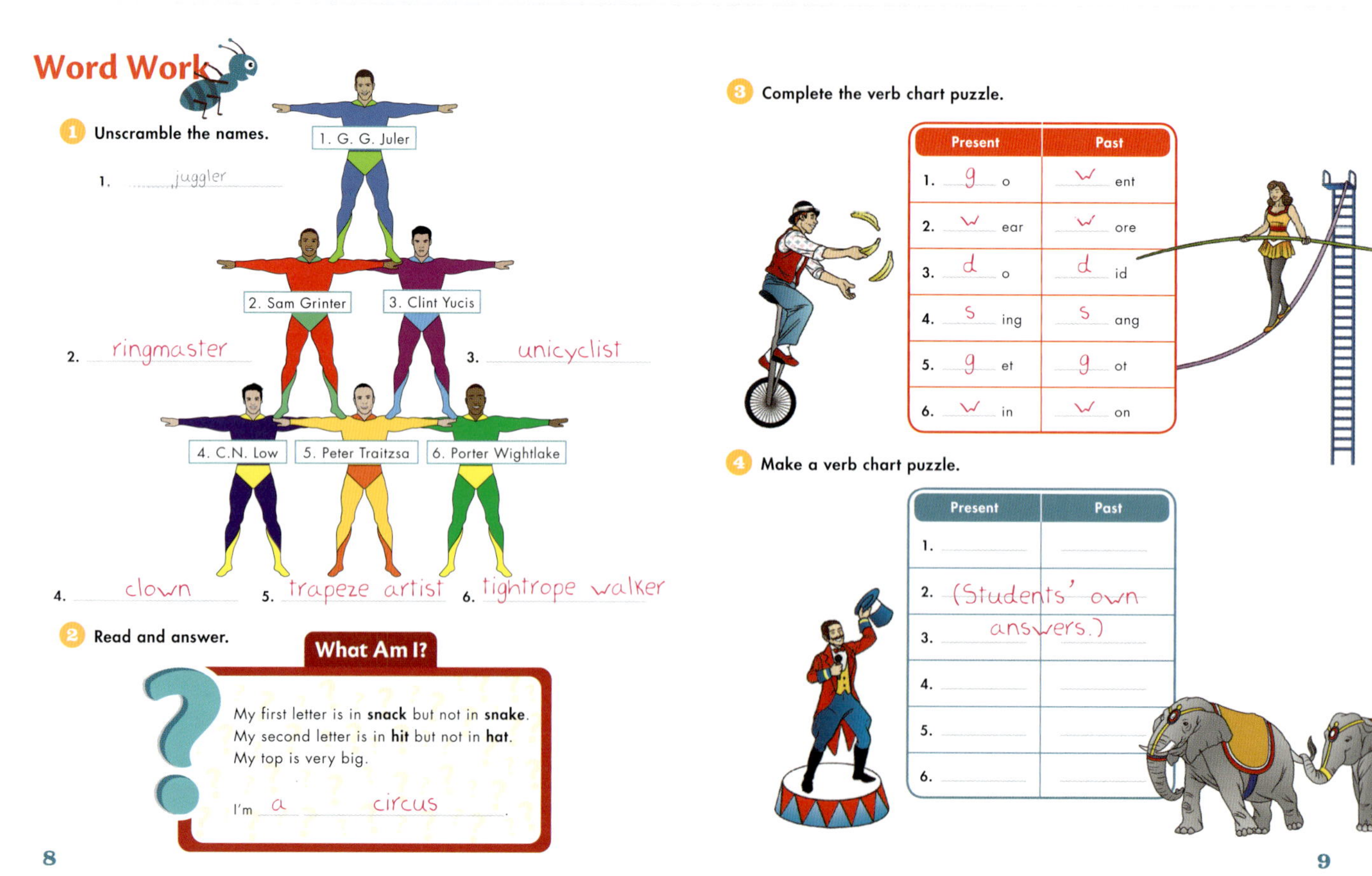

Word Work

1 Unscramble the names.

1. G. G. Juler — 1. juggler
2. Sam Grinter — 2. ringmaster
3. Clint Yucis — 3. unicyclist
4. C.N. Low — 4. clown
5. Peter Traitzsa — 5. trapeze artist
6. Porter Wightlake — 6. tightrope walker

2 Read and answer.

What Am I?

My first letter is in **snack** but not in **snake**.
My second letter is in **hit** but not in **hat**.
My top is very big.

I'm a circus.

8

3 Complete the verb chart puzzle.

	Present	Past
1.	g o	w ent
2.	w ear	w ore
3.	d o	d id
4.	s ing	s ang
5.	g et	g ot
6.	w in	w on

4 Make a verb chart puzzle.

	Present	Past
1.		
2.	(Students' own	
3.	answers.)	
4.		
5.		
6.		

9

Skills Book

Picture Talk

Lesson Objective: Describe two pictures by finding differences between them.

Start the Class

5 min

Brainstorm words related to movies with the class. Write them on the board.

1 Look at the pictures. Find the differences. Then complete.

20 min

Tell students to look carefully at Picture A and Picture B on **Page 11**. Have students work in pairs to find and circle everything in Picture B that is different from Picture A.

Have a volunteer read the example sentences. Have students work individually to write similar sentences about the other differences between the pictures. Then review the answers with the class. Ask students to point to the differences in the pictures and read the sentences they wrote.

2 Talk about the pictures.

15 min

Have volunteers read the example dialogue in the speech bubbles on **Page 11**.

Have students work in groups of three or four. Tell them to point to details in the pictures—such as people, objects, or actions—and describe them to the group. Tell students that they can also use their imaginations to speculate about the picture, for example, *The astronaut was hot in his costume.* Students may have difficulty with vocabulary, so walk around the classroom to provide help as needed. Make sure students are talking about the picture in the past tense as much as possible.

Finish the Class

10 min

Have each group create a title for the movie in the pictures. Write all the titles on the board and take a class vote for the best one.

UNIT 2 Picture Talk

1 Look at the pictures. Find the differences. Then complete.

1. Picture A: The scene had white stars.
   Picture B: The scene had yellow stars.
2. Picture A: The movie star was a man.
   Picture B: The movie star was a woman.
3. Picture A: The director wore a hat.
   Picture B: The director wore a cap.
4. Picture A: The camera was black.
   Picture B: The camera was blue.
5. Picture A: The microphone was short.
   Picture B: The microphone was long.

2 Talk about the pictures.

Skills Book

Happy Reader

Lesson Objectives: Identify the sequence of events in a nonfiction text. Recall details.
Materials: Audio **Track 53**

Start the Class

5 min

Ask students to name jobs that are involved in making a movie. Elicit or suggest *producer* if students haven't already thought of this job. Explain that a producer oversees the production of a movie.

1 53 Read and listen.

15 min

Tell students they are going to read and listen to a text about a movie producer and his crew. Explain that a *crew* is a team of people. Play **Track 53**. Ask students to read and listen again. As they read, have them underline all the crew members that are mentioned.

2 Number the producer's jobs in order.

10 min

Ask volunteers to read the directions and the descriptions of the producer's jobs. Tell students to read the text again and number the jobs in order according to the text. Check answers by having volunteers read the phrases in order while they point to the corresponding sentences in the text.

Page 52 Happy Writer

15 min

Have students look at the movie crew jobs listed in the box. Explain that they will choose a job and write about it. Remind students to describe what their crew members did to contribute to the movie production. Then have volunteers share their ideas with the class.

Finish the Class

5 min

Ask each student to write a sentence describing a movie crew member, but not to write the name of the job. Have students take turns reading their sentences aloud for the class to guess the correct jobs.

Happy Reader

1 53 Read and listen.

Meet the Crew

1
Movie studios have many jobs for people with different skills. I am a movie producer. A producer has a really important job. I think about the cost of the movie and find people to write the movie. I also find the right director.

2
For my latest movie, I needed screenwriters. The screenwriters wrote the script. I helped the screenwriters with the idea for the movie. The idea had to be great! Next, I met with the director. The director read the script and gave many ideas. Then we called the movie stars. They also read the script. Then the director rehearsed lines with them.

3
Next, we made the movie. The makeup artist was very creative. She made a young actor look old. She also painted big muscles on a thin actor. All of the actors looked very different.

The cameraman filmed the scenes and followed the director's instructions. The director said, "Positions, please." The cameraman was ready to record. The director said, "Action!" The cameraman recorded the scene. Then the director said, "Cut!" Finally, the cameraman stopped recording.

Everyone saw their names on the movie screen at the end of the movie. They felt very happy. It was fun to make this wonderful movie.

2 Number the producer's jobs in order.

3 help the screenwriters	4 call the movie stars	5 make the movie
2 find the right director	1 think about the cost	

Happy Writer Page 52

12 13

Page 52 (Students' own answers)

Skills Book

Word Work

Lesson Objectives: Categorize words. Read clues to identify people in a picture. Read clues to identify words.
Materials: a list of words from the unit for a Spelling Bee

Start the Class

10 min

Write *ate, went,* and *got* on the left side of the board and *yesterday, last week, last month,* and *last year* on the right side. Say *I ate pizza last week. I went to the circus last year.* Have students make sentences about themselves using the verbs and time expressions on the board.

1 Color the word that's different and write why. Then make your own puzzle.

15 min

Explain that one word in each pie chart is different from the other two words and students must use their own reasoning to determine why. Review the example answer for Item 1 as a class. Tell students to complete the activity in pairs by coloring in the words that are different and writing sentences explaining why. Have volunteers read their answers aloud.

2 Read. Then write the answers.

10 min

Explain that students will read sentences about the people in the illustration, find the people's names on their T-shirts, and write sentences about their jobs. Have students work individually, then check answers with the class.

3 Read and answer.

5 min

Have students read the *What Am I?* riddle and discuss the answer in pairs. Check the answer with the class.

Finish the Class

10 min

Use the unit vocabulary to have a team Spelling Bee. Students may discuss the answers within their teams, but a different student must say the answer each time.

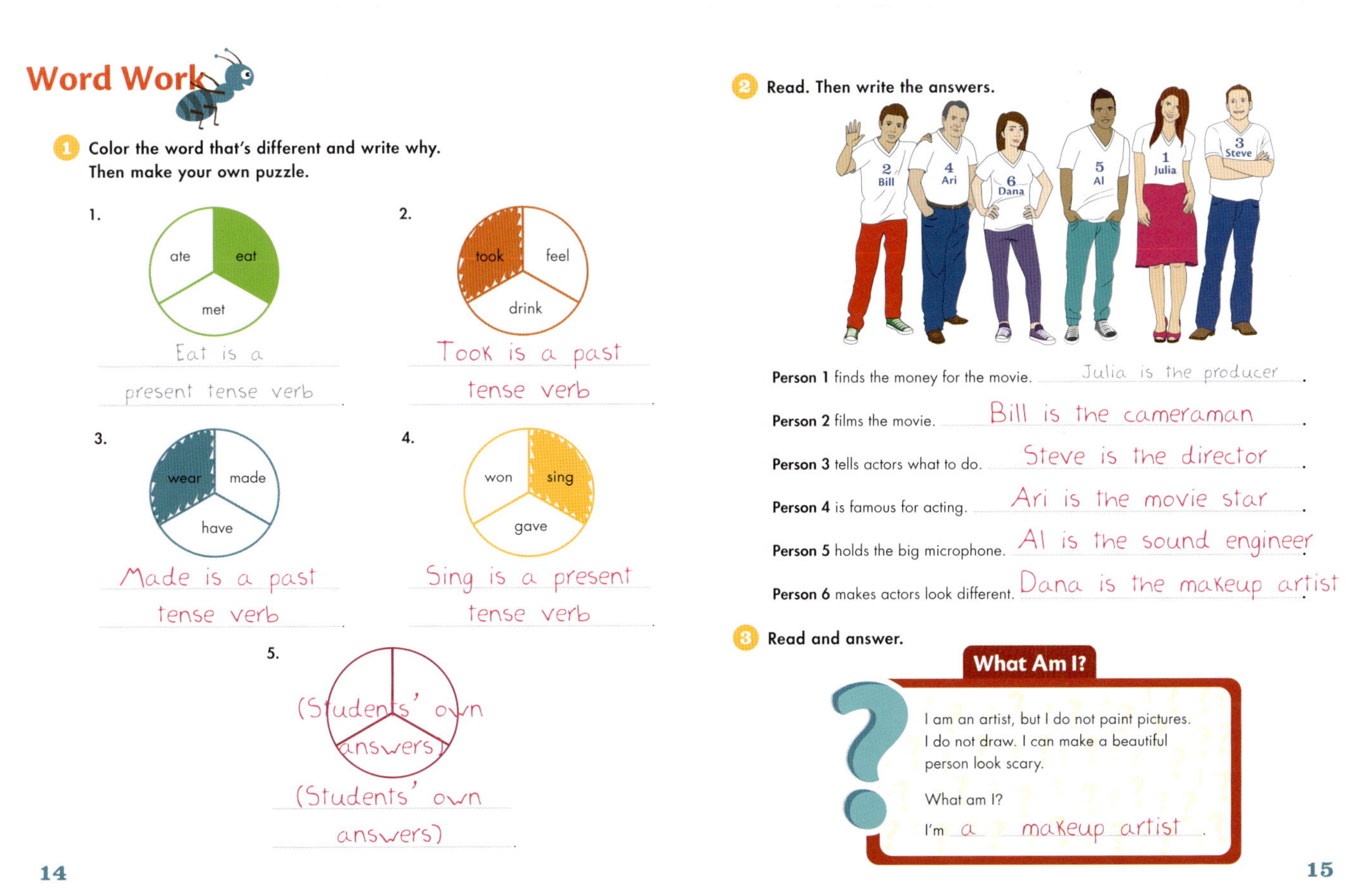

Word Work

1 Color the word that's different and write why. Then make your own puzzle.

1. ate / eat / met — Eat is a present tense verb
2. took / feel / drink — Took is a past tense verb
3. wear / made / have — Made is a past tense verb
4. won / sing / gave — Sing is a present tense verb
5. (Students' own answers) — (Students' own answers)

2 Read. Then write the answers.

Person 1 finds the money for the movie. Julia is the producer.
Person 2 films the movie. Bill is the cameraman.
Person 3 tells actors what to do. Steve is the director.
Person 4 is famous for acting. Ari is the movie star.
Person 5 holds the big microphone. Al is the sound engineer.
Person 6 makes actors look different. Dana is the makeup artist.

3 Read and answer.

What Am I?

I am an artist, but I do not paint pictures. I do not draw. I can make a beautiful person look scary.

What am I?

I'm a makeup artist.

14 15

Unit 3 Skills Book Picture Talk

Lesson Objective: Make statements about a picture and respond.

Start the Class
5 min

Write *US$100 =* on the board. Ask students if they know roughly how much US$100 is in the currency of their country. Tell students the exchange rate if they don't know (use an approximate, round figure). Write the figure on the board after the equals sign.

1 Look at the picture. Find and complete.
20 min

Tell students to look carefully at the window display on **Page 17**. Ask *How much is the blue vest?* to make sure students notice the price tags.

Tell students to look at the text on **Page 16**. Have them complete the text about Wendy by looking at the picture on **Page 17**.

2 Talk about the picture.
15 min

Have volunteers read the example dialogue in the speech bubbles on **Page 17**. Have students work in pairs to look at the picture and talk about what Wendy bought according to the text on **Page 16**. Encourage students to use the past tense verb *got* in their sentences.

Finish the Class
10 min

Play a Chain Memory Game (see **Page T 53**) with items of clothing. For example, say *I went to Cool Clothes and I got a vest.* Then the first student repeats your sentence and adds a new item of clothing: *I went to Cool Clothes and I got a vest and a hoodie.* Continue until all students have participated.

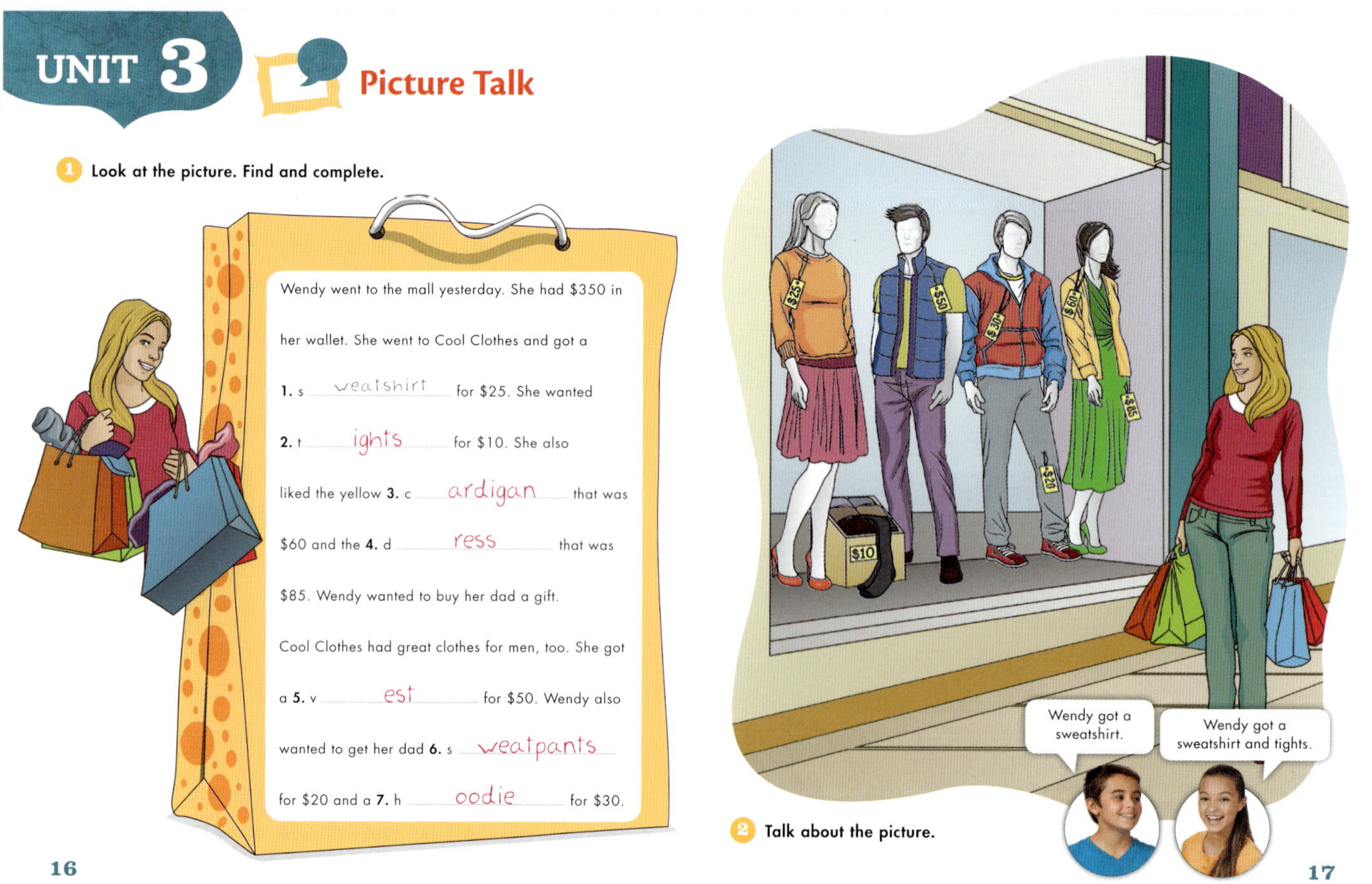
UNIT 3 Picture Talk

1 Look at the picture. Find and complete.

Wendy went to the mall yesterday. She had $350 in her wallet. She went to Cool Clothes and got a **1.** s weatshirt for $25. She wanted **2.** t ights for $10. She also liked the yellow **3.** c ardigan that was $60 and the **4.** d ress that was $85. Wendy wanted to buy her dad a gift. Cool Clothes had great clothes for men, too. She got a **5.** v est for $50. Wendy also wanted to get her dad **6.** s weatpants for $20 and a **7.** h oodie for $30.

2 Talk about the picture.

16

17

Skills Book
Happy Reader

Lesson Objectives: Recall details in a fiction text. Recall details.
Materials: Audio **Track 54**

Start the Class
10 min

Ask students if they have ever been to a school play or performed in one. If so, have students describe the experience of being in a play, using L1 if necessary. Have students say in English what theater actors must do before a performance, for example, *learn lines* and *rehearse*.

1 54 Read and listen.
15 min

Tell students they are going to read a story about students preparing for a school play. Play **Track 54** and have students read and listen. Then have students work in pairs to take turns reading paragraphs of the text. Monitor and help with pronunciation.

Tell students you are going to say *true/false* statements about the story. They have to respond by saying *true* or *false*. If the statement is false, have them correct it. Say, for example, *It was the first week of classes.* Elicit *False, it was the last week of classes.*

2 Circle *True* or *False*.
5 min

Have students complete the activity individually. Have volunteers read their answers aloud to check answers.

Page 53 Happy Writer
15 min

Ask a volunteer to read the directions. Have volunteers give examples from the story to explain why the class was worried about Nick. Then have students complete the activity individually.

Finish the Class
5 min

Ask the class to say what Nick *did* do right for the play. Have students give their impressions of Nick.

Page 53 (Students' own answers)

Happy Reader

1 54 Read and listen.

The End-of-Year Play

1
It was the last week of classes, and the sixth grade had a surprise for the rest of the school—an end-of-year play! Everyone wanted to make the play a success. They rehearsed the scenes at lunchtime, they stayed up late to learn their lines, and they read the script carefully. Everyone worked really hard every day—except Nick!

"I don't think we're ready," Lisa said. "Let's rehearse the scene one more time. And Nick, please pay attention to the script!"

"Don't worry," Nick said. "Everything is going to be fine."

Nick never remembered his lines. He was always late, and he wasted a lot of time. The rest of the class was very worried. And Nick was the only student who didn't have his costume.

"Nick, the clothes are really important in our play—it's all about clothes!" Simon said.

"Don't worry," Nick said. "Everything is going to be fine."

That night, everyone went home. They went to bed early to get a good rest. But Nick didn't.

The day of the performance arrived. The whole school gathered in the gym for the school play.

18

2
Everyone was excited. The sixth graders got into their costumes and rehearsed their lines one more time.

"Where's Nick?" Jenna asked.

"I don't know," Karl said. "He wasn't in the boys' dressing room."

It was time to go on stage! The curtains went up, and the audience clapped. Nick walked out in a beautiful costume and said his lines. They were perfect.

"Nick was right! Everything is going to be fine," Simon said.

2 Circle *True* or *False*.

1. Nick rehearsed his lines at lunchtime.	True	(False)
2. Nick was the only student who didn't have his costume.	(True)	False
3. Nick didn't go to bed early to get a good rest.	(True)	False

Happy Writer Page 53

19

Skills Book Word Work

Lesson Objectives: Categorize words. Recognize spelling patterns. Read clues to identify words.
Materials: flashcards of clothes

Start the Class

5 min

Put flashcards of clothes on the board. Point to the clothes and have students say the corresponding parts of the body (where each clothing item is worn).

1 Color the word that's different and write why. Then make your own puzzle.

20 min

Do Item 1 as a class, suggesting that leggings are different because you wear them on your legs. Have students complete the activity in pairs. Tell them to make their own puzzles for Item 5 for their partners to solve.

2 Unscramble the names. Then write what each person says.

10 min

Explain that each person's name is a scrambled command and that students must unscramble the words and write the commands on the blanks. Do Item 1 as a class. Have the class complete the activity individually and then have volunteers read their answers.

3 Read and answer.

5 min

Have a student read the *What Am I?* puzzle aloud. Have students work in pairs to read the clues and write the answer. Have a volunteer say his or her answer. Ask the rest of the class if they agree. Ask students how they figured out the answer.

Finish the Class

10 min

Play Simon Says. Tell students you will give them commands, but they must only follow them if you start the command by saying *Simon says ...* If you say, for example, *Simon says stand up,* students should stand up. If a student follows a command when you don't say *Simon says,* he or she is out of the game.

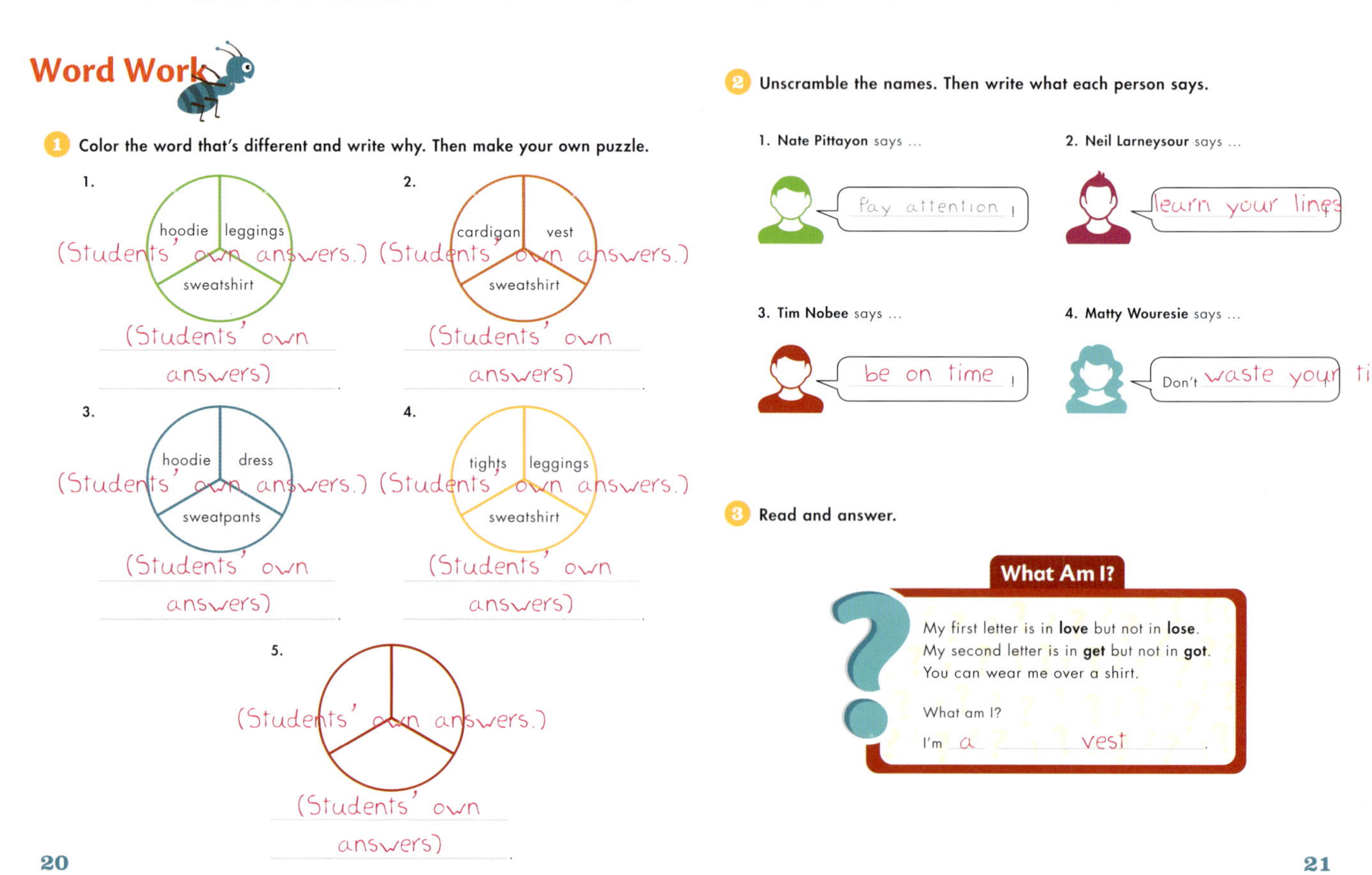

Word Work

1 Color the word that's different and write why. Then make your own puzzle.

1. hoodie | leggings | sweatshirt — (Students' own answers.) (Students' own answers)
2. cardigan | vest | sweatshirt — (Students' own answers.) (Students' own answers)
3. hoodie | dress | sweatpants — (Students' own answers.) (Students' own answers)
4. tights | leggings | sweatshirt — (Students' own answers.) (Students' own answers)
5. (Students' own answers.) (Students' own answers)

2 Unscramble the names. Then write what each person says.

1. Nate Pittayon says ... Pay attention !
2. Neil Larneysour says ... learn your lines
3. Tim Nobee says ... be on time !
4. Matty Wouresie says ... Don't waste your time

3 Read and answer.

What Am I?

My first letter is in **love** but not in **lose**.
My second letter is in **get** but not in **got**.
You can wear me over a shirt.

What am I?

I'm a vest.

20

21

Lesson Objective: Ask and answer questions about a picture.

Start the Class

10 min

Tell students that you went to the movies last night and they have to figure out the movie you saw by asking questions, for example, *Is it a comedy? Is it scary? Who are the movie stars?* Students are not allowed to ask the name of the movie!

1 Look at the pictures. Find and complete.

20 min

Tell students to look the picture on **Page 23** and study the movie billboards. Then have students look at the sentences on **Page 22** and explain that they must identify the movie genre for each movie title by looking at the corresponding billboard on **Page 23**. Have a volunteer read the example answer and explain how we know *Big Bats* is a documentary. Elicit *the movie billboard*. Have students complete the activity individually. Check answers with the class.

2 Ask and answer.

10 min

Have volunteers read the example dialogue in the speech bubbles on **Page 23**. Have two volunteers read the example dialogue. Have students work in pairs to ask and answer about the names of the movies the children saw, when they saw them, and what types of movies they saw.

Finish the Class

10 min

Ask students to think who their favorite movie stars are. Ask a student to come to the board and pretend to be his or her favorite movie star. Explain that the class is going to ask questions to find out who the movie star is. Encourage students to ask as many questions as possible, for example, *Are you Spanish? Do you act in westerns?* When students have guessed the movie star, repeat with different students.

UNIT 4 Picture Talk

1 Look at the pictures. Find and complete.

DKM Cinemas

western action movie musical documentary horror science fiction

DKM Cinemas

1. Danny watched *Big Bats*. It was a documentary.
2. Tim watched *Red Sun*. It was a western.
3. Lou watched *Lost in Time*. It was a science fiction movie.
4. Claire watched *Jump Up*. It was an action movie.
5. Mo watched *Eyes at Night*. It was a horror movie.
6. Karen watched *Sunny Sunday*. It was a musical.

Ticket-000

2 Ask and answer.

Skills Book Happy Reader

Lesson Objectives: Draw conclusions in a fiction text. Write an opinion.
Materials: Audio **Track 55**

Start the Class
5 min

Ask students if they have cell phones. If they do, ask when and where they use them. Ask students if there are any places they don't use their cell phones.

1 55 Read and listen.
15 min

Have students look at the letter. Ask *Who did Polite Paul send his letter to?* Elicit *an editor*. Explain that editors work to make books, newspapers and magazines.

Play **Track 55**. Ask *What was the problem in the theater?* Play **Track 55** again and have students answer, *A woman used her cell phone in the movie theater and an older man was angry.*

2 Circle how Paul feels about using cell phones in the movie theater.
5 min

Have one student read each of the options. Group students into pairs to discuss the options and circle the best answer. Check the answer with the class.

Page 53 Happy Writer
15 min

Have students write how each person feels based on their expressions in the photos. Then have volunteers share their opinions with the class.

Finish the Class
10 min

Put students in pairs to make lists of the good and bad things about cell phones. Have pairs share their lists with the class.

Page 53 (Students' own answers)

Happy Reader

1 55 **Read and listen.**

A Letter to the Editor

July 15

Dear Editor:

1
Cell phones are amazing. You can get a lot of information from cell phones. You can talk to anyone in the world right now. You don't even need to be at home. You can make calls from anywhere. You can send people messages or play games. But sometimes it's better to put your phone away.

Many people use their cell phones in movie theaters. This is not polite. Last week, when I was at the movie theater, a woman used her cell phone in the middle of the movie.

An older man in the theater was angry. He saw the light from the phone and heard the woman talking. He yelled at the woman to put her phone away. The woman said, "Don't be silly. It's just a quick phone call."

2
Then the older man said, "I'm not silly. You're rude. Put your phone away or leave the movie theater."

It wasn't polite for the older man to yell in the movie theater. But was the woman rude to use her cell phone? There was time before the movie to make a call. There was time after the movie, too. It's more polite to wait.

You can talk to anyone, anywhere, at any time. But, it's important to be polite when you use your phone.

Sincerely,

Polite Paul

2 **Circle how Paul feels about using cell phones in the movie theater.**

a. Cell phones are good. You can talk to anyone.

b. Cell phones are bad. People send texts at the movies.

c. Cell phones are good, but people need to think about where and when to use them.

Happy Writer Page 53

Lesson Objectives: Identify multi-syllable words. Recognize spelling patterns. Read clues to identify words.

Start the Class
5 min

Write the following words on the board: *Who, What, Where,* and *When*. Have students think about a movie they went to see in the theater. Then put students in pairs to ask each other questions about their experiences using the words on the board. For example, *Who did you go with? What did you see?*

1 Say the words. Count the syllables. Write.
15 min

Have students read the words in the word bank. Explain that they will count the syllables in each word and write the words in the correct boxes based on how many letters are in each syllable.

Clap out the syllables together for the example. Then have students work in pairs to complete the activity. Tell students to clap out the syllables. Then review the answers with the class.

2 Use the key to write the adjectives. Then draw the faces.
15 min

Tell students to look at the key. Explain that students will use the key to find the letter that each number represents. Have students complete the activity in pairs by looking at the key. Then check answers with the class.

3 Read and answer.
10 min

Have a student read the *What Am I?* riddle. Then have students work in pairs to solve the riddle. Have a pair share their answer with the class. Ask the rest of the class to confirm.

Finish the Class
5 min

Give clues using the adjectives from this unit for students to guess. For example, say *A comedy isn't serious*. Students should respond by saying *It's silly!*

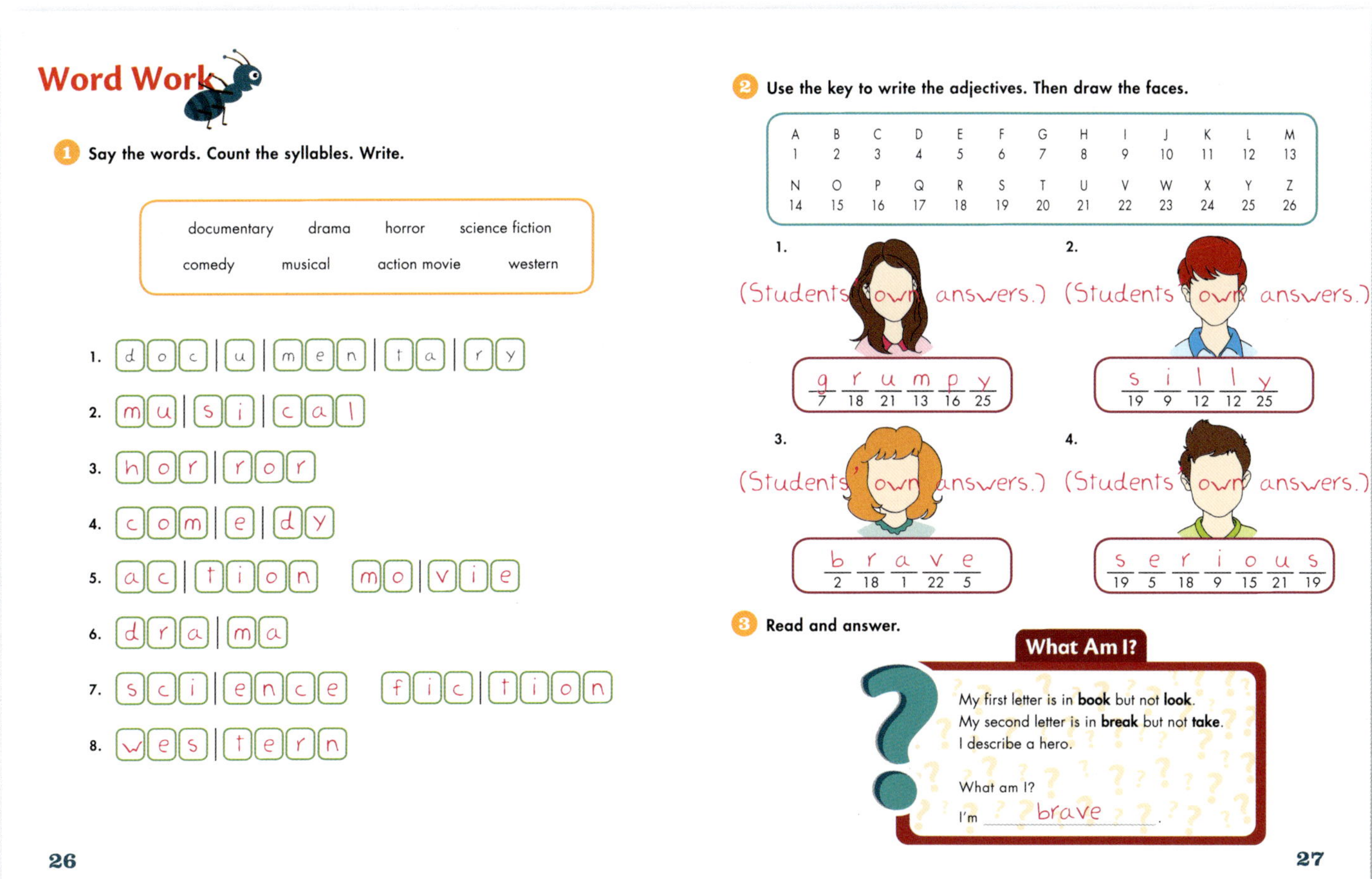

Word Work

1 Say the words. Count the syllables. Write.

documentary drama horror science fiction
comedy musical action movie western

1. d o c | u | m e n | t a | r y
2. m u | s i | c a l
3. h o r | r o r
4. c o m | e | d y
5. a c | t i o n   m o | v i e
6. d r a | m a
7. s c i | e n c e   f i c | t i o n
8. w e s | t e r n

2 Use the key to write the adjectives. Then draw the faces.

A	B	C	D	E	F	G	H	I	J	K	L	M
1	2	3	4	5	6	7	8	9	10	11	12	13
N	**O**	**P**	**Q**	**R**	**S**	**T**	**U**	**V**	**W**	**X**	**Y**	**Z**
14	15	16	17	18	19	20	21	22	23	24	25	26

1. (Students' own answers.) g r u m p y — 7 18 21 13 16 25
2. (Students' own answers.) s i l l y — 19 9 12 12 25
3. (Students' own answers.) b r a v e — 2 18 1 22 5
4. (Students' own answers.) s e r i o u s — 19 5 18 9 15 21 19

3 Read and answer.

What Am I?

My first letter is in **book** but not **look**.
My second letter is in **break** but not **take**.
I describe a hero.

What am I?
I'm brave.

26 27

Unit 5 Skills Book Picture Talk

Lesson Objective: Ask and answer questions about a picture.

Start the Class

5 min

Dictate facts about the planets from the unit, such as *It's a hot planet*, without saying the name of the planet. Ask students to guess which planet you are describing.

1 Look at the picture. Find and write.

15 min

Tell students to study the picture on **Page 29**. Have students say what information the chart provides about the planets: *temperature*, *size*, and *distance from the sun*.

Have students read the sentences about the planets on **Page 28**. Then have students work in pairs to write the names of the planets next to the corresponding descriptions. Then check answers with the class.

2 Ask and answer.

15 min

Have volunteers read the example dialogue in the speech bubbles on **Page 29**. Have students work in the same pairs as Activity 1. Tell them to take turns giving clues about planets and identifying them. Walk around the classroom to provide help as necessary. Have pairs say some of their questions and answers for the class.

Finish the Class

15 min

Put students in groups of three to imagine an ideal planet. Tell the class that the imaginary planet cannot be Earth. Have them write three or four sentences about the imaginary planet. Encourage them to be imaginative, for example, *People can fly on our planet*. Have groups take turns presenting their planets to the class.

UNIT 5 Picture Talk

1 Look at the picture. Find and write.

1. Saturn — It has the largest rings.
2. Mercury — It's the nearest planet to the Sun.
3. Jupiter — It's the biggest planet.
4. Mercury — It's the hottest planet.
5. Neptune — It's the coldest planet.
6. Earth — It's the greenest planet.

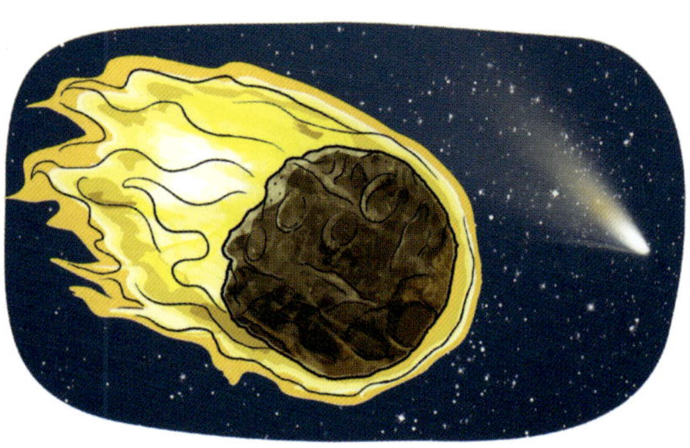

Planet Name	Temperature	Size	Distance from the Sun
Mercury	167°C	4,829 km	57.9 million km
Earth	15°C	12,104 km	149.6 million km
Jupiter	−115°C	142,984 km	778.6 million km
Saturn	−140°C	120,536 km	1433.5 million km
Neptune	−200°C	49,528 km	4495.1 million km

2 Ask and answer.

28

29

Skills Book
Happy Reader

Lesson Objectives: Identify the sequence of events in a fiction text. Recall details.
Materials: Audio **Track 56**

Start the Class

5 min

Draw a big circle on the board to represent the moon, but don't say what it is. Give students clues, such as *It moves around the Earth. You see it at night.* Have students say what it is. Ask students to tell the class anything else they know about the moon.

1 56 Read and listen.

15 min

Tell students to look at the story title and pictures, and ask them to predict what the story is going to be about. Play **Track 56**. Ask the class if their predictions were correct.

Have students read the story again silently. Check understanding by asking questions, for example, *Why did the boys go to the Oak Street Library? What did they find out about the craters on the moon? What caused the biggest crater on their model of the moon?*

2 Number the events from the story in order.

10 min

Have students read the sentences and work in pairs to number the events in the order that they occurred in the story. Check answers with the class.

Page 54 Happy Writer

15 min

Tell students that they will write a paragraph about what Eddie and Tyler did to make their science project. Remind students that they can refer to the story. Have volunteers share their ideas in the class.

Finish the Class

5 min

Ask students to draw a large circle in their notebooks. Have them write *the moon* in the center of the circle and then add all the information they can think of about the moon inside the circle.

Happy Reader

1 56 Read and listen.

The Craters on the Moon

1
Eddie and Tyler had a science project for school. They wanted to build a model of something in space. First, they went to the library.

"Where is the closest library to your house?" Tyler asked.

"There are three libraries that are close, but the Oak Street Library is the closest to my house," Eddie said.

The boys decided to build a model of the moon. They looked at pictures of the moon from very powerful telescopes. Then they drew sketches of the moon and its craters.

2
Eddie and Tyler learned that the craters on the moon are from meteors and comets that crash into it. They watched a video about comets on the website "Ask an Astronomer." Eddie and Tyler learned that comets and meteors are not the same. Meteors are rocks, but comets are ice.

After the library, Eddie and Tyler got a large ball and green paint to make a model of the moon. Tyler used a knife to make the largest craters. Eddie made the smallest craters. They painted the ball and put it outside to dry.

3
The next morning, Eddie went outside to get the moon model, but it wasn't there! He saw green footprints in front of his house. He followed the footprints up a tree. He saw an opossum eating the moon model!

4
Eddie took the moon model back and met Tyler at school for their presentation. They laughed about the opossum. Then they told the class about how their moon model got the biggest crater of all!

2 Number the events from the story in order.

4 An opossum took the moon model.

2 They looked at pictures of the moon and watched a video about comets.

3 They made a model of the moon.

5 Eddie and Tyler told the class about their moon model.

1 Eddie and Tyler went to the library.

Happy Writer Page 54

Page 54 (Students' own answers)

Skills Book Word Work

Lesson Objectives: Recognize spelling patterns. Categorize words. Read clues to identify words.

Start the Class

5 min

Write a sentence on the board with mistakes that your students typically make. Ask students to find and correct the mistakes. Then write the correct sentence on the board.

1 Unscramble the planets.

10 min

Tell students to work in pairs to read the sentences and unscramble the planet words. Then have them label the planets. Check answers with the class.

2 Number from smallest to largest.

5 min

Have students work in pairs to look at the pictures and number them from the smallest (number 1) to the largest (number 6). Check answers with the class.

3 Color the word that's different and write why. Then make your own puzzle.

15 min

Do Item 1 as a class, suggesting that Earth is different because it is a planet. Have students work in pairs. Tell them to make their own puzzles for Item 4 for their partners to solve.

4 Read and answer.

5 min

Ask a volunteer to read the *What Am I?* puzzle. Have students write the answer individually, then check the answer with the class.

Finish the Class

10 min

Play I Spy. Say *I spy something beginning with the letter "T."* Students guess the object you are thinking of. Have students take turns using different letters.

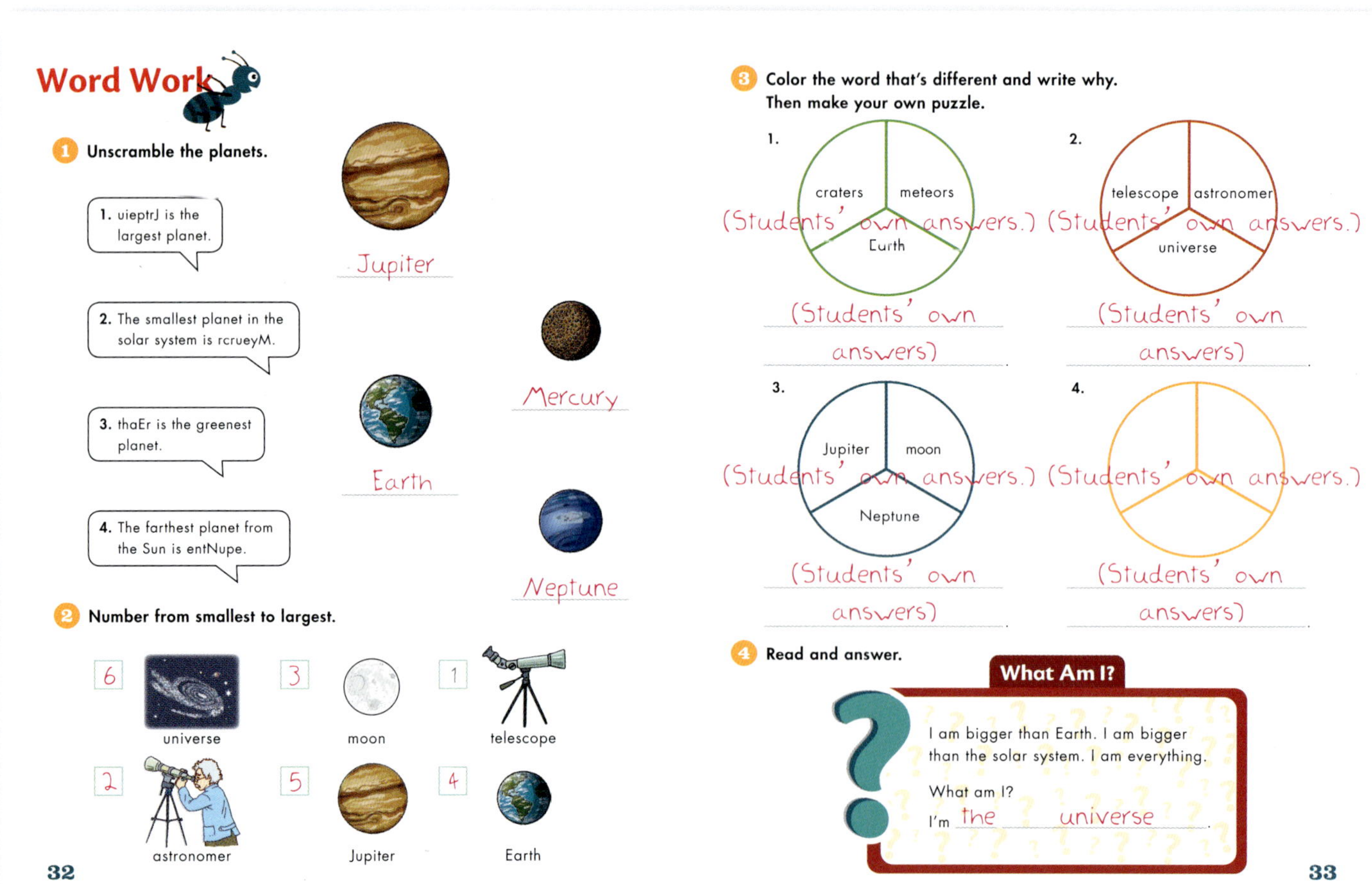

Word Work

1 Unscramble the planets.

1. uieptrJ is the largest planet. — Jupiter
2. The smallest planet in the solar system is rcrueyM. — Mercury
3. thaEr is the greenest planet. — Earth
4. The farthest planet from the Sun is entNupe. — Neptune

2 Number from smallest to largest.

6 universe | 3 moon | 1 telescope
2 astronomer | 5 Jupiter | 4 Earth

32

3 Color the word that's different and write why. Then make your own puzzle.

1. craters, meteors, Earth — (Students' own answers.) (Students' own answers)
2. telescope, astronomer, universe — (Students' own answers.) (Students' own answers)
3. Jupiter, moon, Neptune — (Students' own answers.) (Students' own answers)
4. (Students' own answers.) (Students' own answers)

4 Read and answer.

What Am I?

I am bigger than Earth. I am bigger than the solar system. I am everything.

What am I?

I'm the universe.

33

Lesson Objective: Ask and answer questions about a picture.

Start the Class

10 min

Put the class in two teams. Ask a volunteer from each team to come to the board. Whisper one of the technology vocabulary words to them so the rest of the class can't hear. Then each volunteer draws the item on the board. The first team to correctly guess the item wins a point. Repeat with other volunteers and vocabulary items.

1 Look at the pictures. Find and complete. Then match.

15 min

Ask students to study the picture on **Page 35** and the descriptions of the items. Ask a volunteer to read the example answer on **Page 34**. Explain that students must look at the advertisement's prices and descriptions on **Page 35** to complete the sentences. Draw students' attention to the clues in the descriptions. Ask students to share their answers with the class.

2 Ask and answer.

15 min

Have volunteers read the example dialogue in the speech bubbles on **Page 35**. Have students work in pairs to take turns asking and answering questions about the picture. Walk around the classroom to monitor and help if necessary. Have pairs share their conversations with the class.

Finish the Class

10 min

Ask students which items in the store they would most like to own. Ask students why they want the items, how much the items cost, whether the items are expensive or not, and what they want to use them for. Encourage students to discuss their choices and express their opinions.

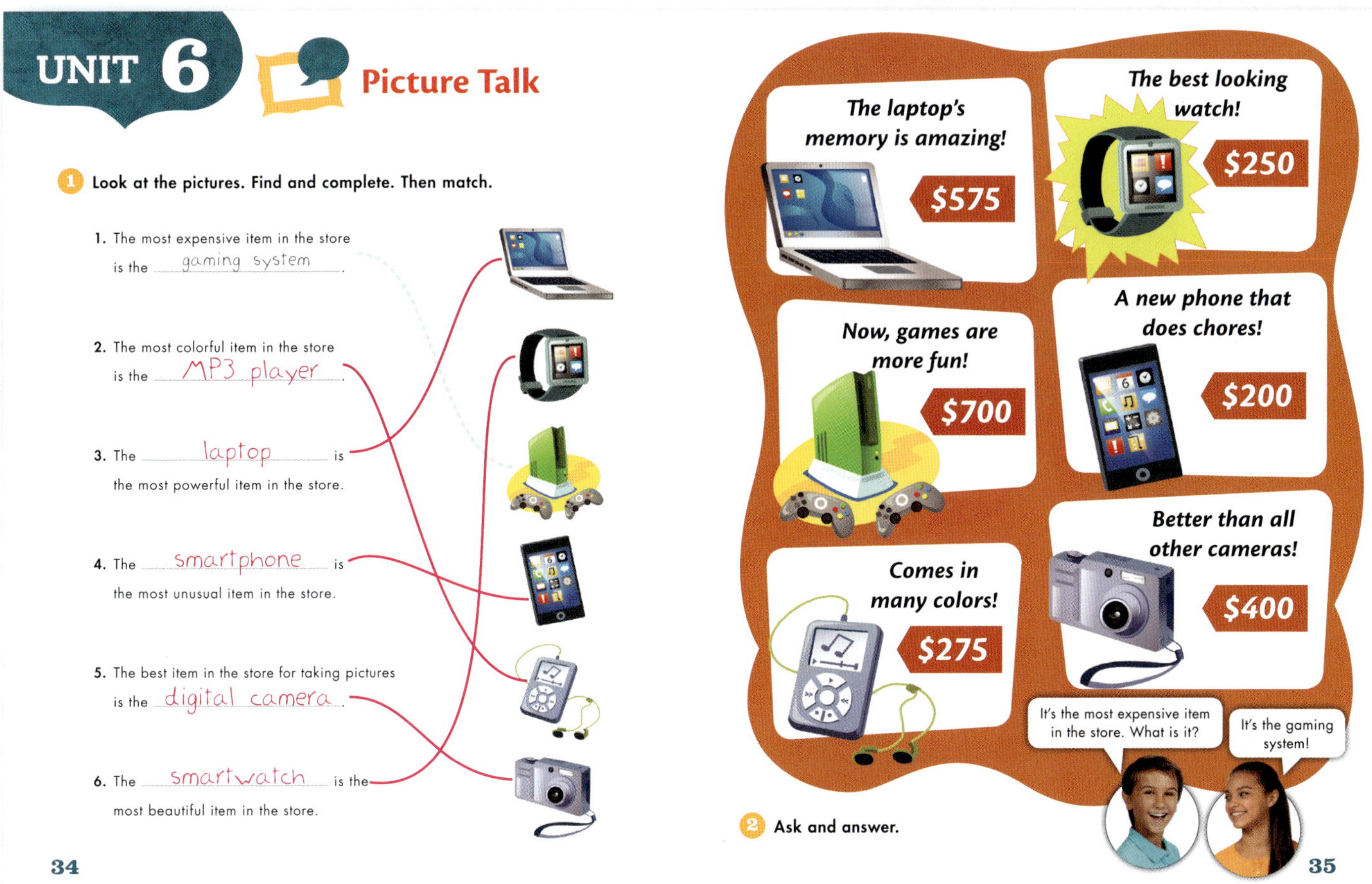
UNIT 6 Picture Talk

1 Look at the pictures. Find and complete. Then match.

1. The most expensive item in the store is the gaming system.
2. The most colorful item in the store is the MP3 player.
3. The laptop is the most powerful item in the store.
4. The smartphone is the most unusual item in the store.
5. The best item in the store for taking pictures is the digital camera.
6. The smartwatch is the most beautiful item in the store.

2 Ask and answer.

34 35

Skills Book

Happy Reader

Lesson Objective: Recall details in a nonfiction text.
Materials: Audio **Track 57**

Start the Class
10 min

Write a text message on the board in abbreviated English: *How r u?* (*How are you?*). Elicit what kind of message it is (*a text message*), and what is special about text messages, for example, *we send them by phone*, *they are short*, and *they often have abbreviations, numbers, or symbols instead of words.* Ask the class if they can guess what the message on the board means. Provide help if needed.

1 57 Read and listen.
15 min

Ask students to look at the title and pictures and predict what the text is going to be about. Then tell them to read and listen to see if their predictions were correct. Play **Track 57**.

Tell students to read and listen to the text again. Play **Track 57** again.

2 Circle *True* or *False*.
5 min

Have students complete the activity individually. Then play **Track 57** again for students to check their answers. Check answers with the class.

Page 54 Happy Writer
15 min

Tell students that they will list the five coolest things a smartphone can do. Encourage them to look at the text on **Pages 36 and 37** for ideas, but suggest that they can come up with their own ideas as well. Have volunteers share their answers with the class.

Finish the Class
5 min

Have a Spelling Bee competition to review vocabulary from the text.

Page 54 (Students' own answers)

Happy Reader

1 57 Read and listen.

How Smart Are Smartphones?

1
What makes smartphones smart? All cell phones make calls and send text messages. But smartphones can get the Internet. We use smartphones to get information and answer questions. We use them to read the news. Smartphones are an amazing invention.

Smartphones can do many things. They can talk to your TV. They can tell your TV to record shows. They can even turn the TV off when you're not home.

You can also use smartphones at school. You can use your smartphone on your own or share it in a group. It can help you study and learn new things. Smartphones can also take you on virtual visits to museums, parks, and other places around the world!

36

2
Some of the newest smartphones talk to toy cars and toy helicopters! You can use smartphones to tell toys what to do. Both children and adults like to play with these toys.

There are many apps for smartphones made for children. You can play games with your friends or share pictures.

Smartphones are great for all people young and old. They are fun, they can help, and there are new things smartphones can do every day.

2 Circle *True* or *False*.

1. All phones are smartphones. True (False)
2. Smartphones help you at school. (True) False
3. Smartphones are only for young people. True (False)

Happy Writer Page 54

37

Skills Book Word Work

Lesson Objectives: Read clues to identify words. Identify one- and multi-syllable words.

Start the Class

10 min

Play the Shark Game (see **Page T 28**) with technology words.

1 Read the clues. Then choose and write.

10 min

Have a volunteer read Item 1. Ask the class which item you can wear. Elicit *smartwatch*. Have students complete the activity in pairs.

2 Make your own puzzles.

10 min

Tell each student to choose a picture for each item and write a clue for it. Have each student switch with a partner to solve the puzzle aloud.

3 Say the words. Count the syllables. Write.

10 min

Say *generous* and ask students to repeat. Then ask how many syllables it has. Elicit *three*. Have students work in pairs to count the syllables for each word and write the words in the correct boxes. Check answers with the class.

4 Read and answer.

5 min

Have a volunteer read the *What Am I?* puzzle. Have students write the answer individually. Check the answer with the class.

Finish the Class

5 min

Tell students to write two sentences using superlative adjectives about their best friends. Have students share their descriptions with the class.

Word Work

1 Read the clues. Then choose and write.

1.

You can wear this.

smartwatch

2.

This doesn't take pictures.

gaming system

3.

This has a keyboard.

laptop

4.

You can read a book with this.

tablet

2 Make your own puzzles.

1.

(Students' own answers)

2.

(Students' own answers)

38

3 Say the words. Count the syllables. Write.

thoughtful	careful	best
generous	peaceful	worst

1. g e n | e r | o u s
2. w o r s t
3. p e a c e | f u l
4. b e s t
5. t h o u g h t | f u l
6. c a r e | f u l

4 Read and answer.

What Am I?

I always give to everyone. I think about other people. I am nice and good.

What am I?

I'm generous.

39

Lesson Objective: Ask and answer questions about a picture.

Start the Class

10 min

Brainstorm weather words with the class. Write them in random order on the board. Then ask the class to help you organize them into a mind map, for example, all the words referring to cold weather should go together.

1 Look at the picture. Find and write.

20 min

Ask students to cover the picture on **Page 41** with a sheet of paper. Ask students to move the paper down below the day of the week so that the clouds and suns are visible. Have students describe what they can see in the picture so far. Then have students remove the piece of paper. Have different students describe what else they can see.

Tell students to look at Activity 1 on **Page 40**. Have a volunteer read the example question and answer. Then have students work in pairs to read and answer the other questions by referring to the picture on **Page 41**.

2 Ask and answer.

10 min

Have volunteers read the example dialogue in the speech bubbles on **Page 41**. Then have pairs take turns to ask and answer questions about the picture. Monitor and help if necessary. Have volunteers ask and answer about the picture for the class. Prepare for the Finish the Class activity, by writing questions and answers from Activity 1 on the board in random order, with the questions and answers separated.

Finish the Class

10 min

Have students come to the board and match a question and answer, and read them aloud. If a student is correct, he or she erases the question and answer from the board. Continue until the board is empty.

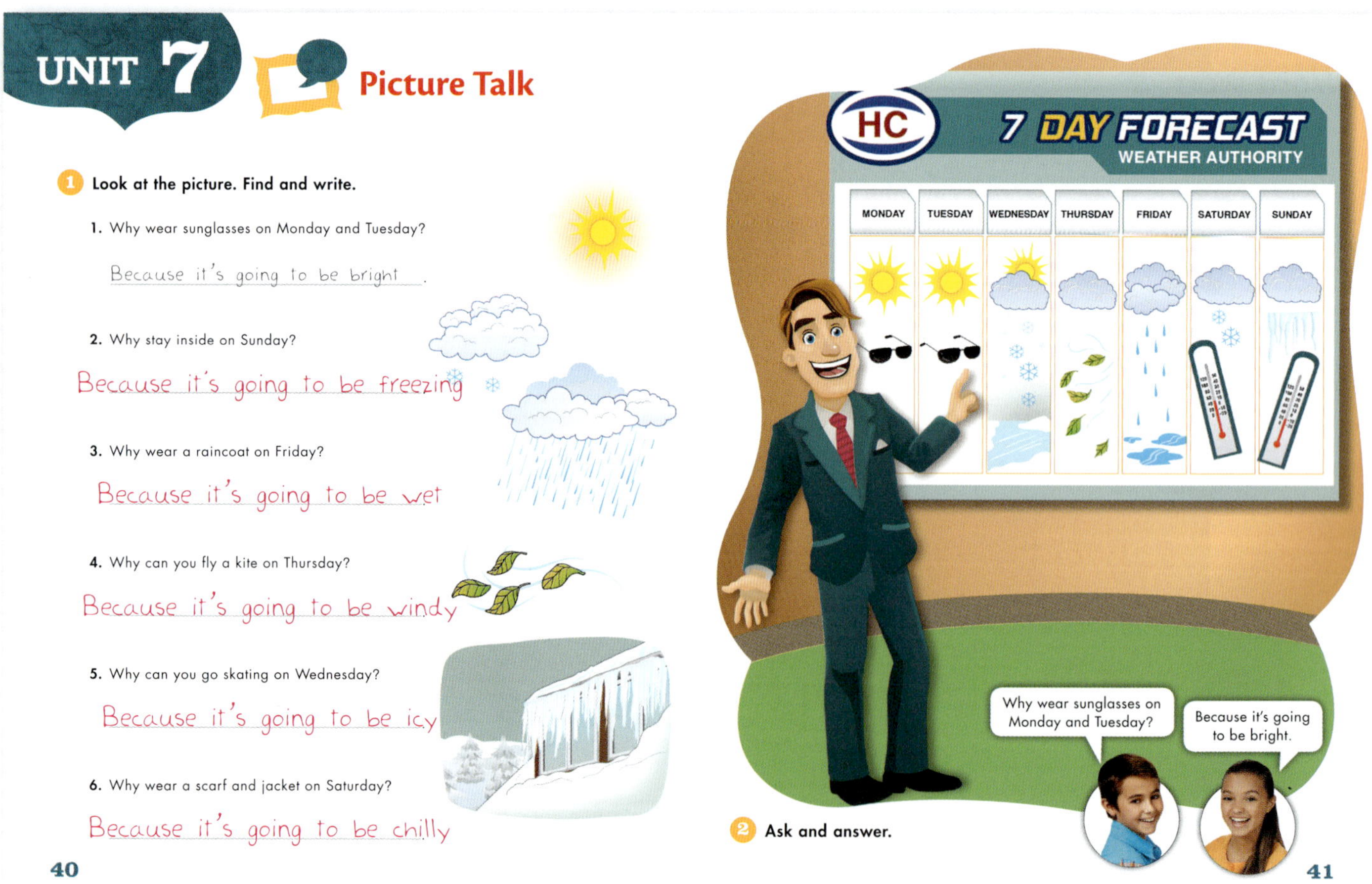

UNIT 7 Picture Talk

1 Look at the picture. Find and write.

1. Why wear sunglasses on Monday and Tuesday?
   Because it's going to be bright.
2. Why stay inside on Sunday?
   Because it's going to be freezing
3. Why wear a raincoat on Friday?
   Because it's going to be wet
4. Why can you fly a kite on Thursday?
   Because it's going to be windy
5. Why can you go skating on Wednesday?
   Because it's going to be icy
6. Why wear a scarf and jacket on Saturday?
   Because it's going to be chilly

40

2 Ask and answer.

41

Skills Book Happy Reader

Lesson Objectives: Draw conclusions in a fiction text. Write an opinion.
Materials: Audio **Track 58**

Start the Class
5 min

Ask students if they have ever been on a camping trip. Ask them to tell the class where they went and who they went with. Then ask if they enjoyed it and why.

1 58 Read and listen.
10 min

Ask students to look at the story title and pictures and make predictions about what the story is going to be about. Write a few ideas on the board.

Tell students to read the story as they listen to the track. Play **Track 58**. Ask students if their predictions were correct.

2 Circle how Linda felt about the camping trip.
10 min

Have students read the answer options aloud. Then have them work in pairs to complete the activity. Ask a volunteer pair to say the answer, and then ask the class to discuss whether or not they agree.

Page 55 Happy Writer
15 min

Tell students they will write about whether or not they like the story title. Ask them to consider if the title accurately describes the story, if the storm was the main event in the story, and whether or not the story title is misleading. If they dislike the title, have students suggest an alternative title. Have volunteers share their ideas with the class.

Finish the Class
10 min

Tell students to work in pairs and tell their partners about something exciting that happened on a vacation. Then have volunteers share with the class.

Page 55 (Students' own answers)

Happy Reader

1 58 Read and listen.

A Terrible Storm

1
Every year Linda goes on a camping trip with her dad and her sister, Laura. This year they went to Rock River Park. "How was the camping trip, Linda?" Mom asked.

"It was great!" Linda said. "It was mild, so we slept under the stars. We ate food that we cooked over a fire. We didn't bring our phones or computers. We just enjoyed nature."

"It was the best camping trip ever!" Laura said. "We went to the top of a mountain. It was the highest place in the park. We saw everything from there."

42

2
"Why was it the best camping trip?" Mom asked.

"Because there was a big storm!" Linda said. "We were scared and it was so rainy and very chilly. There was also a lot of wind. But then Dad took us to a cave. It was a great place to go. We sat together inside the cave because Dad said it was safe. The storm was so close. It was much better than TV!"

"That's so exciting. I'm glad everyone was OK," Mom said.

3
"After the storm we walked back to the campsite," Linda said. "The forest looked very different. The strong wind made some trees fall onto the trail. We climbed over the tree trunks and tree branches. We jumped in the puddles and got mud all over each other. It was great!"

"A big storm and mud puddles? I'm happy I stayed home!" Mom said.

2 Circle how Linda felt about the camping trip.

a. We just enjoyed nature. **b.** (It was great!) **c.** There was a big storm.

Happy Writer Page 55

43

Skills Book Word Work

Lesson Objectives: Recognize rhyming words. Read clues to identify words. Categorize words

Materials: a list of words from the unit for a Spelling Bee

Start the Class

10 min

Have a Spelling Bee competition with the unit vocabulary words.

1 Choose the words that sound the same. Then complete.

10 min

Have a volunteer read the sentence for Item 1. Say the word *pet* aloud and ask students to find the rhyming word in the word bank that completes the sentence. Elicit *wet*. Then have students work in pairs to complete the other sentences with the correct words from the word bank. Check answers with the class.

2 Read and answer.

5 min

Tell students to look at the *What Am I?* riddle. Ask a volunteer to read it. Then have students work in pairs to solve the riddle. Ask for a pair to share their answer and then check the answer with the class.

3 Color the word that's different and write why. Then make your own puzzle.

15 min

Do Item 1 as a class, suggesting that *freezing* is different because it is an adjective, not a noun. Have students complete the activity in pairs. Tell them to make their own puzzles for Item 5 for their partners to solve.

Finish the Class

10 min

Explain to students that they are going to work in pairs to make a weather forecast for the next two days. Have them illustrate the forecast, using the illustration on **Page 41** as an example. Then have each pair present their forecast to another pair.

Word Work

1 Choose the words that sound the same. Then complete.

bright windy wet foggy chilly

1. Don't walk your **pet** when it's wet.
2. Don't be **silly**, wear a sweater when it's chilly.
3. Late at **night**, it isn't bright.
4. Let's fly a kite with **Cindy** when it's windy.
5. Where's my **doggy**? I can't see because it's foggy.

2 Read and answer.

What Am I?

I visit in the fall or winter.
I'm not freezing or icy.
What am I?
I'm chilly.

3 Color the word that's different and write why. Then make your own puzzle.

1. trunk, branch, freezing (Students' own answers.)
(Students' own answers)

2. wet, bright, puddle (Students' own answers.)
(Students' own answers)

3. mud, chilly, windy (Students' own answers.)
(Students' own answers)

4. freezing, mild, icy (Students' own answers.)
(Students' own answers)

5. (Students' own answers.)
(Students' own answers)

Lesson Objective: Ask and answer questions about a picture.

Start the Class

5 min

Play the Chain Memory Game (see **Page T 53**). Start by saying *I'm packing my tickets.* Then the first student repeats your sentence and adds a new item. Continue around the class with students repeating and adding new items.

1 Look at the picture. Find and match.

15 min

Ask students to look at the main picture on **Page 47** and describe it in as much detail as they can.

Have students look at the pictures of the people in Activity 1. Have a volunteer read the first sentence. Tell students to look at the example answer matching the girl to the sentence. Then tell students to work in pairs to read the other sentences and refer to the main picture to decide who is saying each sentence. Check answers with the class.

2 Ask and answer.

15 min

Have volunteers read the example dialogue in the speech bubbles on **Page 47**. Then have students work in pairs to ask and answer about the picture.

Finish the Class

15 min

Ask students to think about a job they want to do when they grow up. Write on the board *I work in a/an ____. I need ____ to do my job. I don't need ____ to do my job.* Tell students to think about the jobs they chose and complete the sentences in their notebooks. Have students say their sentences for the rest of the class to guess the jobs.

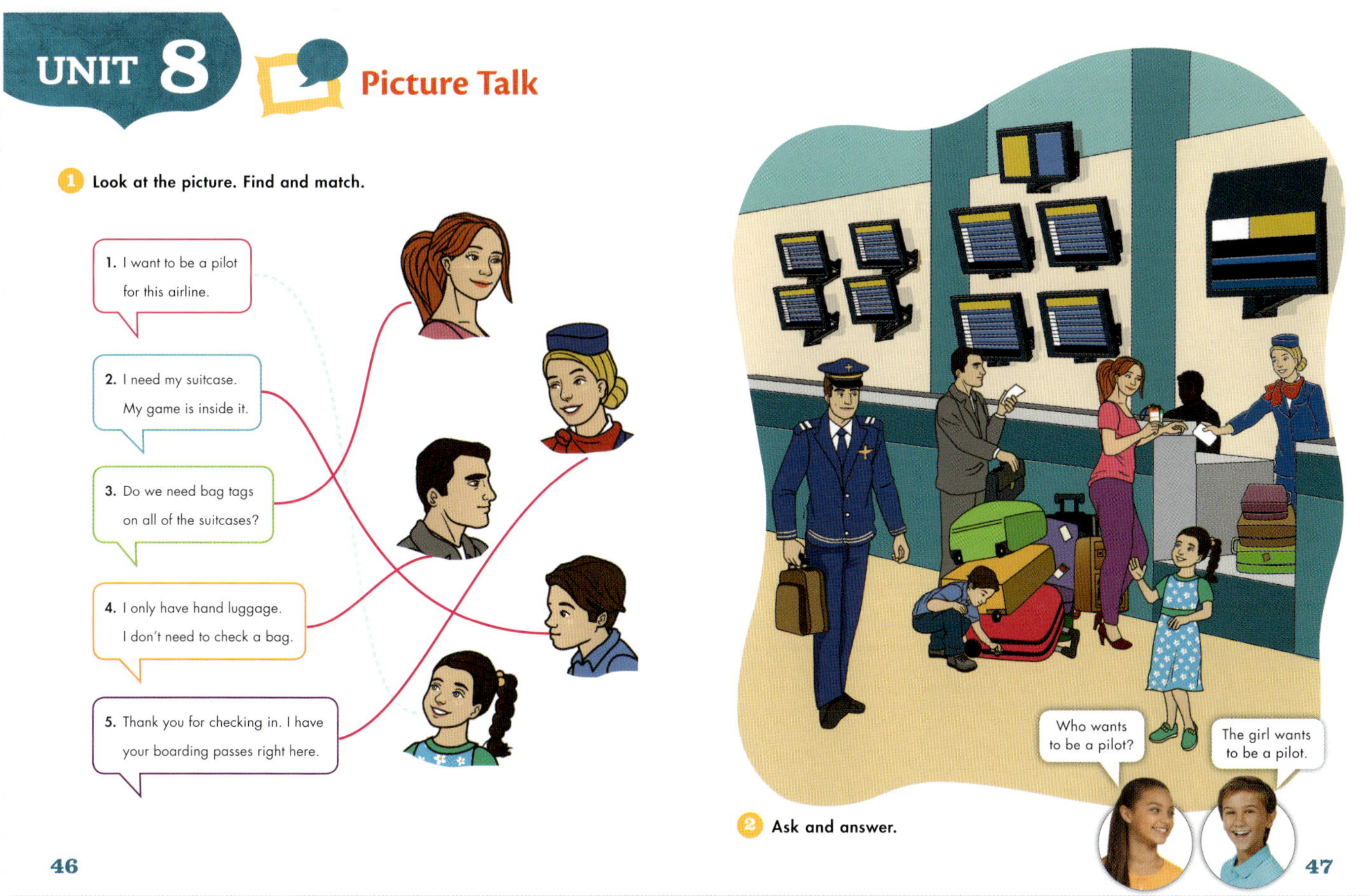

Skills Book

Happy Reader

Lesson Objective: Recall details in a nonfiction text.
Materials: Audio **Track 59**

Start the Class

5 min

Ask the class if anyone wants to be a flight attendant in the future. If they do, ask them why. If they don't, ask them why not. Brainstorm all the things that flight attendants do as part of their job, for example, *give safety instructions, bring food and drinks, show people to their seats*, and so on.

1 59 Read and listen.

15 min

Ask students to look at the photos and describe what the flight attendants are doing in each one.

Tell students to read the text as they listen. Play **Track 59**. Ask questions to check comprehension, for example, *Why do flight attendants have a great job? What do flight attendants bring you if you are cold?*

Put students in groups of four. Assign a paragraph of the text to each student and have them read their paragraphs in their groups.

2 Circle *True* or *False*.

5 min

Have students work in pairs to read the text again and complete the activity. Check answers with the class.

Page 55 Happy Writer

15 min

Tell students they will complete the sentences about flight attendants. Have students refer back to the text on **Pages 48 and 49** for ideas. Then have volunteers share their sentences with the class.

Finish the Class

10 min

Play the Shark Game (see **Page T 28**) with profession words.

Page 55 (Students' own answers)

Happy Reader

1 59 **Read and listen.**

Flight Attendants

1
What do you want to be when you're older? Do you want to be a flight attendant? Flight attendants have a great job. They travel around the world. They see new people and new places all the time.

Every airline wants to have the best flight attendants, so the training is difficult. They also want flight attendants who can prepare food and drinks for passengers. Flight attendants have to be friendly, but they have to be strong, too. Did you know they take care of people in an emergency? Airlines teach flight attendants how to help people if there is a problem on the plane.

2
Flight attendants greet you at the gate. They check your boarding pass and help you find your seat on the airplane. On the flight, you can ask a flight attendant for a blanket if you are cold. Flight attendants tell you how to wear your seat belt. They check the aisles and emergency exit rows on the airplane. Hand luggage can't be in the aisles because people have to walk there. Flight attendants bring you drinks or food if you're thirsty or hungry.

It is a flight attendant's job to keep people happy. They want you to enjoy your flight, but they want you to be safe, too. Isn't it exciting to be a flight attendant?

2 **Circle *True* or *False*.**

1. Flight attendants help people on a flight. (True) False
2. Flight attendants do not keep people happy. True (False)

Happy Writer Page 55

48 49

Skills Book Word Work

Lesson Objectives: Read clues to identify words. Identify one- and multi-syllable words. Use visual clues to identify words.
Materials: a list of words from the unit for a Spelling Bee

Start the Class
10 min

Write each half of the following compound nouns randomly on the board: *hand luggage, bag tag, flight attendant, window seat, boarding pass.* Have volunteers come to the board and match parts of the words by drawing lines.

1 Write.
10 min

Explain that students will read the clues and write the unit vocabulary words they describe. Have students complete the activity individually. Then check answers with the class.

2 Read and answer.
5 min

Ask a volunteer to read the *What Am I?* riddle. Then have students work in pairs to solve the riddle. Check the answer with the class.

3 Say the words. Count the syllables. Write.
10 min

Say *aisle* and ask how many syllables it has. Elicit *one.* Have students work in pairs to say the words, count the syllables, and write them in the correct boxes. Check answers with the class.

4 Complete the chart.
5 min

Elicit the words for the pictures. Then have students complete the chart by writing the words in the correct columns. Check answers with the class.

Finish the Class
10 min

Have a Spelling Bee competition to review the Level 6 vocabulary words.

Word Work

1 Write.

1. You take this on the airplane with you. hand luggage
2. This is where you sit on the airplane. window seat
3. This shows who the suitcase belongs to. bag tag
4. This is what you buy to fly on the airplane. ticket
5. This is what you pack your clothes in for your trip. suitcase
6. This is a company that has many airplanes. airline

2 Read and answer.

What Am I?

You can wear me in a car. You can wear me on an airplane. I keep you safe. I am a belt, but I am not on your clothes.

What am I?

I'm a seat belt.

50

3 Say the words. Count the syllables. Write.

seat belt luggage attendant emergency aisle

1. a i s l e
2. l u g | g a g e
3. e | m e r | g e n | c y
4. a t | t e n d | a n t
5. s e a t | b e l t

4 Complete the chart.

One Word	Two Words
ticket	bag tag
airlines	hand luggage
suitcase	window seat

51

Macmillan Education
4 Crinan Street
London N1 9XW
A division of Macmillan Publishers Limited

Companies and representatives throughout the world

ISBN 978-0-230-47371-3

First published 2015

Teacher's Edition Credits:
Designed by Nancy Ortega Cruz
Cover design by Roberto Martínez
Cover illustration by Donald Wu
Cover photograph by © Getty Images/Kemter
Picture research by Penelope Bowden, Proudfoot Pictures and Tessa Hammond (cover photo)

The authors and publishers would like to thank the following for permission to reproduce their photographs: Getty Images/Kemter (p. iii), Malcolm Llanas (pp. T 17, T 71, T 89, T 107), Jaclyn Maffiore (pp. T 35, T 53, T 125, T 143)

Commissioned photographs by George Contorakes, pp. ii, iii, v, T 16, T 34, T 52, T 70, T 88, T 106, T 124, T 142

Student Book Credits:
Text, design and illustration © Macmillan Publishers Limited 2015
Written by Angela Llanas and Libby Williams
The authors have asserted their rights to be identified as the authors of this work in accordance with the Copyright, Designs and Patents Act 1988.

Designed by Pronk Media Inc.
Student Book pages illustrated by Charlene Chua (vocabulary: pp. 8, 15, 16, 23, 24, 31, 32, 40–41, 47, 48, 55, 56, 63, 64, 71); Russ Daff (stories: pp. 20–21, 36–37, 52–53, 68–69); Jennifer McCormick (pp. 24–25 (store background), 28); Pronk Media Inc. (pp. 62, 72); Donald Wu (comic strips: pp. 6–7, 10–11, 18–19, 26–27, 34–35, 42–43, 50–51, 58–59, 66–67)
The Language Lodge pages illustrated by: Charlene Chua (pp. 1, 4–5, 6, 7, 8, 13, 17, 18–19, 21, 22, 25, 29);
Pronk Media Inc. (pp. 3, 10–11, 15, 27, 28, 30)
Cover design and illustration by Roberto Martínez
Cover photograph by George Contorakes
Picture research by Penelope Bowden, Proudfoot Pictures

The authors and publishers would like to thank the following for permission to reproduce their photographs: **Alamy**/fStop Images GmbH pp. 16, 17(background), Alamy/Imageroller pp. 14(t), 22(t), 30(t), 38(t), 46(t), 54(t), 70(t), Alamy/Mar Photographics p. 12(bl), Alamy/MPVHistory p. 60(t); **Corbis** p. 44(br), Corbis/JACOPIN/BSIP p. 44(l), Corbis/Roger Ressmeyer pp. 40, 41(background), Corbis/Pete Saloutos p. 12(br); **FLPA**/Bob Gibbons p. 28(t); **Fotolibra**/James W Fowler p. 28(br), Fotolibra/World History Archive p. 44(c); **Getty Images**/Mordolff pp. 48, 49(background), Getty Images/Dolores Rodriguez p. 13, Getty Images/Spencer Rowell/VCL p. 12(tl), Getty Images/Science & Society Picture Library p. 60(b), Getty Images/Chris Walsh p. 45, Getty Images/Peter Zelei pp. 56, 57(background); **Glow Images**/Hans Blossey p. 12(tr); **Superstock**/Christian Hütter/imagebroker/imagebroker.net p. 29, Superstock/Iberfoto p. 44(tr), Superstock/Minden Pictures p. 28(l); **Thinkstock**/Joel Blit/iStock p. 61, Thinkstock/Swilmore/iStock pp. 8, 9(background), Thinkstock/Tomasz Wyszołmirski pp. 64, 65(background), Thinkstock/Andrew Zarivny/iStock pp. 32, 33(background)

Commissioned photographs by George Contorakes, pp. 5, 9, 14, 22, 24, 30, 32, 38, 46, 49, 54, 57, 62, 64, 70

Props for commissioned photographs by Luise Johnson-Dailey, Bluwave Creative

The authors and publishers wish to thank the following for their help with the photo shoot: Karen Greer Models, LLC; World of Kids, Inc.; Alyssa; Haylie; Mario; and Max

Skills Book Credits:
Text, design, and illustration © Macmillan Publishers Limited 2015
Written by Jill McEnery
The author has asserted her right to be identified as the author of this work inaccordance with the Copyright, Designs and Patents Act 1988.

Original design by Pronk Media Inc.
Page make-up by Victory Productions, Inc.
Illustrated by Charlene Chua (pp. 34, 35, 38); Jennifer McCormick (pp. 36, 37); Pronk Media Inc. (icons throughout); Victory Productions, Inc. (pp. 4–33, 39–55)
Cover design and illustration by Roberto Martínez
Picture research by Penelope Bowden, Proudfoot Pictures

The author and publishers would like to thank the following for permission to reproduce their photographs: **Corbis** pp. 12(bl), 25(t), 53(l, r); **Getty Images**/bluecinema/E+ p. 13(tr), Getty Images/Gene Chutka pp. 48 (t, m, b), 49(m), 55(t), Getty Images/Digital Vision pp 49(b), 55(b), Getty Images/Jens Lennartsson/Mascot p. 12(tr), Getty Images/Neustockimages p. 49(t); **Thinkstock**/audioundwerbung/iStock p. 13(br), Thinkstock/indigolotos/iStock p. 25(b), Thinkstock/Dennis Sabo/iStock pp. 12–13(background)

Commissioned photographs by George Contorakes, pp. 4, 5, 11, 17, 23, 29, 35, 41, 47

The author and publishers wish to thank the following for their help with the photo shoot: Karen Greer Models, LLC; World of Kids, Inc.; Alyssa; Haylie; Mario; and Max

Printed and bound in Thailand

2019 2018 2017 2016 2015
10 9 8 7 6 5 4 3 2 1